Margory Niblock

Crime could never flourish if there were more community-minded persons like yourself.

Best wishes!

Andy Suter
Dec. 1977

Criminal Justice and Law Enforcement Books

of

WEST PUBLISHING COMPANY

St. Paul, Minnesota 55102

July, 1976

CONSTITUTIONAL LAW

Maddex's Cases and Comments on Constitutional Law by James L. Maddex, Professor of Criminal Justice, Georgia State University, 816 pages, 1974.

CORRECTIONS

Burns' Corrections—Organization and Administration by Henry Burns, Jr., Professor of Corrections, The Pennsylvania State University, 578 pages, 1975.

Kerper and Kerper's Legal Rights of the Convicted by Hazel B. Kerper, Late Professor of Sociology and Criminal Law, Sam Houston State University and Janeen Kerper, Attorney, San Diego, Calif., 677 pages, 1974.

Killinger and Cromwell's Selected Readings on Corrections in the Community by George G. Killinger, Director of the Institute of Contemporary Corrections, Sam Houston State University and Paul F. Cromwell, Jr., Member, Texas Board of Pardons and Paroles, 579 pages, 1974.

Killinger and Cromwell's Readings on Penology—The Evolution of Corrections in America by George G. Killinger and Paul F. Cromwell, Jr., 426 pages, 1973.

Killinger, Cromwell and Cromwell's Selected Readings on Issues in Corrections and Administration by George G. Killinger, Paul F. Cromwell, Jr. and Bonnie J. Cromwell, San Antonio College, 644 pages, 1976.

Killinger, Kerper and Cromwell's Probation and Parole in the Criminal Justice System by George G. Killinger, Hazel B. Kerper and Paul F. Cromwell, Jr., 374 pages, 1976.

Krantz' The Law of Corrections and Prisoners' Rights in a Nutshell by Sheldon Krantz, Professor of Law and Director, Center for Criminal Justice, Boston University, 353 pages, 1976.

Model Rules and Regulations on Prisoners' Rights and Responsibilities, 212 pages, 1973.

Rubin's Law of Criminal Correction, 2nd Edition (Student Edition) by Sol Rubin, Counsel Emeritus, Council on Crime and Delinquency, 873 pages, 1973.

CRIMINAL JUSTICE BOOKS

CORRECTIONS—Continued

Smith & Berlin's Introduction to Probation and Parole by Alexander B. Smith, Professor of Sociology, John Jay College of Criminal Justice and Louis Berlin, Chief, Training Branch, New York City Dept. of Probation, 250 pages, 1975.

CRIMINAL JUSTICE SYSTEM

Kerper's Introduction to the Criminal Justice System by Hazel B. Kerper, 558 pages, 1972.

CRIMINAL LAW

Dix and Sharlot's Cases and Materials on Basic Criminal Law by George E. Dix, Professor of Law, University of Texas and M. Michael Sharlot, Professor of Law, University of Texas, 649 pages, 1974.

Ferguson's Readings on Concepts of Criminal Law by Robert W. Ferguson, Administration of Justice Dept. Director, Saddleback College, 560 pages, 1975.

Gardner and Manian's Principles, Cases and Readings on Criminal Law by Thomas J. Gardner, Professor of Criminal Justice, Milwaukee Area Technical College and Victor Manian, Milwaukee County Judge, 782 pages, 1975.

Heymann and Kenety—The Murder Trial of Wilbur Jackson: A Homicide in the Family by Philip Heymann, Professor of Law, Harvard University and William Kenety, Instructor, Catholic University Law School, 340 pages, 1975.

Loewy's Criminal Law in a Nutshell by Arnold H. Loewy, Professor of Law University of North Carolina, 302 pages, 1975.

CRIMINAL PROCEDURE

Davis' Police Discretion by Kenneth Culp Davis, Professor of Law, University of Chicago, 176 pages, 1975.

Dowling's Teaching Materials on Criminal Procedure by Jerry L. Dowling, Professor of Criminal Justice, Sam Houston State University, 544 pages, 1976.

Ferdico's Criminal Procedure for the Law Enforcement Officer by John N. Ferdico, Assistant Attorney General, State of Maine, 372 pages, 1975.

Israel and LaFave's Criminal Procedure in a Nutshell, 2nd Edition by Jerold H. Israel and Wayne R. LaFave, 372 pages, 1975.

Johnson's Cases, Materials and Text on The Elements of Criminal Due Process by Phillip E. Johnson, Professor of Law, University of California, Berkeley, 324 pages, 1975.

Kamisar, LaFave and Israel's Cases, Comments and Questions on Basic Criminal Procedure, 4th Edition by Yale Kamisar, Professor of Law, University of Michigan, Wayne R. LaFave, Professor of Law, University of Illinois and Jerold H. Israel, Professor of Law, University of Michigan, 790 pages, 1974. Supplement Annually.

Uviller's the Processes of Criminal Justice—Adjudication by H. Richard Uviller, Professor of Law, Columbia University, 991 pages, 1975.

Uviller's the Processes of Criminal Justice-Investigation by H. Richard Uviller, 744 pages, 1974.

CRIMINAL JUSTICE BOOKS

EVIDENCE

Klein's Law of Evidence for Police by Irving J. Klein, Professor of Law and Police Science, John Jay College of Criminal Justice, 416 pages, 1973.

Rothstein's Evidence in a Nutshell by Paul F. Rothstein, Professor of Law, Georgetown Law Center, 406 pages, 1970.

INTRODUCTION TO LAW ENFORCEMENT

More's The American Police—Text and Readings by Harry W. More, Jr., Professor of Administration of Justice, California State University at San Jose, 278 pages, 1976.

Police Tactics in Hazardous Situations by the San Diego, California Police Department, 228 pages, 1976.

Schwartz and Goldstein's Law Enforcement Handbook for Police by Louis B. Schwartz, Professor of Law, University of Pennsylvania and Stephen R. Goldstein, Professor of Law, University of Pennsylvania, 333 pages, 1970.

Sutor's Police Operations—Tactical Approaches to Crimes in Progress by Captain Andrew Sutor, Philadelphia, Pennsylvania Police Department, about 270 pages, 1976.

INVESTIGATION

Markle's Criminal Investigation and Presentation of Evidence by Arnold Markle, The State's Attorney, New Haven County, Connecticut, about 350 pages, 1976.

JUVENILE JUSTICE

Faust and Brantingham's Juvenile Justice Philosophy: Readings, Cases and Comments by Frederic L. Faust, Professor of Criminology, Florida State University and Paul J. Brantingham, Professor of Criminology, Florida State University, 600 pages, 1974.

Fox's Law of Juvenile Courts in a Nutshell by Sanford J. Fox, Professor of Law, Boston College, 286 pages, 1971.

Johnson's Introduction to the Juvenile Justice System by Thomas A. Johnson, Professor of Criminal Justice, University of Kentucky, 492 pages, 1975.

LAW ENFORCEMENT SUPERVISION

Wadman, Paxman and Bentley's Law Enforcement Supervision—A Case Study Approach by Robert C. Wadman, Rio Hondo Community College, Monroe J. Paxman, Brigham Young University and Marion T. Bentley, Utah State University, 224 pages, 1975.

POLICE-COMMUNITY RELATIONS

Cromwell and Keefer's Readings on Police-Community Relations by Paul F. Cromwell, Jr., and George Keefer, Former F.B.I. Agent, 368 pages, 1973.

PSYCHOLOGY

Parker and Meier's Interpersonal Psychology for Law Enforcement and Corrections by L. Craig Parker, Jr., Criminal Justice Dept. Director, University of New Haven and Robert D. Meier, Professor of Criminal Justice, University of New Haven, 290 pages, 1975.

CRIMINAL JUSTICE BOOKS

VICE CONTROL

Ferguson's the Nature of Vice Control in the Administration of Justice by Robert W. Ferguson, 509 pages, 1974.

Uelman and Haddox' Cases, Text and Materials on Drug Abuse Law by Gerald F. Uelman, Professor of Law, Loyola University, Los Angeles and Victor G. Haddox, Professor of Criminology, California State University at Long Beach and Clinical Professor of Psychiatry, Law and Behavioral Sciences, University of Southern California School of Medicine, 564 pages, 1974.

POLICE OPERATIONS

TACTICAL APPROACHES TO CRIMES IN PROGRESS

By
ANDREW P. SUTOR
Professor, Community College of Philadelphia

CRIMINAL JUSTICE SERIES

ST. PAUL, MINN.
WEST PUBLISHING CO.
1976

COPYRIGHT © 1976
By
WEST PUBLISHING CO.
All rights reserved

Library of Congress Catalog Card Number: 76–16911

Sutor Police Operations Cr.J.S.

This book is dedicated to the first "street-cop" of record: "St. Michael the Archangel" and to those officers who followed in his endless task. His followers, to whom this is also dedicated, are those brave men and women in blue who patrol the streets, every hour of every day, to keep the lions from devouring the lambs.

PREFACE

This handbook is, I believe, the first comprehensive collection of effective tactical police operations from police departments throughout the United States. Its purpose is to provide a broad reference source for those responsible for developing police tactics to combat the crime problem.

Although the science of police operations is not new, the concept of using special anti-crime tactical forces to combat crime is relatively new and this handbook is, in effect, a state-of-the-art report on the subject.

As our society suffers more and more from the crime problem, the need for effective police operations becomes more critical, not only to achieve increased levels of organizational efficiency but also to achieve higher levels of self-satisfaction for the individual officer. We have come to recognize that what's good for the organization, is, in the long run, good for its people. Those officers most satisfied with their jobs are those who are using their fullest abilities to make real and identifiable contributions in the war on crime.

A good police officer should have a working knowledge of all police tactics so that he can use the most suitable for each situation. Police tactics are, of course, undergoing rapid change and each officer should maintain continual contact with the field. Yet, he should also be careful about using unproven methods since the police operations field seems prone to embrace fads which may have limited merit. This handbook, you'll note, reflects a cautious attitude toward accepting new methods merely because they're new, or because of pressures to be "in" with the newest gimmick.

"Tactical Approaches to Crimes in Progress" is concerned with situations the working police officer faces on patrol every hour of every day across the United States.

PREFACE

The book was written because there is a critical need for information on theory and methods of police patrol that is not satisfied by contemporary works on the subject.

The approach to the crime problem emphasized as a proactive * apprehension-oriented, legalistic-style, form of policing that is certain to become the accepted approach to the crime problem in the United States in the future.

Traditionally, the criminal justice system has operated mostly on a reactive approach to crime. Under this approach, less than 20 percent of reported "street crimes" are cleared (solved) by police and the conviction rate is appallingly low.

The proactive approach involves "Special Crime Tactical Forces" as recommended in the recent report of the National Advisory Commission on Criminal Justice Standards and Goals. Police use of stakeouts, surveillances, special alarm systems, intelligence information, police "decoys", computer informational systems, grid systems, resource allocation, deployment and technology (including helicopters on patrol) are the integral elements of the proactive approach to crime.

The text encompasses five sections and twenty-four units, a true one-semester course, leaving time for outside readings if the instructor chooses.

The principles in this work have been proven in the "real world" and have the potential for making police services in America more effective in dealing with the crime problem.

Since the handbook has been quite a few years in preparation, to my family goes my thanks for their endurance and forbearance. I must also thank Messrs John Eldred, Fred Fletcher, Jacob Haber, Robert Hurst, James Ramp, George Sinnott, Jeff Slemrod and Jude Walsh for their contributions.

* Proactive, used here, refers to an action-oriented, pre-planned approach to the crime problem as opposed to the traditional "reactive" approach. For more details refer to Unit 8 Reactive vs. Proactive Response to Crime.

PREFACE

And finally I must thank my many students from my police operations classes and workshops at Philadelphia Community College and the University of Delaware for their contributions to this work, which I hope serves its purpose well.

Andrew P. Sutor

Philadelphia, Pa.
June, 1976

SUMMARY OF CONTENTS

SECTION 1. THE CRIME PROBLEM

Unit		Page
1.	Crime in America	1
2.	Part I. Offenses—Violent Crimes	9
3.	Part I. Offenses—Crimes Against Property	28
4.	Victims	36
5.	Police Victims	47
6.	Crime Reporting and Clearance	55

SECTION 2. ROLE OF THE POLICE

7.	The Goals of Police Service	67
8.	Reactive vs. Proactive Response to Crime	78
9.	A Day Without Police	84
10.	Role Implementation	89

SECTION 3. POLICE OPERATIONS

11.	Resource Allocation	109
12.	Communications	131
13.	Holdup Information Systems	147
14.	Surveillances	160
15.	Searches	178

SECTION 4. PROACTIVE CRIME FIGHTING TACTICS

16.	Special Crime Tactical Forces	201
17.	Model Tactical Units	214
18.	Use of Decoys	229
19.	Tactical Holdup Alarm Systems	256
20.	Management of Special TAC Units	279
21.	Helicopters on Patrol	290

SUMMARY OF CONTENTS

SECTION 5. TACTICAL APPROACHES TO SELECTED CRIMES

Unit	Page
22. Tactical Approaches to Robbery	301
23. Tactical Approaches to Burglary	307
24. Tactical Approaches to Auto Theft	317
Index	325

TABLE OF CONTENTS

SECTION 1. THE CRIME PROBLEM

	Page
UNIT 1. CRIME IN AMERICA	1
1. Types of Crime	2
2. Part I. Offenses—The Crime Index	3
3. Crime and Population	6
4. Summary	7
5. Questions for Discussion	8
UNIT 2. PART I. OFFENSES—VIOLENT CRIMES	9
1. Murder and Non-Negligent Manslaughter	9
A. Murder Volume, Trend and Rate	10
B. Nature of Murder	10
C. Murder Circumstances	12
D. Clearances	12
E. Murder Projection	13
2. Forcible Rape	15
A. Rape Volume, Trend and Rate	15
B. Nature of Rape Offenses	15
3. Robbery	17
A. Robbery Volume, Trend and Rate	19
B. Nature of Robbery	19
C. Robbery Clearances	21
D. Persons Arrested for Robbery	21
4. Aggravated Assault	22
A. Aggravated Assault Volume and Trend	22
B. Nature of Aggravated Assault	23
C. Aggravated Assault Clearances	23
5. Summary	25
6. Questions for Discussion	26
UNIT 3. PART I. OFFENSES—CRIMES AGAINST PROPERTY	28
1. Burglary	28
A. Burglary Volume and Trend	28

TABLE OF CONTENTS

UNIT 3. PART I. OFFENSES—CRIMES AGAINST PROPERTY—Continued

1. Burglary—Continued | Page
   B. Nature of Burglary | 28
   C. Burglary Clearances | 29
2. Larceny—Theft | 30
   A. Larceny Volume and Trend | 32
   B. Nature of Larceny—Theft | 32
3. Auto Theft | 32
   A. Auto Theft Volume and Trend | 32
   B. Nature of Auto Theft | 32
4. Summary | 34
5. Questions for Discussion | 35

UNIT 4. VICTIMS | 36
1. The Case of Mrs. Slawnyk | 36
2. The Case of Mr. Rauer | 39
3. Victimization of Inner City Residents | 41
4. Victimization by the Criminal Justice System | 42
5. Summary | 45
6. Questions for Discussion | 46

UNIT 5. POLICE VICTIMS | 47
1. Law Enforcement Officers Killed | 48
   A. Circumstances Surrounding Deaths | 51
   B. Weapons Used | 51
   C. Types of Assignments | 53
2. Assaults on Law Enforcement Officers | 53
3. Summary | 54
4. Questions for Discussion | 54

UNIT 6. CRIME REPORTING AND CLEARANCE | 55
1. Clearance of Crime | 57
2. Elements of Crime | 58
3. Repressible Crimes | 62
4. Summary | 63
5. Questions for Discussion | 65

XIV

TABLE OF CONTENTS

SECTION 2. ROLE OF THE POLICE

	Page
UNIT 7. THE GOALS OF POLICE SERVICE	67
1. The English Model	68
2. Kansas City Patrol Study	71
3. Styles of Policing	74
4. Summary	75
5. Questions for Discussion	76
UNIT 8. REACTIVE vs. PROACTIVE RESPONSE TO CRIME	78
1. Detective Work	79
2. Study on Detective vs. the Robbers	79
3. Criminal Intelligence—Enhancing the Proactive Response	80
4. Summary	82
5. Questions for Discussion	82
UNIT 9. A DAY WITHOUT POLICE	84
1. Summary	88
2. Questions for Discussion	88
UNIT 10. ROLE IMPLEMENTATION	89
1. Development of Goals and Objectives	89
A. National Advisory Commission Commentary	90
B. Workable Goals and Objectives	91
C. Development of Goals and Objectives	92
D. Internal Publication of Goals and Objectives	93
E. Review and Revision of Goals and Objectives	94
2. Establishing the Role of the Patrol Officer	94
A. National Advisory Commission Commentary	95
3. Patrol Service Priorities	97
A. Response Time	98
B. Informing Personnel of Priorities	98
4. Enhancing the Role of the Patrol Officer	99
A. National Advisory Commission Commentary	100
B. Classification and Pay System	101
C. Status and Recognition	102

TABLE OF CONTENTS

UNIT 10. ROLE IMPLEMENTATION—Continued Page
4. Enhancing the Role of the Patrol Officer—Continued
   D. Investigation _____ 103
   E. Incentives _____ 104
   F. Training _____ 105
5. Summary _____ 106
6. Questions for Disscussion _____ 107

SECTION 3. POLICE OPERATIONS

UNIT 11. RESOURCE ALLOCATION _____ 109
1. Manpower _____ 110
2. Limiting Non-Emergency Services _____ 111
3. RDO Volunteers _____ 115
4. Stack Cars _____ 116
5. Deployment of Patrol Officers _____ 116
   A. National Advisory Commission Commentary __ 118
   B. Workload Study _____ 120
   C. Collection and Analysis _____ 121
   D. Personnel Allocation System _____ 122
   E. Determining Shift Hours _____ 124
   F. Distribution of Personnel by Shifts _____ 125
   G. Distribution of Field Policemen by Day of Week 126
   H. Distribution of Field Policemen by Beats _ 126
   I. Fixed Posts, Availability and Relief _____ 127
   J. Deployment System Procedures _____ 129
6. Summary _____ 130
7. Questions for Discussion _____ 130

UNIT 12. COMMUNICATIONS _____ 131
1. Radio _____ 131
2. Dispatchers _____ 131
3. Telephones _____ 132
4. Signal Lights _____ 134
5. Alarm Systems _____ 134
   A. A Better Criminal Mousetrap _____ 135
      (1) Purpose of Study _____ 135
      (2) Hidden Key _____ 136
      (3) Clearances _____ 138
      (4) False Alarm Rate _____ 139

XVI

TABLE OF CONTENTS

UNIT 12. COMMUNICATIONS—Continued   Page
- 6. Roadblock Networks 141
  - A. Operation F.I.N.D. 141
    - (1) Organization 141
    - (2) Plan of Action 142
    - (3) Operations 143
    - (4) Apprehension 143
    - (5) Program Proves Successful 144
- 7. Summary 145
- 8. Questions for Discussion 145

UNIT 13. HOLDUP INFORMATION SYSTEMS 147
- 1. Response Time 147
- 2. Observation and Description 153
  - A. Observation 153
  - B. Description of Persons 155
  - C. Description of Vehicles 157
- 3. Summary 158
- 4. Questions for Discussion 158

UNIT 14. SURVEILLANCES 160
- 1. Surveillance Definitions 160
- 2. Uses of Surveillance 161
- 3. Preparation for a Surveillance 161
- 4. Information Regarding the Locality of the Surveillance 162
- 5. Equipment Needed 163
- 6. Moving Surveillance 164
- 7. Fixed Surveillance 165
- 8. Foot Surveillance 166
- 9. Specific Situations 166
  - A. Restaurant 166
  - B. Public Conveyance 167
  - C. Elevator 167
  - D. Taxi 167
  - E. Telephone Booth 167
  - F. Hotel 168
  - G. Contact 168

TABLE OF CONTENTS

UNIT 14. SURVEILLANCES—Continued
9. Specific Situations—Continued   Page
    H. Tricks Used by Subject ___ 168
    I. Testing for a Make ___ 169
10. Automobile Surveillance ___ 170
    A. One Surveillance Vehicle ___ 171
    B. Two Surveillance Vehicles ___ 172
    C. Three Surveillance Vehicles ___ 173
    D. Test for Auto Surveillance ___ 174
11. Do's and Don'ts of Surveillance ___ 174
12. Summary ___ 176
13. Questions for Discussion ___ 177

UNIT 15. SEARCHES ___ 178
1. General Guidelines for all Searches ___ 178
    A. Objective ___ 178
    B. Planning ___ 178
    C. Organizing ___ 179
    D. Communications ___ 179
    E. Control ___ 180
2. Mechanics of the Search of Buildings ___ 180
3. Building Searches ___ 182
4. Searching a Building With a Warrant of Arrest ___ 182
5. Searching a Building for Suspects Known to be Inside ___ 185
    (1) Preparation for Entry Into the Building ___ 187
    (2) Entry Into the Building ___ 198
    (3) Entering the Room ___ 199
6. Summary ___ 200
7. Questions for Discussion ___ 200

SECTION 4. PROACTIVE CRIME FIGHTING TACTICS
UNIT 16. SPECIAL CRIME TACTICAL FORCES ___ 201
1. National Advisory Commission Commentary ___ 202
2. Deployment ___ 203
3. TAC Force Organization, Staff and Command ___ 205
4. Part-time Units ___ 207

TABLE OF CONTENTS

UNIT 16. SPECIAL CRIME TACTICAL FORCES—Continued

Page

5. Experimental Arm of the Police Department   208
6. Answer to Corruption and Brutality   208
7. TAC Unit Activity   210
8. Location of TAC Unit Headquarters   211
9. TAC Unit Operations Room   211
10. TAC Unit Weapons   211
11. Summary   212
12. Questions for Discussion   212

UNIT 17. MODEL TACTICAL UNITS   214
1. Philadelphia P.D. Stakeout Unit   214
   A. Equipment Recommended for TAC Units   215
2. Los Angeles P.D. Metropolitan Division   221
   A. Organization   221
   B. Purpose   221
   C. Functions   221
   D. Personnel Selection   222
   E. Equipment   222
   F. Uniform   222
   G. Training   223
   H. Los Angeles Police Department Special Weapons and Tactics Section   223
      (1) Purpose   223
      (2) Organization   223
      (3) Deployment   224
      (4) Personnel and Training   224
      (5) Equipment   226
      (6) Logistics   226
3. New York P.D. Street Crime Unit   226
4. Summary   227
5. Questions for Discussion   227

UNIT 18. USE OF DECOYS   229
1. Entrapment   229
2. Types of Decoys   232
   A. General Considerations   247

TABLE OF CONTENTS

UNIT 18. USE OF DECOYS—Continued
2. Types of Decoys—Continued   Page
   B. Insuranceman Decoy   248
     (1) Equipment   248
     (2) Communications   249
     (3) The Decoy   249
     (4) Working the Street   250
     (5) The Act . . . Robbery   252
3. Summary   254
4. Questions for Discussion   255

UNIT 19. TACTICAL HOLDUP ALARM SYSTEMS   256
1. A New Anti-holdup System   256
2. Tactical Advantages   263
3. Summary   263
4. Questions for Discussion   278

UNIT 20. MANAGEMENT OF SPECIAL TAC UNITS   279
1. Selection of TAC Unit Personnel   279
2. Leadership   280
3. High Trust—A Key to High Performance   281
4. Incentives   285
   A. Monetary Incentives   286
     (1) Paid Overtime (Especially Court)   286
     (2) Incentive Pay   287
   B. Personal Car Program   287
   C. 4 x 10 Plan   287
5. Summary   288
6. Questions for Discussion   288

UNIT 21. HELICOPTERS ON PATROL   290
1. Surveillances   291
2. Advantages and Disadvantages   292
   A. Advantages of Police Helicopter Patrol   292
   B. Disadvantages of Police Helicopter Patrol   293
3. Turbine Helicopters Found More Cost-Effective   294
4. Arrest/Helicopter Response Time   295
5. Police Patrol in Fixed Winged Aircraft   296
   A. STOL Aircraft   296
     (1) Cost Effectiveness   298

TABLE OF CONTENTS

UNIT 21. HELICOPTERS ON PATROL—Continued Page
6. Summary 299
7. Questions for Discussion 299

SECTION 5. TACTICAL APPROACHES TO SELECTED CRIMES

UNIT 22. TACTICAL APPROACHES TO ROBBERY 301
1. Helpful Techniques 303
2. Responding to a Robbery in Progress 303
3. Summary 305
4. Questions for Discussion 306

UNIT 23. TACTICAL APPROACHES TO BURGLARY 307
1. Burglars 307
2. The "Professional" Burglar 307
3. Casing the Job 308
4. Potential Burglar Tools 310
5. Planning 310
6. Vehicles Used 311
7. The Burglary 311
8. Responding to a Burglary in Progress 312
9. Tips for the Police to Aid in Apprehension .. 313
10. Truancy and Burglary 314
11. Curfew and Burglary 314
12. Summary 314
13. Questions for Discussion 315

UNIT 24. TACTICAL APPROACHES TO AUTO THEFT 317
1. Proactive Approach to Auto Theft 317
2. High-Speed Pursuits 320
   A. Problems Involved in Pursuits 320
   B. Controls for High-Speed Pursuits 321
3. Summary 323
4. Questions for Discussion 324
Index 325

XXI †

POLICE OPERATIONS: TACTICAL APPROACHES TO CRIMES IN PROCESS

SECTION I

THE CRIME PROBLEM

UNIT I

CRIME IN AMERICA

Before considering tactical approaches to crimes in progress, it is of paramount importance to appraise the crime problem in the United States. O. W. Wilson ranks criminality second to war as an immediate threat to life and property in our society.[1] Our Declaration of Independence espouses the right to "life, liberty and the pursuit of happiness", yet we see our citizens denied these basic rights because of the crime problem. Nearly 20,000 United States citizens are murdered each year and many others permanently disabled—thus deprived of "life". In addition to economic losses people spend vast sums protecting their homes and businesses against intruders. In our urban areas iron bars and special locks are prevalent on the windows and doors of many homes and businesses-literally making prisoners of our citizenry.

1. O. W. Wilson, Police Administration, (New York, N. Y.: McGraw-Hill Book Co., 1972) p. 3.

Amusements and small businesses either close down completely or have daylight hours because of the crime problem. Thus our people are deprived both of "liberty and the pursuit of happiness".

In comparing crime to medicine it can be said that we have been witnessing an epidemic of crime in the United States during the past decade. If you agree, it may help you decide on the proper remedy for the crime epidemic as we discuss alternative approaches to the crime problem in a chapter on "Role of the Police". Is it time for "preventive medicine", "surgery", or both?

I. TYPES OF CRIME

According to former Attorney General of the United States, Ramsey Clark, crime in America has many faces: [2]

White—collar crime converts billions of dollars annually in tax evasion, price fixing, embezzlement, swindling and consumer fraud.

Organized crime reaps hundreds of millions in gambling, loansharking, drug traffic, extortion, prostitution with the subsequent corruption of officials. Force, including murder when necessary is used to accomplish its purposes.

Crime in the streets, as we have come to call it, encompassing a wide variety of crimes against people and against property —robbery, mugging, burglary, larceny, theft and looting— produces millions of dollars for its perpetrators.

Crimes of passion, includes most murders, rapes and assaults. Conduct once deemed immoral and made criminal—gambling, prostitution, alcohol and drug abuse, profanity, abortion, homosexuality, fornication and obscenity—is a pervasive face of crime accounting for hundreds of thousands of arrests annually.

Violations of regulations designed to protect the public health, safety and convenience—traffic control, building

---

2. Ramsey Clark, Crime in America, 3 (New York, N. Y.: Simon and Schuster, 1970) p. 20.

codes, fire ordinances, minimum standards of quality, mandatory safety precautions, misrepresentation—involve highly anti-social conduct in mass society causing hundreds of thousands of deaths each year.

Revolutionary crime and illegal conduct intended to alter institutions impose rioting, mob violence, unlawful confrontation, arson and trespass on a weary society. Terrorist actions—sniping, bombing and ambushing—common in parts of the world, are an ever increasing risk in America.

Corruption in public office—bribes, payoffs, fixes, conflicts of interest—occur in every branch of government, legislative, executive, judicial, administrative, and at every level, federal, state and local.

Police crime—wrongful arrest, brutality and blackmail is not unknown.

Society has marshalled forces to combat crime. The Securities and Exchange Commission and Internal Revenue Service are examples of agencies specifically concerned with white-collar crime. The FBI investigates crimes against the United States Code. The Treasury Department handles smugglers and counterfeiters among other duties. Although these crimes have a tremendous deleterious effect on the quality of life in our society, they are not the crimes that deprive our citizenry of the aforementioned rights "to life, liberty and the pursuit of happiness". Perhaps these crimes are even the "root causes" of other crimes. It is the other crimes—street crimes—to which your attention is directed. These crimes, mainly known in law enforcement circles as Part I Crimes or the Crime Index, will be the primary target of this book.

2. PART I. OFFENSES—THE CRIME INDEX

The offenses of murder, forcible rape, robbery, aggravated assault, burglary, larceny and auto theft are used to establish an Index in the Uniform Crime Reporting Program to measure the trend and distribution of crime in the United States.[3] These crimes are counted by law enforcement agencies as they become known and are reported on a monthly basis. The Crime Index offenses were selected as a measuring device because, as a group, they represent the most common local crime problem. They are all serious crimes, either by their very nature or due to the volume in which they occur. The offenses of murder, forcible rape, aggravated assault, and robbery make up the violent crime category. The offenses of burglary, larceny and auto theft make up the property crime category.

Law enforcement officials do not purport to know the total volume of crime because of the many criminal actions which are not reported to official sources. Estimates as to the level of unreported crime can be developed through costly victim surveys (see "Crime Reporting and Clearance" in Unit 6) which serve to illustrate the reluctance of the victim to report many criminal actions to law enforcement agencies. In light of this situation, the crime picture must be drawn from information available to law enforcement agencies. The crimes listed in the Crime Index are those considered to be the most constantly reported and provide the capability to compute meaningful crime trends and crime rates. However they are not necessarily the most serious crimes. Arson, kidnapping, hijacking and blackmail are examples of crimes that are certainly more serious than auto theft. However, they are not common enough to be included in the Crime Index. Part I Crimes can best be compared to the Dow Jones Index which measures the stock market by tracking the rise and fall of selected stocks. Like the Dow Jones Index, the Crime Index charts the rise and fall of crimes in our communities. They are universal—a burglary in California is recorded in the same manner as a burglary in New York even though legal terminology may differ.

The crime counts used in the Crime Index are based on actual offenses established by police investigation. When the law en-

3. Uniform Crime Reports for the United States, (Washington D. C.: Federal Bureau of Investigation, 1973) All crime statistics are taken from this source.

Unit 1 CRIME IN AMERICA 5

forcement agency receives a complaint of a criminal matter and the follow-up investigation discloses no crime occurred it is "unfounded". On a national average police investigations "unfound" 4 percent of the complaints concerning Crime Index offenses. These unfounded complaints are eliminated from the crime counts.

There was an average of over eight million Crime Index offenses reported annually to law enforcement agencies during this decade. This amounted to 19 serious crimes each minute. Refer to Chart #1.1 for frequency of Crime in America.

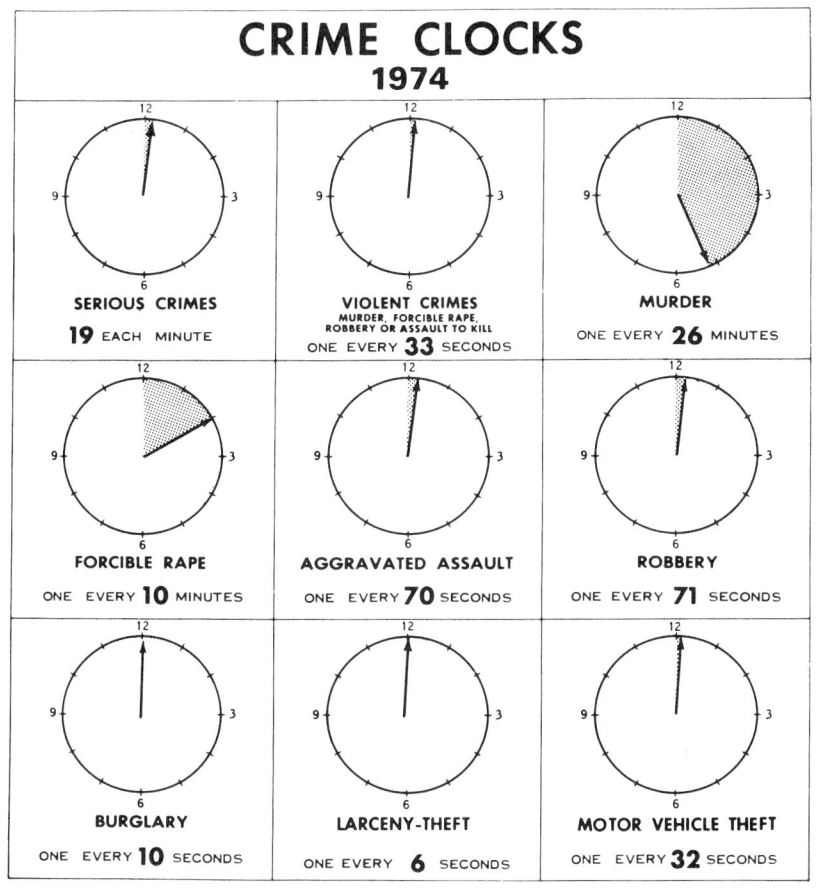

CRIME CLOCKS
1974

SERIOUS CRIMES	VIOLENT CRIMES	MURDER
19 EACH MINUTE	MURDER, FORCIBLE RAPE, ROBBERY OR ASSAULT TO KILL ONE EVERY 33 SECONDS	ONE EVERY 26 MINUTES
FORCIBLE RAPE	AGGRAVATED ASSAULT	ROBBERY
ONE EVERY 10 MINUTES	ONE EVERY 70 SECONDS	ONE EVERY 71 SECONDS
BURGLARY	LARCENY-THEFT	MOTOR VEHICLE THEFT
ONE EVERY 10 SECONDS	ONE EVERY 6 SECONDS	ONE EVERY 32 SECONDS

CHART 1.1 FBI CHART

3. CRIME AND POPULATION

Crime rates relate the incidence of crime in population. A crime rate should be considered a victim risk rate in that it demonstrates the risk of becoming a victim of crime. See Chart #1.2.

CRIME AND POPULATION
1969 - 1974
PERCENT CHANGE OVER 1969

CRIME = CRIME INDEX OFFENSES
CRIME RATE = NUMBER OF OFFENSES PER 100,000 INHABITANTS

CRIME UP **38%**
CRIME RATE UP **32%**
POPULATION UP **5%**

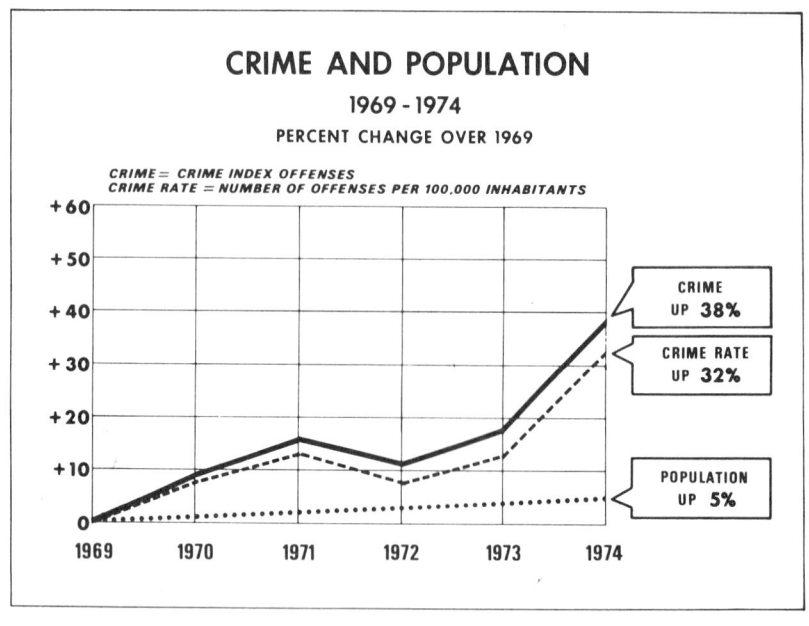

CHART 1.2   FBI CHART

The Crime Index rate of the United States in 1974, was nearly 5,000 per 100,000 inhabitants. This means that you have 1 chance in 20 of being a victim of a serious crime. The national crime rate, or the risk of being a victim of one of these crimes, has increased 32 percent since 1969. This rate is likely to rise at an accelerated pace during the mid 70's because of adverse economic conditions. Unless there is an intervention this crime problem is likely to grow. This is one of the underlying principles of this book.

The following two units contain many statistics on the crime problem in the United States. They are placed in the front of this work intentionally, because it is necessary to know the extent of the crime problem and some specifics about crime in order to combat it.

Once the reader has internalized the extent of the crime problem in the United States he could refer to the annual Uniform Crime Reports to see how his own community fares.

Only by a clear understanding of the extent of the crime problem will individuals involved in the criminal justice system be able to effectively master it.

4. SUMMARY

Everyone knows America is having acute crime problems. Before developing police operations and tactics to deal with the crime problem it is necessary to know more facts about crime.

First, the seriousness of the crime problem must be internalized. It is not enough just to "know" there is a lot of crime. It takes commitment on the part of the community and police to effectively deal with it. Secondly, we must identify the types of crime that are causing the problem. This becomes of paramount importance because, as you will see later, police resources are "spread too thin".

This unit then focuses in on the crimes that are the primary responsibility of the police—Part I Crimes.

Although police operations cannot affect all Part I Crimes equally because of the nature of the offense and location of occurrence, certain crimes can be dealt with effectively. Fortunately, these crimes, as you will see later, are crimes that cause much of the loss and fear in our society.

Author's note:
1974 crime statistics are used in this book for several reasons. First, they are the latest data to date. Secondly, 1974 crime statistics reflect the midpoint of the crime experience for this decade and provide a reasonable data base for the reader.

One fact remains. If nothing new is done about the crime problem, it will continue to deprive citizens of the right to "life, liberty and the pursuit of happiness".

5. QUESTIONS FOR DISCUSSION

1. How has the crime problem affected the quality of life in your neighborhood?
2. List the crimes that people fear most. Compare the list with the Part I Crimes and identify the types of crimes that are the responsibility of the police.
3. Since police resources (namely manpower and equipment) are limited, which crime would you attempt to control first if you were Chief? Why?
4. Arson and kidnapping are serious crimes but they are not listed among Part I Crimes. Why?
5. Explain the functions of the Crime Index in relation to the total crime problem.
6. Define "actual crime count" and "crime rate". Explain how a city with only a few crimes may be more dangerous than, say, New York.
7. Discuss the impact of the economy on crime during the mid 70's. What can the police do about it?

UNIT 2

PART I. OFFENSES—VIOLENT CRIMES

1. MURDER AND NON-NEGLIGENT MANSLAUGHTER

This Crime Index offense is defined in Uniform Crime Reporting as the willful killing of another. The classification of this

MURDER AND NONNEGLIGENT MANSLAUGHTER

WITH GUN

WITH CLUB

WITH KNIFE

WITH FISTS

COUNT ONE OFFENSE FOR EACH PERSON KILLED BY ANOTHER.

offense, as in all of the other Crime Index offenses, is based solely on police investigation as opposed to the determination of a court, medical examiner, coroner, jury, or other judicial body.

Deaths caused by negligence, suicide, accident, or justifiable homicide are not included in the count for this offense classification. Attempts to murder or assaults to murder are scored as aggravated assaults and not as murder.

A. MURDER VOLUME, TREND AND RATE

In 1974 there were over 20,000 murders committed in the United States.

An analysis of murder by month shows that the summer months had the greatest frequency of murder as compared to any other period of the year.

The number of murders increased 40 percent in the past five years. (Chart #2.1)

In 1974 there were 10 victims of murder for every 100,000 inhabitants in the Nation. This means you have about one chance in 10,000 of being killed this year. You should note that if you are male and live in an urban area your chances of being murdered increase tremendously.

B. NATURE OF MURDER

The law enforcement agencies which participate in Uniform Crime Reporting cooperate in providing additional information regarding homicide so that a more in-depth analysis of this offense can be made. Through a supplemental reporting system, information is provided regarding the age, sex, and race of the victim; the weapon used in the murder; and the circumstances surrounding the offense.

The victims of murder in 1974 were male in approximately three out of four instances. This ratio of male to female victims is similar to the experience in the last several years. Approximately 48 out of 100 murder victims were white, 50 were Negro and 2 percent other races.

Chart #2.2 shows a breakdown of weapons used in 1974 murders.

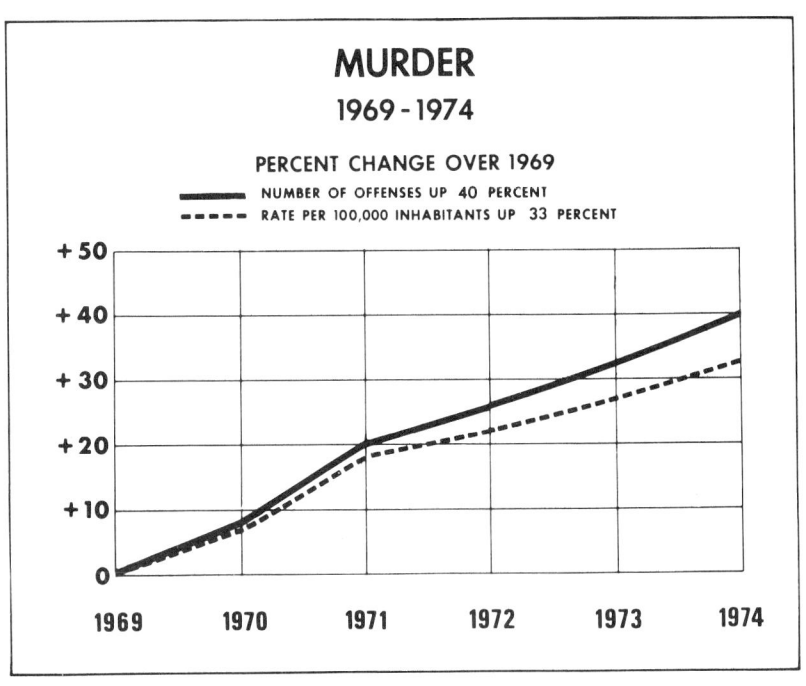

Unit 2   VIOLENT CRIMES   11

MURDER
1969-1974

PERCENT CHANGE OVER 1969
━━━ NUMBER OF OFFENSES UP 40 PERCENT
━ ━ ━ RATE PER 100,000 INHABITANTS UP 33 PERCENT

CHART 2.1   FBI CHART

MURDER
BY TYPE OF WEAPON USED
1974

Weapon	Percent
HANDGUN	54%
RIFLE	5%
SHOTGUN	9%
CUTTING OR STABBING	18%
OTHER WEAPON (CLUB, POISON, etc.)	7%
PERSONAL WEAPON (HANDS, FISTS, FEET, etc.)	8%

DUE TO ROUNDING, DOES NOT ADD TO 100%

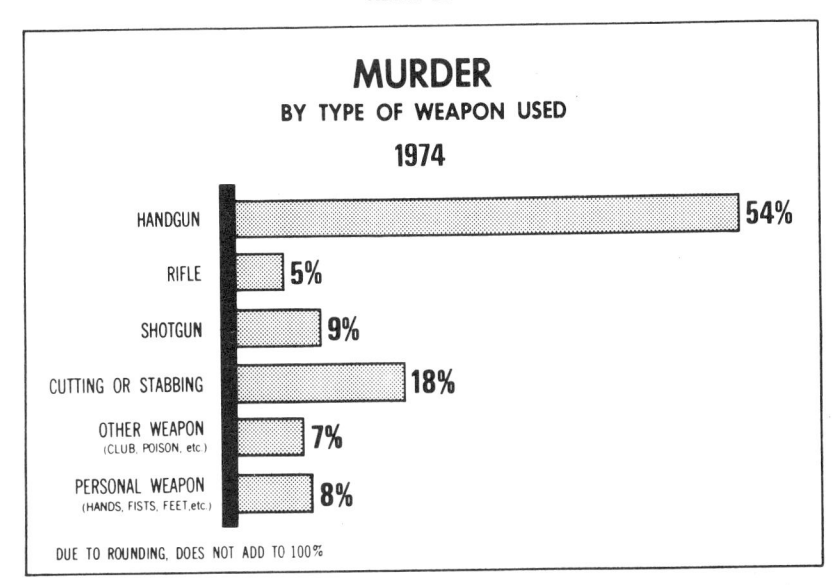

CHART 2.2   FBI CHART

Sutor Police Operations Cr.J.S.—3

C. MURDER CIRCUMSTANCES

The circumstances which result in murder vary from family arguments to felonious activities. Criminal homicide is largely a societal problem which is beyond the control of police. The circumstances of murder serve to emphasize this point. In 1974, murder within the family made up approximately one-fourth of all murder offenses. Over one-half of these family killings involved spouse killing spouse. The remainder were parents killing children and other in-family killings.

Felony murder in Uniform Crime reporting is defined as those killings resulting from robbery, sex motive, gangland slaying, and other felonious activities. Felony type and suspected felony type murders in 1974 constituted 28 percent of all murder, whereas these two categories accounted for 27 percent of total murder in 1969.

D. CLEARANCES *

Nationally, police continue to be successful in clearing or solving by arrest a greater percentage of homicides than any other Crime Index offense.

Since 1969, the clearance rate, nationwide, in homicide has decreased from 86 per 100 offenses to 80 per 100 offenses in 1974. Although the clearance rate is high, homicide is not the easiest crime to clear. The complainant and main witness is dead. The high clearance rate is the result of the large amount of police resources expended on this most serious of all crimes. This fact becomes of paramount importance in allocation of police resources dealt with later in this book.

* Clearance of a crime generally means identification and arrest of an offender. For a more detailed explanation of clearances refer to Unit 6 "Crime Reporting and Clearance".

Unit 2　　　　　　VIOLENT CRIMES　　　　　　13

E. MURDER PROJECTION

In March, 1974, the Massachusetts Institute of Technology released a study of murder in the 50 largest cities of the United States. Among the more startling findings are the following:

—A child born in 1974 has a slightly higher chance of being murdered than an American soldier had of being killed in World War II.

—The American murder rate, which doubled in the past eight years, may soon surpass the American auto accident fatality rate.

Table 2.1 lists your chances of becoming a murder victim in the nation's 50 largest cities. The cities are listed in order of murder

YOUR CHANCES OF GETTING MURDERED IN THE
NATION'S 50 LARGEST CITIES *

CITY & SIZE	Current Chances	Projected Chances
1. Atlanta (25)	28	11
2. Detroit (5)	35	14
3. Cleveland (10)	35	14
4. Newark (32)	37	15
5. Baltimore (7)	38	15
6. Washington, D. C. (9)	40	16
7. St. Louis (17)	40	16
8. Miami (39)	51	21
9. Birmingham (45)	52	21
10. Ft. Worth (30)	53	21
11. Dallas (8)	55	22
12. Houston (6)	56	23
13. New Orleans (18)	58	23
14. Oakland (36)	59	24
15. Louisville (35)	60	24
16. Chicago (2)	60	24
17. Philadelphia (4)	62	25
18. Tampa (47)	65	26

* M.I.T. Study.

YOUR CHANCES OF GETTING MURDERED IN THE NATION'S
50 LARGEST CITIES—Continued

CITY & SIZE	Current Chances	Projected Chances
19. New York (1)	67	27
20. Memphis (16)	78	31
21. Kansas City (24)	79	32
22. Boston (15)	79	32
23. Denver (23)	81	33
24. Los Angeles (3)	82	33
25. Cincinnati (27)	82	33
26. San Antonio (13)	89	35
27. Buffalo (26)	91	36
28. Norfolk (44)	104	42
29. San Francisco (12)	106	42
30. Akron (49)	108	43
31. Long Beach (37)	113	45
32. Oklahoma City (34)	113	45
33. Columbus (20)	114	46
34. Phoenix (19)	117	47
35. Pittsburgh (22)	123	49
36. Rochester (46)	133	53
37. Tulsa (40)	139	56
38. Honolulu (41)	139	56
39. Minneapolis (29)	158	63
40. Toledo (31)	165	66
41. Seattle (21)	170	67
42. Milwaukee (71)	179	71
43. Omaha (38)	195	78
44. Portland (Ore.) (33)	198	79
45. Tucson (50)	229	91
46. St. Paul (43)	232	92
47. Wichita (48)	241	96
48. San Diego (14)	276	110
49. San Jose (28)	279	111
50. El Paso (42)	322	128

TABLE 2.1

Unit 2 VIOLENT CRIMES 15

rates, most dangerous cities first, safest cities last. The number in parentheses after the name of each city indicates its relative size; thus, New York is (1) and Tucson is (50). Current chances: indicates the odds of a child born today would stand one chance in 28 of being murdered some day during its expected lifetime. Projected chances: indicates the odds of a child born now of being murdered if the murder rate in that city continues to increase at its current rate.

2. FORCIBLE RAPE

Forcible rape, as defined under Uniform Crime Report is the carnal knowledge of a female through the use of force or the threat of force. Assaults to commit forcible rape are also included; however, statutory rape (without force) is not counted in this category.

A. RAPE VOLUME, TREND AND RATE

During 1974 there were over 55,000 forcible rapes reported to police.

The volume of forcible rape offenses in 1974 increased 49 percent over 1969. See Chart #2.3.

A crime rate, in its proper perspective, is a victim risk rate since it equates the number of crimes per unit of population. Rape, however, is measured by offenses per 100,000 females. In 1974, 51 out of every 100,000 females in this country were reported rape victims.

B. NATURE OF RAPE OFFENSES

In 1974, 74 percent of all forcible rape offenses were actual rapes by force while the remainder were attempts or assaults to commit forcible rape. This offense is a violent crime against the person, and of all the Crime Index offenses, law enforcement administrators recognize this offense as the most under-reported crimes due primarily to fear and/or embarrassment on the part of the victims. As a national average, 15 percent of all forcible

16 THE CRIME PROBLEM Sec. 1

FORCIBLE RAPE
1969 - 1974

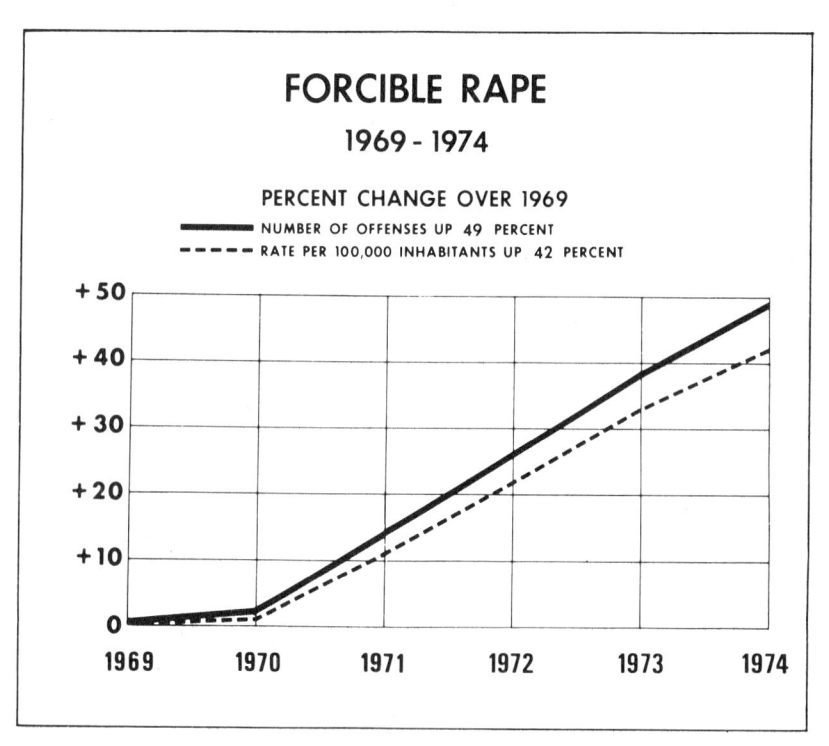

PERCENT CHANGE OVER 1969
— NUMBER OF OFFENSES UP 49 PERCENT
- - - - RATE PER 100,000 INHABITANTS UP 42 PERCENT

CHART 2.3   FBI CHART

RAPE LOCATIONS

28%	Victim's home
18%	Outside (not auto or abandoned building)
12.8%	Auto
12%	Rapist's home
8%	Abandoned building
8%	House known to offender/victim
6%	Public building—school, museum, etc.
5%	Other

Source: A study of 150 rape cases, between November 1972 and January 1973 treated at Philadelphia General Hospital, completed by the Center for Rape Concern.

CHART 2.4

Unit 2　VIOLENT CRIMES

rapes reported to police were determined by investigation to be unfounded. In other words, the police established that no forcible or attempted rape occurred. This is caused primarily due to the question of whether the use of threat of force occurred and is often complicated by a prior relationship between victim and offender. This fact becomes a particularly important consideration in use of police firearms to apprehend suspected rapists.

Most rapes occur away from the streets. Therefore, this crime is not as "repressible" as robbery, burglary or auto theft. See Chart #2.4 for locations of rapes. Studies of rape have shown that most rapists (82 percent) don't stray from their own neighborhoods to seek out victims.

3. ROBBERY

Robbery is a vicious type of crime which takes place in the presence of the victim to obtain property or a thing of value from a person by use of force or threat of force. Assault to commit

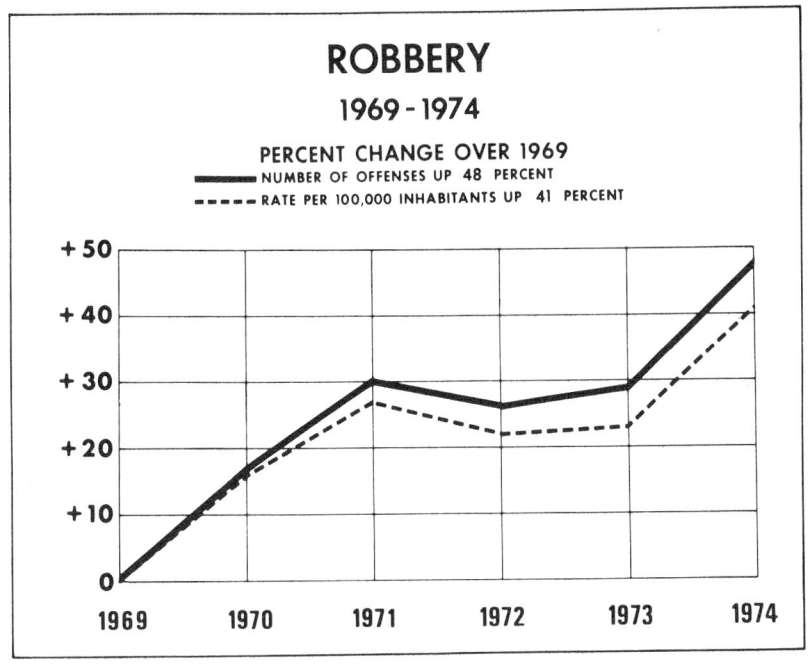

ROBBERY
1969 - 1974
PERCENT CHANGE OVER 1969
—— NUMBER OF OFFENSES UP 48 PERCENT
- - - - RATE PER 100,000 INHABITANTS UP 41 PERCENT

CHART 2.5　　　　FBI CHART

robbery and attempts are included in this category. This is a violent crime and frequently results in injury to the victim. For purposes of crime reporting information concerning robbery is collected in cases of armed robbery where any weapon is used, and strong-arm robbery where no weapon is used. The latter category includes crimes such as mugging.

ROBBERY
CLASSIFICATION 3

BANK

MUGGING

STICK-UP

PURSE-SNATCHING with force

COUNT ONE OFFENSE FOR EACH DISTINCT OPERATION.

Unit 2 VIOLENT CRIMES 19

A. ROBBERY VOLUME, TREND AND RATE

There were over 400,000 robbery offenses committed in the United States in 1974. Robbery occurs most frequently during the month of December.

Since 1969, robbery has increased 48 percent for a current rate of 209 victims per 100,000 inhabitants. (See Chart #2.5)

Robbery is primarily a large city crime. American cities with more than 250,000 inhabitants accounted for two-thirds of all robberies which occurred in the United States during 1974.

B. NATURE OF ROBBERY

Supplemental robbery information is obtained from cities as a part of the monthly collection of statistical data under the Uniform Crime Reporting Program. In 1974, these figures disclosed that half of the robberies were committed in the street. This will become significant later, when we consider tactics to combat the problem.

The 1969-1974 trends in robbery by type, as illustrated by the following (Chart #2.6) show that chain stores have the largest increase (184 percent). These facts become very important in selecting likely robbery targets for police coverage.

Armed perpetrators were responsible for about two-thirds of robbery offenses while one-third were muggings or other violent confrontations where personal weapons were used by the offender to subdue or overcome the victim.

The full impact of violent crime on the victim cannot be completely measured in terms of dollar loss alone. While the object of the attack is money or property, many victims of the mugger and the strong-arm robber, as well as the armed robber, suffer death or serious personal injury as a result of the attack. Na-

20 THE CRIME PROBLEM Sec. 1

tionally it is estimated that about 10 percent of all willful homicides result from robbery attempts. You can find your local robbery-murder ratio by dividing the known robbery murder cases into the total number of robberies reported.

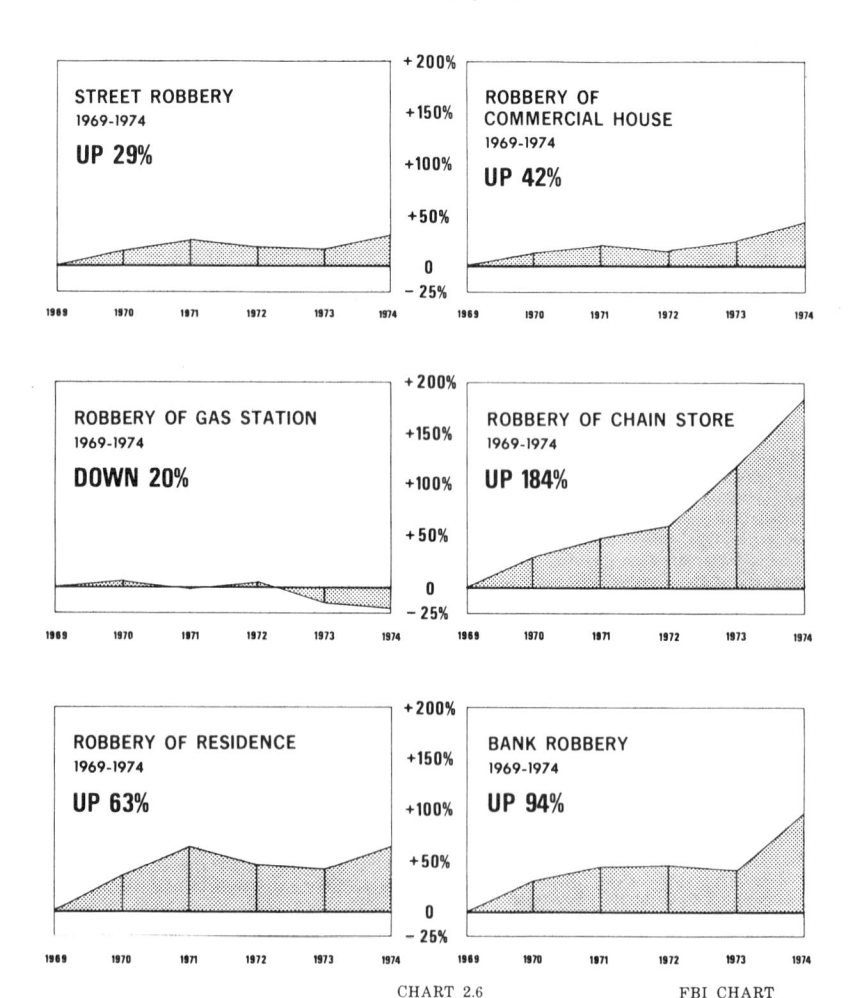

STREET ROBBERY
1969-1974
UP 29%

ROBBERY OF COMMERCIAL HOUSE
1969-1974
UP 42%

ROBBERY OF GAS STATION
1969-1974
DOWN 20%

ROBBERY OF CHAIN STORE
1969-1974
UP 184%

ROBBERY OF RESIDENCE
1969-1974
UP 63%

BANK ROBBERY
1969-1974
UP 94%

CHART 2.6 FBI CHART

C. ROBBERY CLEARANCES

In 1974, law enforcement agencies were successful in clearing 27 percent of the robbery offenses reported.

D. PERSONS ARRESTED FOR ROBBERY

Since robbery is the most frequently repeated crime, increased arrests for robbery has great potential for lowering robbery rates by removing those who continually rob the community.

Examination of arrest data discloses that 76 percent of the persons arrested for robbery were under 25 years of age, and 56 percent were under 21 years of age. Of all persons arrested for robbery, 34 percent were under the age of 18. This greater proportion of youthful arrests, compared to clearances, is accounted for in part by the fact the young age offenders frequently act in groups. Robbery arrests for this young age group and for females have been increasing during recent years. This information is being offered to help you in knowing likely robbery suspects. The more you know about particular criminals the better your "probable cause" in arresting them.

The extent of the robbery problem in United States cities can best be demonstrated by a comparison of robbery statistics of foreign cities. (See Chart #2.7)

Compare the robbery count of U. S. cities with foreign cities of similiar size. Granted, there are many cultural and sociological differences between cities, but can these explain the vast amount of crime suffered by U. S. cities? It seems reasonably sure that foreign criminal justice systems are functioning better than our own. Let's look at it from the robbers point of view. If you were a robber, where would you rather be caught—In Detroit or Hamburg?—In New York or Tokyo? Chances are, if you are not a masochist, you would rather be captured here. The legal "loopholes" are larger and the sanctions are not as severe.

As you progress through this book you will find that police cannot do much about the sanctions, but they can minimize the

ROBBERIES IN LARGE CITIES

CITY	YEAR	POPULATION	NUMBER OF ROBBERIES	ROBBERIES PER 100,000 PERSONS
BERLIN	1969	2,100,000	669	32
CHICAGO	1972	3,367,000	23,531	699
DETROIT	1972	1,511,000	17,170	1,136
HAMBURG	1972	1,780,000	1,363	77
LONDON	1970	7,379,014	2,372	32
MANILA	1970	1,330,788	3,190	240
NEW YORK	1972	7,895,000	78,202	991
TOKYO	1970	8,800,000	472	5
TORONTO	1970	2,300,000	1,374	60
VIENNA	1970	1,600,000	275	17

CHART 2.7

effect of the legal "loopholes" that are largely responsible for "revolving-door justice". As far as criminals go, this can best be achieved by "catching-them-in-the-act". Later chapters will be concerned with precisely how to accomplish this task.

4. AGGRAVATED ASSAULT

Aggravated assault is defined as an unlawful attack by one person upon another for the purpose of inflicting severe bodily injury usually accompanied by the use of weapons or other means likely to produce death or serious bodily harm. Attempts are included since it is not necessary that an injury result when a gun, knife, or other weapon is used which could and probably would result in serious personal injury if the crime were successfully completed.

A. AGGRAVATED ASSAULT VOLUME AND TREND

In calendar year 1974, there were over 450,000 assaults in the Nation.

Unit 2 VIOLENT CRIMES 23

The volume of aggravated assault offenses increased 47 percent over 1969. (See Chart #2.8)

B. NATURE OF AGGRAVATED ASSAULT

Most aggravated assaults occur within the family unit, and among neighbors or acquaintances. The victim-offender relationship, as well as the nature of the attack makes this crime similar to murder.

C. AGGRAVATED ASSAULT CLEARANCES

Law enforcement agencies were successful in solving 63 of each 100 cases of aggravated assault in 1974. This relatively high solution rate is consistent with high solution rates in other

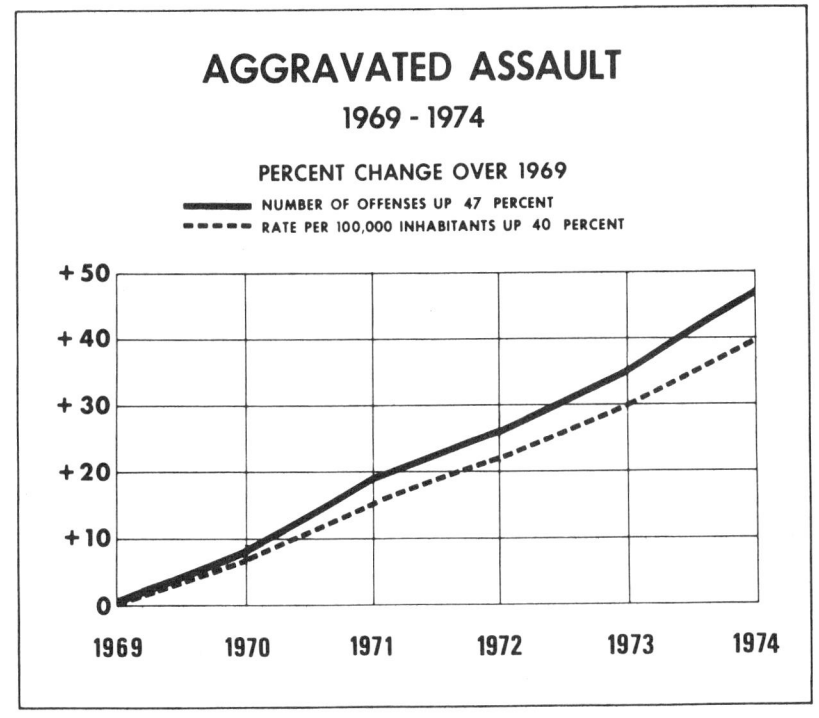

AGGRAVATED ASSAULT
1969 - 1974

PERCENT CHANGE OVER 1969
——— NUMBER OF OFFENSES UP 47 PERCENT
- - - - RATE PER 100,000 INHABITANTS UP 40 PERCENT

CHART 2.8 FBI CHART

crimes against the person. Due to the nature of these crimes, arrests are frequently made upon the response of patrol units. This type of patrol call is hazardous to the officer. Since 1965, 149 officers have lost their lives responding to disturbance-type call, which frequently involve family or neighborhood arguments. (Refer to Unit 4 for more information on police victims.)

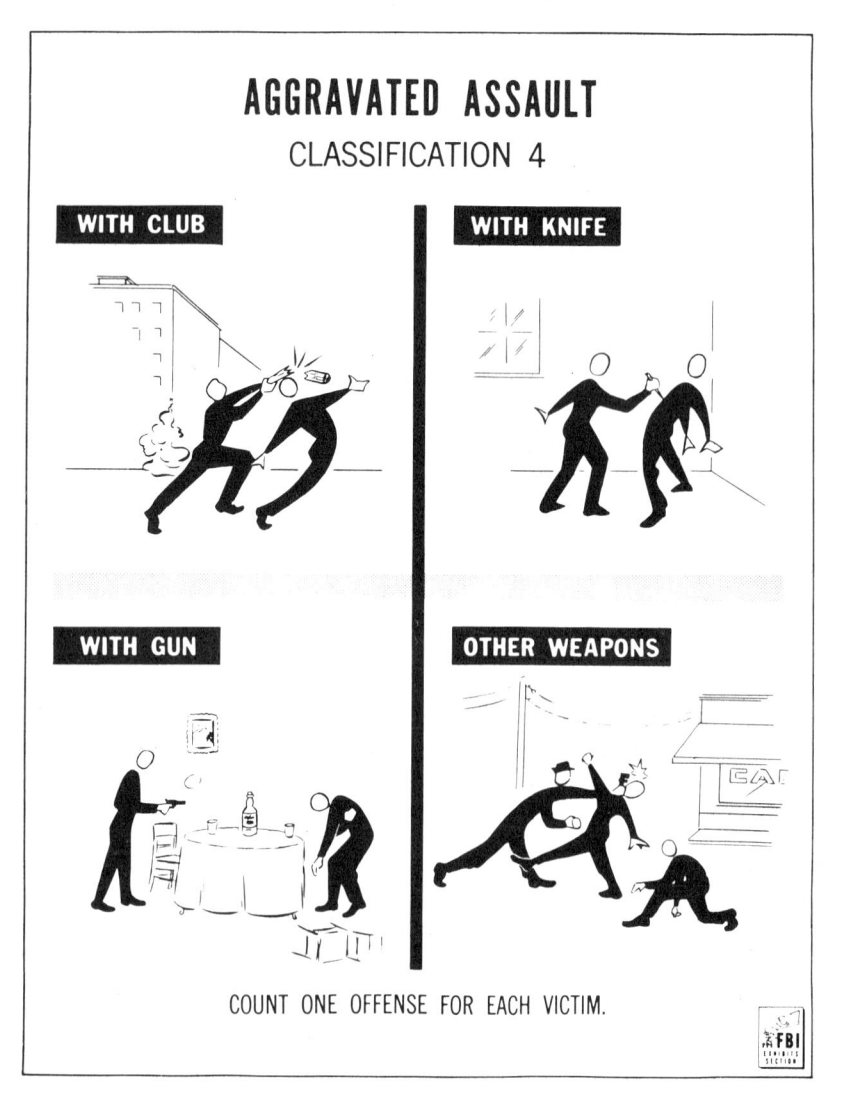

5. SUMMARY

Murder heads the list of Part I Offenses because it is the most serious of all crimes. In reality, murder is actually a theft. A theft of an individual's most cherished possession—his life.

Twenty thousand people will be celebrating New Year's Eve this year and will not be around to do so next year. They will be prematurely deprived of their right to live. How long can our society tolerate this condition?

If you are male, black, and live in an urban area (or any combination of the above) your chances of being murdered increase tremendously.

Many murders occur within families. It has been estimated that as many as 70 percent of the victims knew their attacker. Because of the nature and locale of this crime it is difficult for the police to "repress" them. Murder is largely a sociological problem.

Felony murder, generally between strangers and on the streets or in public places, are the responsibility of the police. A little less than a third of the 20,000 murders a year are felony type murders.

Although the crime of murder has one of the highest clearance rates, (about 80% solved) it is not the easiest crime to solve. The main witness/complainant (the victim) cannot talk or identify the doer. The high clearance rates results from the extensive police resources applied to the problem. This writer is of the opinion that other crimes such as robbery could have similar high clearance rates given the level police resources applied to murder.

Rape rates second only to murder in seriousness. Rape is usually often accompanied by injury and far reaching trauma for the victim. Although over 50,000 rapes are reported to police annually it is one of the most underreported crimes due to fear and/or embarrassment on the part of the victim.

Rape is only moderately repressible because of the nature and locale of the offense. One fact helpful in combatting rape is that statistics have shown that most rapists don't stray from their own neighborhoods to seek out victims.

Refer to Unit 18 for additional details on combatting rape.

Robbery is the highest crime in the hierarchy of Part I Offenses that "belongs" to the police. Robbery is a repressible crime occurring on the streets or places readily accessible to police.

Since robbery is a vicious type crime that often results in injury or death, it deserves considered attention by police. Robbery is a good point to start your anti-crime program. Less than a third of the annual 400,000 robberies reported to police are solved. The police operations and tactics that follow throughout this book are primarily directed against the crime of robbery.

The 400,000 aggravated assaults reported to police each year have a high clearance rate (63%) consistant with crimes against the person. However, this crime is similar to homicide in nature and locale. Thus it is generally not repressible.

6. QUESTIONS FOR DISCUSSION

1. Define the crime of murder and the extent of the problem in your area.
2. How does "felony-type" murders differ from other murders in this crime category? What are the implications for police?
3. Who are the most likely victims of murder? Why?
4. Explain the seasonal effect on the incidence of murder.
5. Is murder "repressible" by police? Explain.
6. Why does murder enjoy a high clearance rate (80%)? Can other crimes be cleared at the same rate?
7. Examine the list of cities in table 2.1. Where does your city (or nearest city) stand? Discuss the relationship of your area with others on the list.

8. How is the rape rate established? Utilizing the appendices compare your local rate with the national rate.
9. Consider the nature and locale of rape and assess its "repressibility" by police.
10. How do you explain the great differences between the robbery rates of Tokyo, Japan and New York?
11. What is the extent of the robbery problem in your community?
12. How can the crime of robbery be reduced?
13. Can police affect the rate of aggravated assaults? Discuss.

UNIT 3

PART I. OFFENSES—CRIMES AGAINST PROPERTY

I. BURGLARY

The Uniform Crime Reporting Program defines burglary as the unlawful entry of a structure to commit a felony or theft, even though no force was used to gain entry. The offense of burglary is broken down into three sub-classifications: forcible entry, unlawful entry where no force is used, and attempted forcible entry.

A. BURGLARY VOLUME AND TREND

Over 3,000,000 burglaries occurred during 1974.

The five year trend, 1969–1974, indicates burglary offenses have risen 53 percent during the period. (See Chart #3.1)

B. NATURE OF BURGLARY

Burglary is generally accepted as a crime of stealth and opportunity. It is committed by both amateurs and professionals. Although burglary rates are expressed in the number of burglaries per 100,000 in population, it is very helpful to develop your local burglary rate in terms of burglaries per 1,000 premises. This reflects the fact that buildings are burglarized, not people.

Daytime burglaries of residences accounted for over half of the residential burglaries. Considering the period 1969–1974, there has been an increase of 67 percent in the volume of daytime residential burglaries.

Prevention and detection of the burglary offense poses a most difficult problem to law enforcement. Volume alone is an overriding factor, particularly as related to the number of officers available for this type investigation. Viewed as a group, nighttime burglary represents 61 percent of all burglaries.

Unit 3 CRIMES AGAINST PROPERTY 29

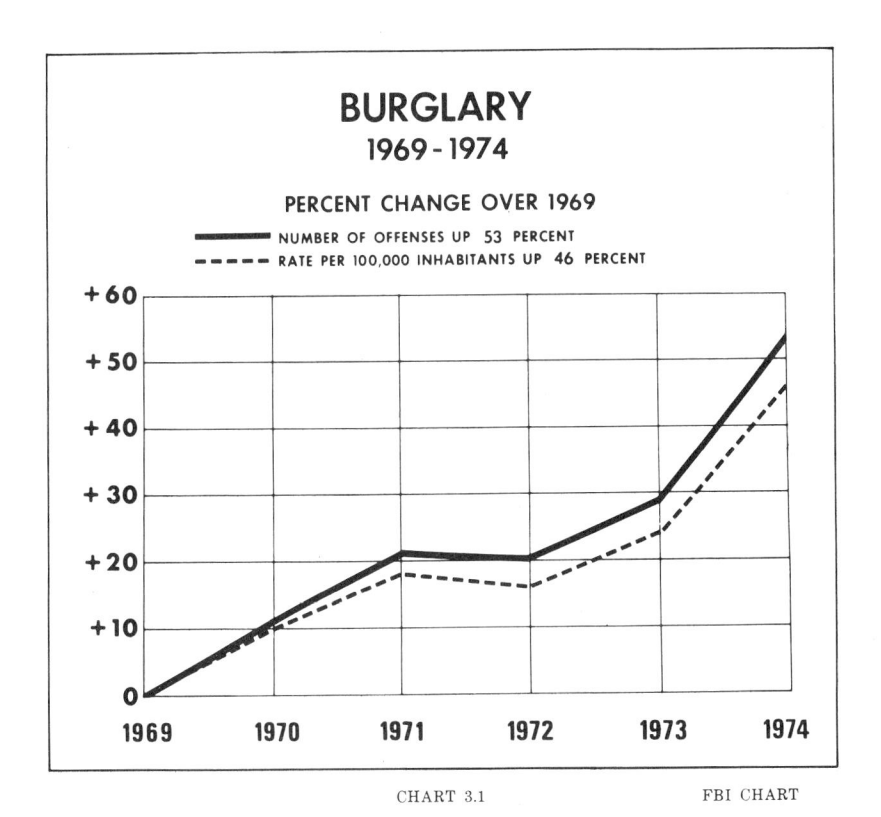

BURGLARY
1969-1974

PERCENT CHANGE OVER 1969
— NUMBER OF OFFENSES UP 53 PERCENT
----- RATE PER 100,000 INHABITANTS UP 46 PERCENT

CHART 3.1   FBI CHART

C. BURGLARY CLEARANCES

As suggested earlier, burglary is a crime of stealth. This characteristic tends to make the detection of the perpetrator more difficult. In 1974 law enforcement was successful in clearing 18 percent of the total burglary offenses. Alarm systems can be a valuable police tool in combating this crime.

30   THE CRIME PROBLEM   Sec. 1

BURGLARY
CLASSIFICATION 5

FORCE

PASSKEY

OPEN DOOR

WAREHOUSE NO. 4

SAFECRACKING

COUNT ONE OFFENSE FOR EACH DISTINCT OPERATION.

2. LARCENY—THEFT

Larceny-theft is the unlawful taking or stealing of property or articles of value without the use of force, violence, or fraud. It

Unit 3   CRIMES AGAINST PROPERTY   31

includes crimes such as shoplifting, pocket-picking, purse-snatching, thefts from auto, thefts of auto parts and accessories, bicycle thefts, etc. In the Uniform Crime Reporting Program this crime category does not include embezzlement, "con" games, forgery, and worthless checks. Auto theft, of course, is excluded from this category for crime reporting purposes inasmuch as it is a separate Crime Index offense.

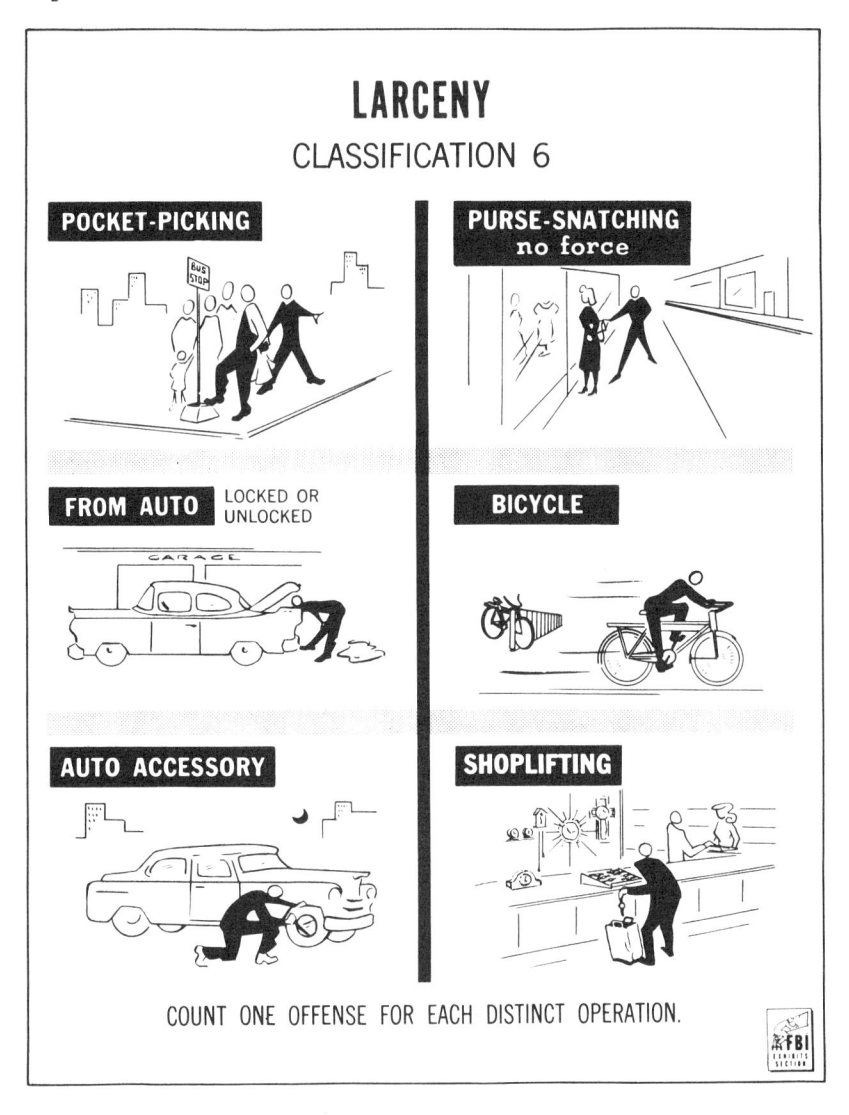

LARCENY
CLASSIFICATION 6

POCKET-PICKING

PURSE-SNATCHING no force

FROM AUTO LOCKED OR UNLOCKED

BICYCLE

AUTO ACCESSORY

SHOPLIFTING

COUNT ONE OFFENSE FOR EACH DISTINCT OPERATION.

FBI

A. LARCENY VOLUME AND TREND

In 1974 there were over 5,000,000 offenses of larceny-theft. From a seasonal standpoint, the volume of larceny is highest during the summer months.

Nationwide this offense has increased 35 percent since 1969.

B. NATURE OF LARCENY—THEFT

Many offenses in this category, particularly where the value of the solen goods is small, never come to police attention.

Cities and suburban areas appear to have similar experience except for pocket-picking and purse-snatching which are considerably less in suburban areas. Although purse-snatching should be counted under the larceny section for Uniform Crime Report purposes, it should be dealt with as robbery for tactical purposes.

The nature of larceny, a crime of opportunity, sneak thievery, and petty unobserved thefts, makes it an extremely difficult offense for law enforcement officers to solve.

3. AUTO THEFT

In Uniform Crime Reporting, auto theft is defined as the unlawful taking or stealing of a motor vehicle, including attempts. This definition excludes taking for temporary use by those persons having lawful access to the vehicle.

A. AUTO THEFT VOLUME AND TREND

In 1974, nearly one million motor vehicles were reported stolen.

The number of auto thefts has increased 11 percent since 1969.

B. NATURE OF AUTO THEFT

Auto theft rates again clearly indicate that this crime is primarily an urban problem, since the highest rates appear in the

Unit 3　　CRIMES AGAINST PROPERTY　　33

most heavily populated sections of the Nation. Since stolen vehicles are used in many other Part I Crimes, it is important to concentrate anti-crime efforts on auto theft.

AUTO THEFT
CLASSIFICATION 7

FOR USE IN OTHER CRIME

FOR TRANSPORTATION

FOR JOY RIDE

FOR SALE OR STRIP

COUNT ONE OFFENSE FOR EACH AUTO STOLEN.

4. SUMMARY

"A man's home is his castle". But not to the friendly neighborhood burglar.

Over 3 million burglaries occur each year in the United States. Only about 18% of burglaries are cleared (solved) by police. Burglary poses a most difficult problem for police because of its volume and the fact that it is a crime of stealth. Once the robbery problem is brought under control the burglary problem should be targeted for corrective police action. Because of the nature and locale of the offense, burglary falls in the "repressible" crime category.

Unit 23 (Tactical Approaches To Burglary) discusses methods of controlling burglary.

Larceny is the largest volume offense with over 4 million reported annually in the United States. Larceny is generally not "repressible" because of the nature and locale of the theft. However, some larcenies such as purse snatching "belong" to the police. Purse snatching should be handled as a street robbery when applying police tactics to the problem.

Other larcenies, particularly from autos or public places, can be effectively combatted by police.

About a million vehicles a year are reported stolen throughout the United States. Because of the nature and locale of the crime it is highly susceptible to police opertaions. However, the clearance rate is generally low (about 16%).

Juveniles are responsible for a large portion of auto thefts and any police program designed to combat this problem should take this into consideration.

Other reasons for combatting the crime of auto theft is that frequently the stolen vehicles are used in other crimes and death or personal injury results from crashes of stolen autos.

Unit 24 (Tactical Approaches To Auto Theft) discusses methods of controlling auto theft.

5. QUESTIONS FOR DISCUSSION

1. Why do crimes against property have a lower clearance rate than crimes against persons?
2. Define the crime of burglary and discuss how it differs from the crime of robbery? When does a crime of burglary become a robbery?
3. If you were Chief, how would you go about lowering crimes against property? Which crime would you deal with first? Why?
4. Discuss the nature of burglary, larceny and auto theft and their "repressibility" by police.
5. List several kinds of larceny and explain the nature of the crimes.
6. Why is it important for police to lower the auto theft problem?
7. Who is responsible for stealing cars? Why?
8. Discuss the role of the community in lowering crimes against property.
9. Consider the effects of crime against property and your homeowners and auto insurance policies.
10. What is the largest problem involving crimes against property in your community?

UNIT 4
VICTIMS

Statistics often do not reflect the human loss and tragedy involved in the crime problem. It is hard to relate to a "crime clock" and we have been numbed by the media's use of numerical "body counts" during Viet Nam War reporting of the past decade. Perhaps a couple of case histories by Philadelphia Bulletin columnist Adrian Lee will bring the statistics into "real world" focus. They are not stories of famous cases such as the "Manson family" murders and "Zebra" killings in California or "Speck's" murder of eight nurses in Illinois. However, they are stories of the everyday tragedies occurring in our crime infested urban areas and they are truly representative of the "real world" as our citizens endure it.

I. THE CASE OF MRS. SLAWNYK

Mrs. Eva Slawnyk's luck ran out the same day Governor Wallace's did. Not to the sound of gunfire. Mrs. Slawnyk's luck ran out with absolute finality. Beaten and robbed seven days before, she died. Wallace didn't.

There wasn't any big commotion over Mrs. Slawnyk's death. Where's the big story in odds and ends like these. An aging immigrant woman trying to exercise the pain of a broken hip with feverish whisperings in an obscure Polish-Russian dialect. She was born, she bore four sons to her husband, a $35-a-week slaughterhouse worker. And she died.

She caught rainwater in six mayonnaise jars in back of her house at 3006 N. Franklin St., and when the jars were full she poured the water on her flowers.

"She said it was 'water from Heaven,' " one of her sons said. But then again, he said maybe she was just trying to save money—"she was careful; we didn't have much."

Mrs. Slawnyk's name shows up just one place the day Wallace was shot; it was Item Three on the Log of Outstanding Events that Philadelphia Police Commissioner O'Neill gets every day. SLAWNYK, EVA, 76—sandwiched in between "holdup inside bar" and "prisoners processed this tour of duty." It reads: "Dead from injuries received 5/8/72 . . 8th and Indiana, strongarm robbery."

If the entry wasn't commonplace, it was still routine for a changing neighborhood where flowering windowboxes and scrubbed steps alternate with broken windows stuffed with rags. Mrs. Slawnyk died just as Wallace was being stitched up after emergency surgery.

A coincidence to make a headline? Hardly . . . But wait a bit. Follow Mrs. Slawnyk the day she was beaten and robbed of $309. Ponder then whether she wasn't being stalked by violence just as surely as Wallace was. She didn't have the protection Wallace had—the massive, shoulder-high lectern, assembled from pieces of an old safe, the small army of Secret Service agents.

If it had taken that, all of it, to deliver her to her door safely, then she was entitled to it, right down to the last pound of iron, the last Secret Service man.

HER RIGHT TO LIVE and safety on the street was just as valid as Wallace's or anybody else's.

Mrs. Slawnyk was alone when she left the Philadelphia Saving Fund Society branch at 11th and Lehigh, no iron shield, no sharpshooters with telescopic sights manning the rooftops. The only precaution she took against robbers and purse-snatchers—the only precaution she could think of—seems almost pitiful. She stuffed the $309 down the front of her blue-flowered print dress.

She didn't carry a purse or package of any kind; her hands were empty. There was nothing to mark out the small, gray-haired woman with rimless glasses as a "good hit." Women don't like to carry purses "around here any more," said her son.

For a fast walker, it is 13½ minutes from the bank to the Slawnyk house. For a woman of Mrs. Slawnyk's age, it would ordinarily be more. But with fear to hurry her on, she could walk the five blocks in less than 15 minutes, her husband John, 71 said.

A quarter of the way home—about 12 minutes from the front door—she passed the Thomas A. Edison High School. The windows and doors are covered with enough heavy steel mesh to suggest a whole gray granite building sheathed in wire. It is here police pick up and later release a 17-year-old suspect in the beating and robbery to come.

EIGHT MINUTES—the rotting elm tree. It probably turned her throat dry, making it difficult to swallow the sudden fear which lodged like a lump behind the purple buttons at the neck of her dress. It was here her husband was beaten and robbed, on the same errand last July.

The robber's hand went unerringly that day to Slawnyk's shirt, ripped it open and snatched the $187 rolled up inside. Lying on his back in the litter of broken glass and trash around the tree, his chest hurting from the robber's fist, Slawnyk wrapped both arms around the trunk to hoist himself to his feet. He swayed a moment under the detached gaze of two men sitting on a doorstep and stumbled home.

THREE MINUTES—a rusting Turn-of-the-Century touch of elegance: a first-floor bay window stamped out of tin, with brown paint peeling from embossed floral wreaths and garlanded columns. Mrs. Slawnyk hurries on, pulling her coat around her. It is chilly, 61 degrees, cloudy, with a threat of rain.

FIFTY SECONDS, give or take a second or two—the house was a short block and two doors away. If Mrs. Slawnyk heard the footsteps behind her, she didn't say so later.

An arm came around her neck, a hand across her mouth. She was thrown to the ground, kicked. Her dress was torn open the way her husband's shirt was. The money was taken. Like her husband, she struggled to her feet, broken hip and all, groping instinctively for her house, the flower pots, the rainwater, the worn, glassless bric-a-brac cabinet with the china inside; a white slipper with a gilded bow, a cat no bigger than a thimble, a rooster with a brilliant red comb.

It was about 10 a m, May 8 and Mrs. Slawnyk's luck had run out in the city her husband described as an "important place—we came here from Poland, and I got right away a job, too."

2. THE CASE OF MR. RAUER

Here are four numbers—3262, 1632, 671 and 3249. There is no particular significance to the order in which they come. As to whether they add up to anything important, you shall be the judge.

The first number, 3262, was prefixed to Edward Rauer's name when he was taken to the morgue ten days ago, dead of a 12-gauge shotgun blast in the back of the neck. His wife, Joyce, 28, didn't know he was dead until the phone rang at 5:10 a m, in their $122-a month Mafair apartment—the Medical Examiner's Office calling: ". . . we got a Rauer here, 35 years old, cab driver, killed in Mt. Airy."

The voice faded into a metallic scratching. Only the S-sounds, the sibilance, were audible to Mrs. Rauer now as she huddled in the chair she had stumbled to.

The red bedside phone dangled at the end of its white cord on the far side of the room. She rocked to and fro: he had always boasted he could "talk himself out of any situation . . if they get in the cab talking rough, I make 'em friends before they get out . . ."

By the bed, the phone was still talking. There was a last flurry of scratchings: ". . . take this number, call police; come on down at 9 a m and identify him . . . click"; the ME's Office had hung up.

Slender, red-haired Mrs. Rauer was alone with the splat-splat of Hurricane Agnes against the tank-shaped basement apartment's only windowpane. The pane was high up in the front wall, to clear the ground, and now at 5:15 a m, to catch the first watery light of a gray, rainswept day.

The Rauers' only child, Dawn, seven, was still asleep. Standing guard at the foot of her bed was the silent sentinel she had left there the day before—a hollow white-plastic dog with a slot in the back for the pennies her father saved from his taxi fares.

In the sideboard were unpaid bills totaling $1,100 for furniture, mail-order bedsheets and pillow cases. Still to come was the last bill, some $1,600 for Rauer's funeral, his grave and the gray coffin he was buried in.

Next number—Pennsylvania House of Representatives bill No. 1632.

It would establish a Crime Victim's Compensation Board, to determine the dollar value of a widow's "emotional hurt," total her unpaid bills, measure the financial support she lost with her husband's murder.

In the proper, lawyerlike language the General Assembly esteems, 1632 tells the board to "swear witnesses, subpoena police records, hold hearings," in making awards of $10,000, $15,000 and up.

But not a dime for Mrs. Rauer.

The bill opens up a whole new vista of patronage for job-famished politicians: the hiring of clerks, stenographers and other jobs the board might "need" and imaginative politicians might devise. It takes care of attorneys; one of the board's first chores is defining a "proper" legal fee for representing applicants for the board's largesse.

As for Mrs. Rauer, her husband got killed too soon; the bill isn't retroactive, as the legislators say. It doesn't reach back to the shotgun blast in Mt. Airy.

Which brings up the third number, No. 671, is loaded with retroactivity. Not for the victims of crimes, but the perpetrators. In this instance, Jones, the appellant in No. 671, sentenced to life for murder in 1930 by a Lancaster County jury.

His sentence was commuted in 1952; he was paroled, jailed again for pulling a gun in an argument, paroled a second time, and again locked up—this time for assault with intent to kill.

But Jones still hadn't exhausted the patience of the Pennsylvania courts.

Acting in February on his last bid for freedom, the Supreme Court reached back 42 years to order another review of his original murder conviction: intervening U. S. Supreme Court rulings not only "warranted" but "mandated" it!

In all this outpouring of retroactivity, sure to reach a torrent with the U. S. Supreme Court ruling on capital punishment, there ought to be some left over for Mrs. Rauer and her child.

The last of the four numbers, 3249, is added by way of postscript. It doesn't change any of the foregoing or, perhaps, even add to it. But it does help illuminate the Rauer apartment for all to see.

No. 3249 was chalked on a paper sack, the kind supermarkets bag groceries in. It sagged with the weight of a blue blazer in brass buttons, a pair of brown chino pants, shoes, underclothes. Mrs. Rauer looked at it listlessly: ". . . the undertaker said it was his clothes; it isn't. Seeing them, I thought for a minute he was still alive."

3. VICTIMIZATION OF INNER CITY RESIDENTS

It took the National Commission on Causes and Prevention of Violence an uncommonly long time to restate what has been common knowledge among law enforcement officials for years, that blacks are arrested much more frequently for violent crimes than whites.

Still, the actual statistics are alarming. According to the commission, blacks are arrested 18 times as often as whites for murder, 12 times as often for forcible rape, 10 times as often for aggravated assault and 16 times as often for robbery.

Like previous reports, this one put the blame for crime and violence on social and economic conditions under which people in the slums are forced to live. And it called for a total effort toward the changing of "demoralizing conditions and life patterns of Negroes, the unequal opportunity and discrimination they confront, and the overcrowding and decay of the urban ghettos."

Had it stopped there, this newest report might not have warranted the time and space—2,436 pages—it required. But it went on to one highly significant point that whites often overlook; that is, that the victims of black crimes are usually blacks, too.

With the exception of robbery, about 70 percent of the victims of violent crimes are blacks. In respect to crimes committed by blacks, 90 percent of the victims are also black.

Crime, thus, is not only a result of slums, it usually occurs in slums, and one of its most fearsome by-products is in causing law-abiding citizens there to lose faith in authority.

To the extent that whites brush aside the crime figures, saying the blacks themselves must solve their problems, society is playing into the hands of terrorists who aim to drive the police away to gain a clear field for their dirty work.

Neglect of slum conditions only brings more crime, and crime brings more polarization and thus neglect. It is a vicious circle, one requiring corrective action.

4. VICTIMIZATION BY THE CRIMINAL JUSTICE SYSTEM

"The system can add insult to injury" claimed Donald E. Santarelli, former head of the Law Enforcement Assistance Administration (LEAA), who gave these excerpts in a talk he delivered to a recent national meeting of state justice planning officials:

We read of Americans being prisoners in their own homes and hear of proposals on how to reduce fear of crime. The fear of crime is very real—and with very good reason. There is only one way to reduce the fear of crime—and that is to substantially reduce crime itself.

We should ask what we can say to the victims of those crimes—to the nearly 400,000 victims of aggravated assaults in 1972, to the more than 46,000 victims of rape, to the families of nearly 20,000 victims of homicide. I don't believe any of us could say we are doing enough.

Our goal is the reduction of crime in America. There are many paths we must follow simultaneously to reach that goal.

One that has been overlooked in the past is the citizen—and the role he can play in helping to fashion advances in crime reduction.

The foremost way in which the criminal justice system can aid citizens is by protecting them, by reducing crime. But we also have to face the fact that in much of the nation today the criminal justice system seems to be operating to serve its own needs, running things to suit its own preferences, carving out spheres of influence to suit its own convenience.

Policemen, judges, correction officials, and prosecutors cannot be in business for themselves. Their job is not to erect empires and operate outside of the gaze and control of the public.

There are two ways in which the criminal justice system can reclaim the trust of the public. The first is by reducing crime in significant and permanent ways. The second is by the criminal justice system treating citizens as though they are what they are—decent, law-abiding people who comprise the heart of our democracy. It is time the criminal justice system began viewing citizens in that fashion—rather than as pawns who can be moved on life's board at the whim of officials who occupy posts only at the public's tolerance.

It is easy to discern the reasons for public disenchantment with the criminal justice system. The odds are better than ever that any citizen who comes into contact with the system will come out of that experience with a sour taste in his mouth, with his or her confidence eroded.

A victim of a criminal can also find he is a victim of the criminal justice system. If he shows up to testify, he can find the case is postponed—and then postponed again and again. That is money out of his pocket, time out of his life. He begins to wonder who the system is supposed to be for— him, the victim, or a host of other people—the defense attorneys, the prosecutors, the judges.

We know that non-cooperation from witnesses is a major factor in prosecutions washing-out, and perhaps responsible for half the cases that are scrubbed. We know that fear of reprisal seems to be the reason in a significant number of cases.

It means that we not only cannot protect huge numbers of our citizens against crime in the first place, but we cannot even instill confidence in significant numbers of citizens that the law can protect them if they testify against the accused.

There is a particular problem, it seems to me, with the ways in which minority groups are treated by the criminal justice system. In many citizens today, police-community relations programs have no more substance or no more relation to reality than the false-front stores erected on the sound stages of a film studio for a western movie.

If some in the criminal justice system interpret my remarks as unfair criticisms, let me say that I certainly do mean to criticize and that it is not unfair. It is no more unfair to criticize bungling public officials than it is to criticize a surgeon who bungles an operation or a public health scientist who fails to detect quickly enough an outbreak of typhoid.

The thing that every single person in the criminal justice system has to understand is that we, too, hold human lives in our hands. And if we fall short, if we fail to protect, then we bear burdens too heavy for even the most hardened conscience.

The views I express are not mine alone. They are the views of the Congress, which created this program to achieve results. They are the views of the people of this nation, whose patience is remarkable—but not endless.

5. SUMMARY

This unit attempts to show the human side of the crime problem. The cases of Mrs. Slawnyk and Mr. Rauer were selected because they are typical robbery-murders. Unlike most other murders, these crimes are the direct responsibility of the police. They occurred where police patrol—on the streets. The victims weren't killed by a relative or friend in some place inaccessible to police patrols. Robbery by strangers contributes highly to the "fear of crime" that is crippling our major urban areas.

Because of the nature of robbery, it is a repressible crime. Also it has a high recidivism rate. Had the robbers who made prey of Mrs. Slawnyk and Mr. Rauer been apprehended on a previous robbery, perhaps these cases would not be available for discussion here. This now, is the main intent of the book: To identify those crimes that police can affect and develop tactics to apprehend criminals so that there will be fewer tragic cases of this sort.

Mrs. Slawnyk and Mr. Rauer have fallen victim to the same pervasive condition that threatens all who dwell in American urban areas—"street crime". Only by considering the actual victims of street crime do the bland crime statistics become meaningful. Once they become meaningful and important the extent of the problem will be realized. Only by full understanding of the problem and its extent will those responsible for rectifying it be able to employ systems and programs to effectively correct it. Correction of the crime problem means a definite reduction of crime incidents with fewer human tragedies such as those of Mrs. Slawnyk and Mr. Rauer.

Civilians aren't the only victims of crime. Police, because of their exposure to crime and violence, often fall victim to criminals. Thus, the next unit will provide insight into the extent of the crime problem as it affects the men who are attempting to deal with it on the street.

6. QUESTIONS FOR DISCUSSION

1. How do the robbery-murder cases in Unit 4 differ from the typical murder?

2. Discuss the responsibility of the police in the different cases listed in Question #1.

3. How do "stranger to stranger" crimes differ from crimes between relatives and acquaintances?

4. Define the much discussed "fear of crime" syndrome affecting our society. What are its effects on the quality of life in our urban areas? On our economy?

5. List the crimes that you think police should combat first. Explain your rationale.

6. How can police combat the robbery-murder cases discussed in Unit 4? What tactics do you think will alleviate the problem?

7. How can police combat the other crimes listed in Question #5? What tactics do you think will alleviate them?

8. Why do inner city residents have higher victimization rates?

9. How does the criminal justice system "add insult to injury" to crime victims? How can this be corrected?

UNIT 5

POLICE VICTIMS

Clarence M. Kelley, Director of the FBI expressed concern for police officers who fall victim to crimes in pursuit of their sworn duties:

Victims are the most neglected consequence of crime. Statistically, the risk of becoming a victim of crime is demonstrated by the rate of lawlessness. But this is only a small part of the full story.

Those whose lives are lost, whose persons are injured, and whose property is taken by crime are not its only victims. Crime is bad enough when its impact is confined to those persons it personally accosts. But lawbreaking is rarely that selective.

Crime often causes far-reaching damage to many innocent persons beyond the scope of its individual acts. This is nothing new to an experienced law enforcement officer. I am, however, painfully reminded of the fact when reviewing the circumstances of the murders of law enforcement officers throughout the Nation.

The record-setting toll of 131 local, county, state, and federal law enforcement officers killed due to felonious acts in 1973 is a sorrowful figure. It is a tragic count. Even more grievous, perhaps, than the loss of these valiant officers' lives is the fact that their deaths left nearly three times their number in immediate family survivors. The fabric of considerably more than 300 lives of men, women, and children was severely torn with the loss of a husband, a father, a son, or a brother. The tentacles of crime had, at the moment of these deaths, seized the loved ones in a terrifying grip which would likely leave its ugly imprint on their heads and minds for the remainder of their lives. And this says nothing of the shattered remnants of their livelihood.

These survivors, as well as any persons similarly affected by the commission of crime, are truly victims. If the number of the officers' survivors is at all representative, society has reason to shudder at the huge group of persons spiritually and functionally impoverished by the more than 18,500 murders, for example, which occurred in 1973.

Yet, we hear very little about the victims of crime. The reports of their loss too often are the sole accounts of their plight or their demise. This is in puzzling contrast to the frequently prolonged, hand wringing appeals made in behalf of those who commit crime. There seems to be no scarcity of spokesmen who will concoct any rationale, from any platform, to excuse persons accused or convicted of crime.

Certainly, our society must not ignore the criminal offender. The community has an obligation to see that he is afforded every protection the law provides and, if convicted, a responsibility to seek his meaningful rehabilitation.

However, I cannot help but wonder if more public attention on the victims of crime would help serve as a strong crime deterrent. Surely, their stories of suffering and mental anguish would better capture the misery and meanness of crime, hopefully to an extent that might even trigger the conscience of all but the worst would-be offenders. Furthermore, it would put lawlessness in its proper perspective—as a clear menace to society rather than a seemingly lifeless event which simply involves prosecutors and the police pitted against an accused.

We should all strive to remember, not forget, the victims of crime.

I. LAW ENFORCEMENT OFFICERS KILLED

It is important to understand the great risk incurred by police officers in performance of their duties. During the ten-year period, 1965–1974, 947 officers were killed. Hopefully, the danger will be recognized and tactics discussed later will be adopted to minimize this loss of life.

Unit 5 POLICE VICTIMS 49

LAW ENFORCEMENT OFFICERS KILLED
by Type of Activity
1965-1974

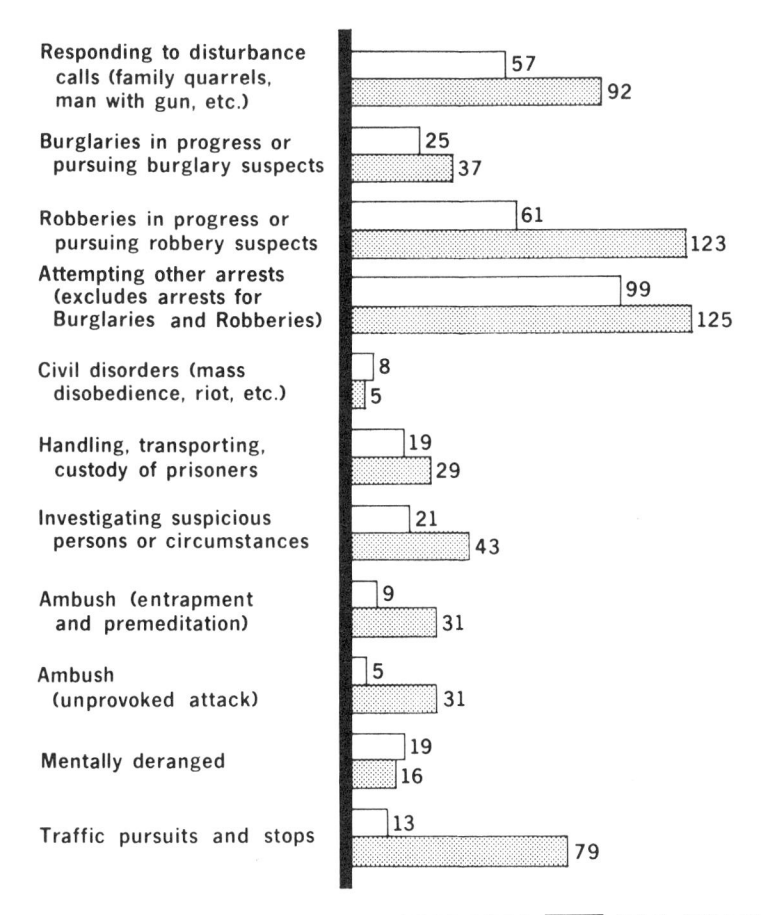

Activity	1965-1969	1970-1974
Responding to disturbance calls (family quarrels, man with gun, etc.)	57	92
Burglaries in progress or pursuing burglary suspects	25	37
Robberies in progress or pursuing robbery suspects	61	123
Attempting other arrests (excludes arrests for Burglaries and Robberies)	99	125
Civil disorders (mass disobedience, riot, etc.)	8	5
Handling, transporting, custody of prisoners	19	29
Investigating suspicious persons or circumstances	21	43
Ambush (entrapment and premeditation)	9	31
Ambush (unprovoked attack)	5	31
Mentally deranged	19	16
Traffic pursuits and stops	13	79

1965-1969 ☐ 336 KILLED
1970-1974 ▨ 611 KILLED
1965-1974 total: 947 KILLED

CHART 5.1 FBI CHART

LAW ENFORCEMENT OFFICERS KILLED
by Hour of Day
1965-1974

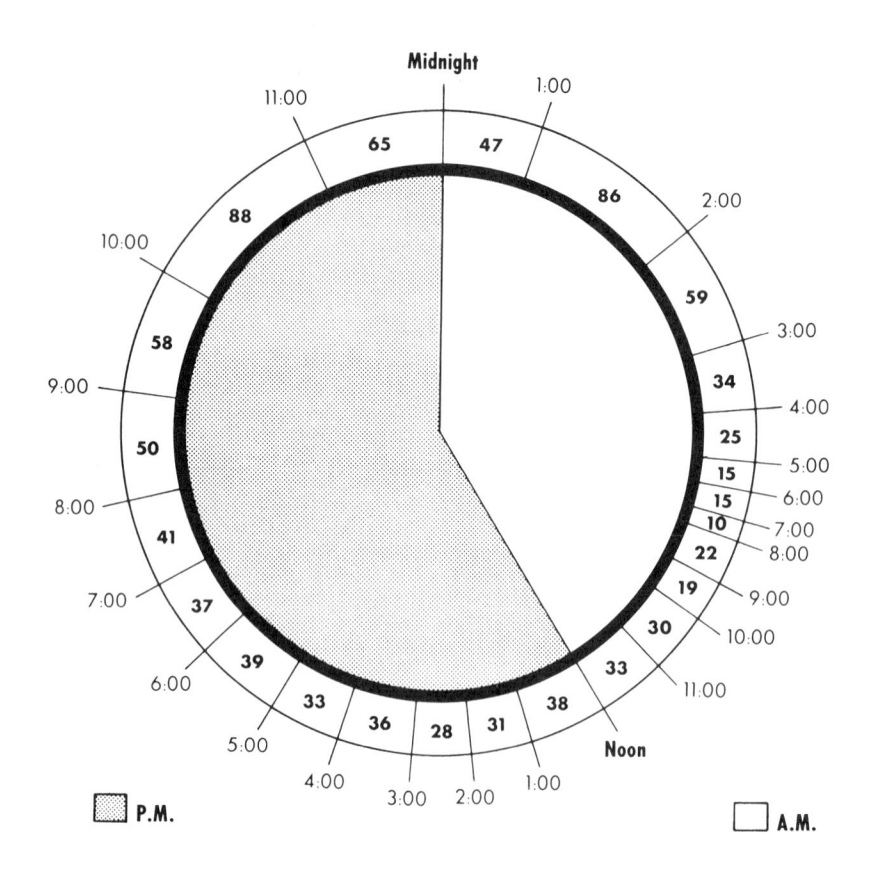

Hour	Count
Midnight	
1:00	47
2:00	86
3:00	59
4:00	34
5:00	25
6:00	15
7:00	15
8:00	10
9:00	22
10:00	19
11:00	30
Noon	33
1:00	38
2:00	31
3:00	28
4:00	36
5:00	33
6:00	39
7:00	37
8:00	41
9:00	50
10:00	58
11:00	88
(to Midnight)	65

P.M.   A.M.

CHART 5.2   FBI CHART

Unit 5 POLICE VICTIMS 51

A. CIRCUMSTANCES SURROUNDING DEATHS

Examination of circumstances under which police officers were slain, continues to disclose a most urgent need for officers to be more alert in connection with all their duties, regardless of how routine these duties may seem or have been in the past. It is essential that officers be extremely alert with all individuals they contact. No arrest situation can be considered routine, as evidenced by the fact that more officers were killed attempting arrests than in any other matter. Chart #5.1 indicates the type of activity being performed by officers when slain. Chart #5.2 indicates the most dangerous time of day for police officers.

**LAW ENFORCEMENT OFFICERS KILLED BY FIREARMS - 1973
DISTANCE BETWEEN VICTIM OFFICER AND OFFENDER**

Feet	Number of Officers
1 - 5	66
6 - 10	27
11 - 20	13
21 - 50	8
Over 50	10

CHART 5.3   FBI CHART

An accompanying table shows the type of weapons used to kill officers from 1964 through 1973. (Refer to table 5.1)

B. WEAPONS USED

One hundred twenty-four of the police killings in 1973 were perpetrated through use of firearms. Chart #5.3 demonstrates that there is often a very close distance between the victim officer and the offender.

Law Enforcement Officers Killed, 1965–1974

[By type of weapon]

Type of weapons	1965-1974 Total Number	1965-1974 Percent	1965-1969 Number	1965-1969 Percent	1970-1974 Number	1970-1974 Percent
Handgun	675	71.3	240	71.4	435	71.2
Shotgun	119	12.6	44	13.1	75	12.3
Rifle	111	11.7	38	11.3	73	11.9
Total firearms	905	95.6	322	95.8	583	95.4
Knife	13	1.4	2	.6	11	1.8
Bomb	3	.3			3	.5
Personal weapons	8	.8	5	1.5	3	.5
Other (clubs, etc.)	18	1.9	7	2.1	11	1.8
Total	947	100.0	336	100.0	611	100.0

TABLE 5.1

C. TYPES OF ASSIGNMENTS

Officers who are assigned patrol duties within law enforcement organizations have the most hazardous type of assignment. During the course of his duties the patrol officer is frequently in contact with suspicious persons. Each of these situations constitutes a threat to the officer's personal safety. The patrol officer is readily identifiable because of his uniform and/or patrol vehicle. He cannot hide his presence or official capacity, and frequently must determine quickly and accurately if a person is involved in a criminal act, and if that person constitutes a danger to his, the officer's personal safety. The patrol officer must react to situations as they occur without the benefit of detailed information or planning and thus places himself in a variety of dangerous situations. The patrol officer also risks attack through frequent encounters with criminal offenders at or near crime scenes. These perils are in a large measure substantiated by the fact that officers assigned to patrol duty are the most frequent targets of the police killer. Officers assigned in other capacities are confronted with equally tense and dangerous types of situations while performing their duties, but not with the same frequency.

2. ASSAULTS ON LAW ENFORCEMENT OFFICERS

The large number of reported assaults on sworn officers is in part due to a prevalent attitude of disrespect for law enforcement in certain elements of our society.

The uniformed officer is the target for persons with real or imagined grievances against the "system". He also is, in many instances, the first person to render aid to mentally deranged individuals, to calm disturbances and quarrels, to offer protection to those threatened or rescue those in peril. The officer is the active representative of a society whose members too often forget their individual responsibilities to their fellow human beings. In this role, he suffers a variety of unsolicited and undeserved abuse.

3. SUMMARY

Each year over 100 officers are slain in the line of duty. Many more are injured, some permanently.

The most dangerous duty a police officer can perform is to respond to a crime in progress and try to apprehend felons. Since that is the topic of the book, it in incumbent upon every officer to recognize the hazards of this type activity and take precautions to minimize the risks involved in the job.

Hopefully the units that follow will help make the officer more effective and safer in these kinds of duties.

4. QUESTIONS FOR DISCUSSION

1. How many police officers were slain in your area of jurisdiction during the past 5 or 10 years? What kinds of activity were they performing at the time? How could any of these deaths have been prevented?

2. List the 3 most hazardous calls coming from your police radio. Discuss how risks can be minimized.

3. How do you feel about protective clothing on patrol? In plainclothes?

4. Explain the variance in times of day that officers are killed. What implications, if any, are there for two man cars during the most dangerous times?

5. What percentage of policemen are killed within the minimum Practical Pistol Course (PPC) training distance? What changes should be made in pistol training based on the distance between the victim officer and offender?

UNIT 6

CRIME REPORTING AND CLEARANCE

A recent survey of 500 residents of a large urban city revealed 80% of those interviewed listed "crime in the streets" as the most pressing problem in their city.[1]

Yet, another study sponsored by the Law Enforcement Assistance Administration revealed that crime in our cities is grossly under reported because of apathy on part of the victims. Chart #6.1 shows the findings in the nation's five largest cities. The survey, concerning the first three months of 1973, was conducted for LEAA by Cenus Bureau Investigators from the Department of Commerce. They questioned 22,000 persons in 10,000 households and about 2,000 businesses in each of the five cities surveyed at a cost of $10 million.

Donald E. Santarelli, LEAA administrator, blamed "public apathy toward its criminal justice institutions bordering on contempt"[2] for the results. But "public apathy" alone cannot be blamed for all erroneous crime reporting. Clark makes the point that "erroneous crime statistics are often used to create the im-

Here are comparisons of the two reports for the five cities (1972)

CITY	UCR	LEAA
PHILADELPHIA	78,457	396,400
NEW YORK	515,121	1,100,100
LOS ANGELES	237,801	693,500
CHICAGO	223,630	621,300
DETROIT	128,996	345,600

CHART 6.1

1. J R P Surveys, Inc. (Philadelphia, Penna: 1973).
2. Scott Heimer, "Crime Five Times What Reported" Philadelphia Daily News, (Phila., Penna: March 21, 1974) p. 3.

pression that the new chief is doing a good job, or to support a movement to add more police".[3]

Statistical measures can be employed to determine the accuracy of a given department's crime reporting. They rest on the reasonable assumption that the more serious the crime the more likely it will be reported accurately. Homicide is the most accurately reported crime—it is difficult to ignore the corpse.

Police administrators have a reporting problem if their homicide rate is high, and other crimes low, in comparison with other comparable jurisdictions. In particular we can consider a homicide victim to be simply an aggravated assault victim that happened to expire. Therefore, one good measure of reporting accuracy would be the ratio of homicides to assault cases. If this ratio is unusually high you probably have either false reporting of assaults or very bad hospital facilities. In large urban areas it is likely to be the former.

Another measure would be to compare the ratio of attempted burglary to successful burglaries. Certainly you do not expect all burglars to be successful. If the incidence of attempts is low, perhaps the malicious mischief file or oval file has become the repository for incidents that should have been reported as burglary attempts.

One other measure would be to compare the clearance rate on larceny cases. If the uncleared cases are significantly higher in loss value than the cleared cases a problem may exist.

The above points address the problem of under-reporting of crime. On the other side of the coin there are those exposing the "labeling theory" of deviance and claiming that the crime problem is overstated. This theory holds that deviance is not an inherent property of certain behaviors, but a label conferred upon some behaviors by people who come into direct contact with it. (e. g. a police officer "labels" certain activity as "crime" that is

---

3. Ramsey Clark, Crime in America, (New York, N. Y.: Simon and Schuster, 1970) p. 29.

Unit 6   CRIME REPORTING AND CLEARANCE

not inherently bad.) It is the author's opinion that the labeling phenomenon may occasionally occur, but not to the extent of causing the crime problem to be overstated. It is mentioned here for the sake of completeness.

Several years ago a professor was lecturing on this theory at a local university. He claimed that crime was manufactured by police and other elements of the criminal justice system to justify their existence. He stated that America was suffering from a crime wave that existed only on paper. Unfortunately for the professor, as he left the lecture, he encountered several youths in the parking lot of the inner-city university who promptly "labeled" him as a victim. They asked him for a cigarette—and shot him in the belly after he could not produce one.

The moral is that the truth lies somewhere between "labeling" (high crime) and false reporting (low crime). In reality, crime reports are fairly accurate on the number of cases brought to the attention of the police. It is important for police and police administrators to have a fair and objective crime reporting system. If they do not, they are only fooling themselves and making their task more difficult. People need to know what the true crime problem is before they can plan, prepare and carry out steps to combat it.

I. CLEARANCE OF CRIME

Police clear a crime when they have identified the offender, have sufficient evidence to charge him, and actually take him into custody. Crime solutions are also recorded in exceptional instances when some element beyond police control precludes the placing of formal charges against the offender, such as the victim's refusal to prosecute after the offender is identified or local prosecution is declined because the subject is being prosecuted elsewhere for a crime committed in another jurisdiction. The arrest of one person can clear several crimes or several persons may be arrested in the process of clearing one crime.

Law enforcement agencies in the Nation cleared 21 percent of Part I Crimes during 1974. See Charts #6.2 and 6.3.

Chart #6.4 lists the percent of repeaters by type of crime. Interestingly enough, robbery, burglary, and auto theft appear near the top of the list of repeaters. Logic holds that these repeaters are not apprehended on their first or only try. All these points suggest that a program designed to apprehend repeaters will have a great effect on lowering the crime rate for "street crimes".

This brings us to the next point. In order to combat (clear) crime it is necessary to break it down to its basic elements.

2. ELEMENTS OF CRIME

Legally, there are two essential constituent parts to every true crime (1) an external physical part, and (2) an internal mental part. The Latin term "actus reus", or "guilty act", is sometimes used to describe the essential physical part; and the term "mens rea", or "guilty mind", to describe the essential mental part.

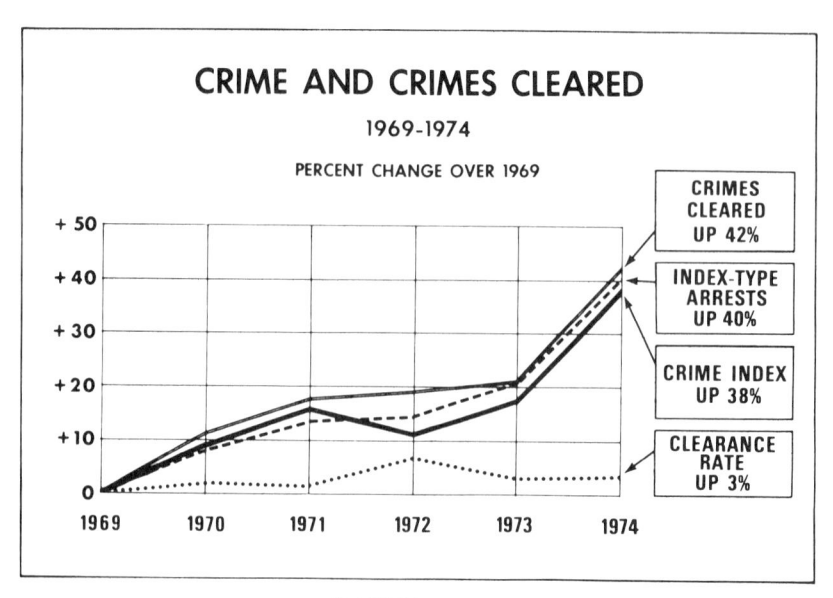

CRIME AND CRIMES CLEARED
1969-1974

PERCENT CHANGE OVER 1969

CRIMES CLEARED UP 42%
INDEX-TYPE ARRESTS UP 40%
CRIME INDEX UP 38%
CLEARANCE RATE UP 3%

CHART 6.2   FBI CHART

Unit 6   CRIME REPORTING AND CLEARANCE   59

These two terms are derived from the most famous of all Latin maxims of the common law of crimes which reads in full "Et actus non fecit reum nisi mens sit rea" meaning "The act of a person does not make him guilty unless he has a guilty mind."

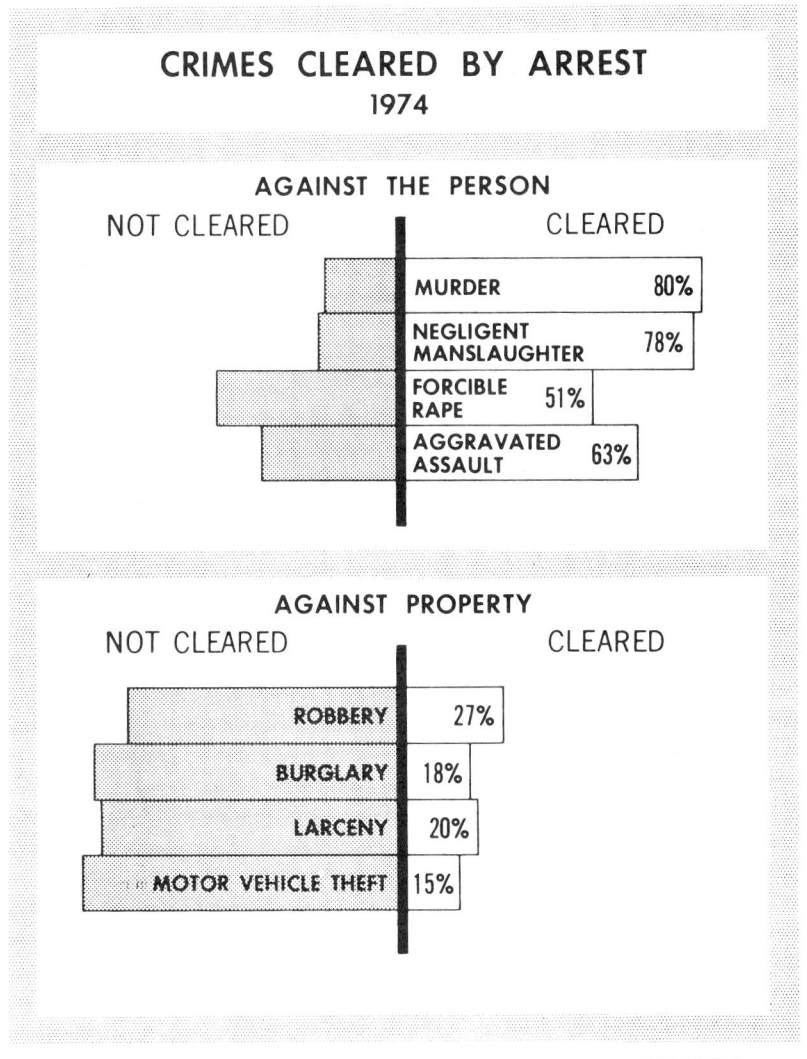

CRIMES CLEARED BY ARREST
1974

AGAINST THE PERSON

NOT CLEARED | CLEARED

MURDER	80%
NEGLIGENT MANSLAUGHTER	78%
FORCIBLE RAPE	51%
AGGRAVATED ASSAULT	63%

AGAINST PROPERTY

NOT CLEARED | CLEARED

ROBBERY	27%
BURGLARY	18%
LARCENY	20%
MOTOR VEHICLE THEFT	15%

CHART 6.3   FBI CHART

PERCENT REPEATERS
BY TYPE OF CRIME
PERSONS ARRESTED, 1970-1972

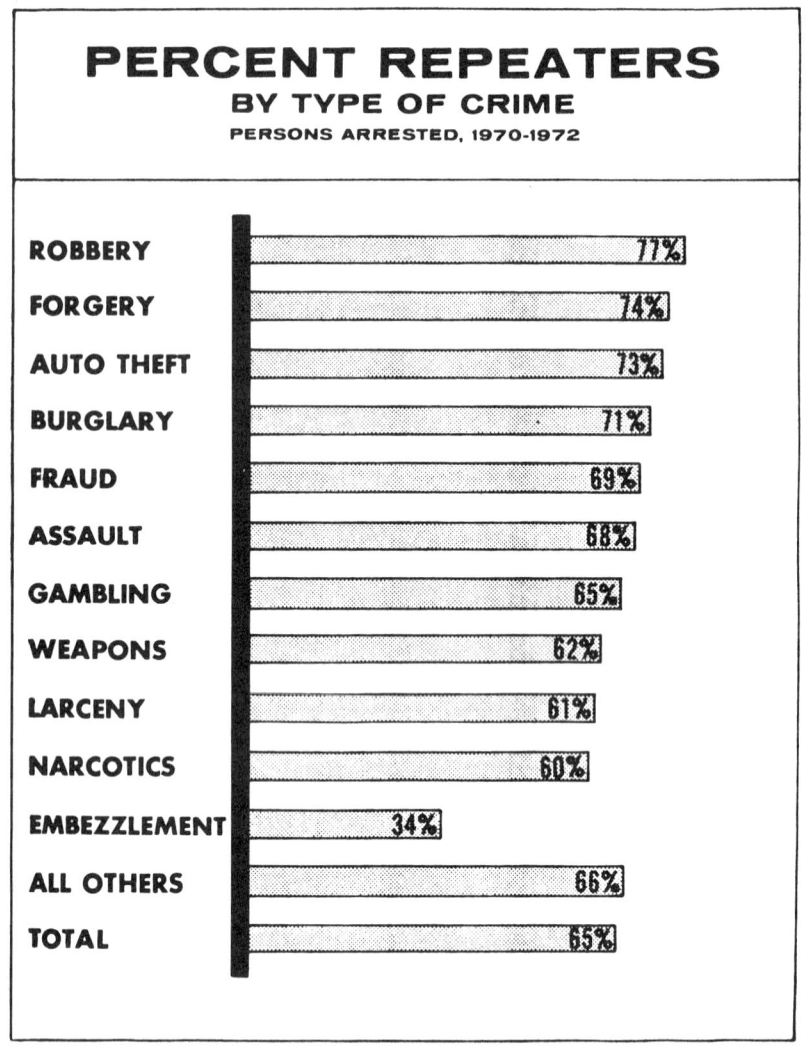

Crime	Percent
ROBBERY	77%
FORGERY	74%
AUTO THEFT	73%
BURGLARY	71%
FRAUD	69%
ASSAULT	68%
GAMBLING	65%
WEAPONS	62%
LARCENY	61%
NARCOTICS	60%
EMBEZZLEMENT	34%
ALL OTHERS	66%
TOTAL	65%

CHART 6.4

The external physical part of a crime consists of the offender's act and its result which the law considers so harmful to the community that it seeks to prevent its occurrence by criminally punishing the person whose conduct is involved. The act forbidden or commanded by the law is set out in the definition of each parti-

Unit 6 CRIME REPORTING AND CLEARANCE   61

cular offense. For example, in the crime of murder it is the death of the victim caused by the offender's unlawful killing. In the crime of larceny, it is the loss of personal property brought about by the offender's trespassory seizing and carrying away. The physical part of a crime generally varies from offense to offense although occasionally it may be the same, e. g. in both murder and manslaughter it is the death of the victim caused by felonious homicide.

The internal mental part of a crime consists of the offender's state of mind toward the act by means of which he causes the forbidden social harm. Just as the physical part generally varies from crime to crime depending upon its definition, so does the mental part. Common to all true crimes, however, is the mental requirement that the offender determine, i. e. actually will, to do the act which the law forbids or commands. This mental requirement is called "general criminal intent". Although general criminal intent suffices for many crimes, there are certain offenses which require additional mental states above and beyond it which vary individually according to their different natures. For example, in the crime of common-law murder, the special mental state is the offender's "malice aforethought" which means usually his knowledge of circumstances showing a strong likelihood that his voluntary, unjustifiable act may cause death. In forgery, it is the forger's intent to defraud when he alters the document involved in his scheme. In common-law larceny, it is the thief's intention to deprive the owner permanently of his goods when he seizes and carries them away.

Without an external act, there can be no crime. If a person possesses a certain criminal mind, but he does nothing to actually carry it out, he does not commit a crime. The external manifestation of his will is essential even though it may not be great, e. g. in libel it is the publication of mere words, and in narcotics violations it is often the mere possession of the forbidden drugs.

Without an internal mental state, there can be no crime. If a person commits an act which would ordinarily constitute the external part of a crime, but he was incapable of entertaining the requisite criminal intent for such reasons as legal insanity, he does not commit a crime.

Not only is an external physical act and an internal mental state essential to every true crime, but it is also necessary that these two parts concur. In other words the forbidden act must be united at one and the same time with the forbidden mind in order for a crime to be committed.

Based on this legal definition, it can be said that a crime has two parts: Intent and Act. Therefore, programs to combat crime must be directed against the intent and/or the opportunity to commit the act. This becomes of particular importance when we consider the "Role of the Police" and basic police functions in the next section.

Police cannot successfully repress all crimes. When considering clearance of crime it is of great importance to know what crimes are more susceptible to police activity. Those crimes which are susceptible are generally known as repressible crimes.

3. REPRESSIBLE CRIMES

Being against crime is like being for apple pie. But having that opinion is not enough. Some activity must be taken against the problem, and it is usually not easy to choose the best activity. When a police administrator is considering certain actions, he knows those actions consume resources (manpower—equipment) and he must recognize that his resources have limitations. Therefore he must deploy them on a "cost-benefit" basis. At this point it is important to note that some crimes are more susceptible to police activity than others. Remember the crime of homicide mentioned earlier in this section? Homicide heads the severity list—but it is difficult to suppress. It is mainly a sociological problem. Frequently a family member slays another family member. Of course police should investigate it and seek out and apprehend the perpetrators, but how do you prevent or deter it? Some measures like the New York Police Department's Family Crisis Intervention Unit and comprehensive gun violation enforce-

Unit 6   CRIME REPORTING AND CLEARANCE

ment programs may help in lowering murder rates, but there are other crimes where police service can have more impact.

Robbery, for example is the highest crime in the hierarchy of Part I offenses that can be successfully influenced by police operations. Chart #6.5 lists the Part I offenses in order of severity and in order of their susceptibility to police tactics and deployment.

Robberies, burglaries and auto theft occur in the police domain. They are truly "street crimes" and that is where the police are supposed to be. This is the area where the police can be most successful in lowering crime rates. The thrust of this book is directed towards these selected crimes. Sections 22, 23 and 24 will deal with Tactical Approaches to Robbery, Burglary and Auto Theft, respectively.

4. SUMMARY

Police often get accused of under or over reporting crime. In reality, the uniform crime reports are a fairly accurate account of crimes known to the police. It behooves police to get an accurate count on their crime problem because it is the basic knowledge necessary prior to mounting anti-crime programs.

Ordered by Seriousness	Ordered by Susceptibility to Patrol
Homicide	Robbery
Rape	Burglary
Robbery	Auto Theft
Aggravated Assault	Rape
Burglary	Larceny
Larceny	Homicide
Auto Theft	Aggravated Assault

CHART #6.5

When in doubt about the veracity of crime statistics, there are several statistical comparisons that can be made to obtain the true picture. An example of one such measure would be to compare the homicide rate with the aggravated assault rate. After all, a homicide victim is simply an aggravated assault victim that happened to die. If homicides are high and aggravated assaults low, you could have a problem. Other such comparisons can be made with other crimes. Also crime counts between cities with like populations and demographics could be made to check the accuracy of crime reports.

A crime is "cleaned" when the perpetrator is arrested or when the case is unfounded or exceptionally cleared. Clearances are a good measure of how police operations are dealing with the crime problem.

Conviction rates are a qualitative measure on the arrests.

In order to combat crime it is necessary to break it down into its basic elements. Every crime consists of the intent and act. Anti-crime programs, as you will see later, should be directed against one or both of these basic elements.

Clearance of crimes against the person are generally higher than those against property. The reasons are several: Face to face confrontation with the offender, nature of the act (e. g. 80% of murder victims knew their assailant), and having application of police resources on crimes against persons.

Volume, recidivism rates and repressibility of particular crimes should determine what target crimes the police should attack first. Fortunately, the most repressible crimes, robbery, burglary and auto theft (all stranger to stranger crimes, largely responsible for 'fear of crime') have the highest recidivism rates. This affords the police with a tremendous opportunity to control these particular crimes. Sound police tactics directed against these crimes are almost sure to be a success. Get a couple of "repeaters" off the street and your crime rates have to come down.

Unit 6 CRIME REPORTING AND CLEARANCE 65

5. QUESTIONS FOR DISCUSSION

1. Are the uniform crime reports accurate? If not, why not?
2. What possible reasons are there for people not reporting crime?
3. Identify and explain the legal elements of crime. How could knowledge of these elements help in combating crime?
4. Which crimes (against persons or property) enjoy the highest clearance rates? Why?
5. What is the clearance rate for homicide? Do you think other crimes against the person could be cleared at the homicide level?
6. Identify the Part I Crimes with the highest rates of recidivism. Explain.
7. Identify the Part I Crimes that are considered "repressible". Explain.
8. Based on your findings in questions 6 and 7, which three Part I Crimes should police target first? In what order? What if the volume at one of the target crimes is not a problem in your area?

*

SECTION 2
ROLE OF THE POLICE

UNIT 7
THE GOALS OF POLICE SERVICE

Ask a five-year-old boy "What does a policeman do?" and the odds are he will reply, "Catch robbers."

Unfortunately for the people who have to live with "street crime" that statement is no longer completely true. Because of a myriad of duties and services in our complex society, only a very small percentage of police are directly engaged in the basic duties of protecting life and property and actively combating street crime. The reader may recall from Unit II that the clearance rate for robbery in the United States is only 27 percent. Also, the incidence of robbery has risen 46 percent in the past five years, and this national disgrace is occurring in the very domain (the streets) that police are sworn to protect.

This section is vitally concerned with the role of the police and its effect on the crime problem. The basic considerations of this section are:

What are the basic principles of law enforcement?

What are the goals of police service?

What are the basic police functions?

Is there a criminal justice sy : n and if there is, where do the police fit in?

What are the basic styles of policing in the United States?

What function or style can best accomplish the goals of police service?

What can the public expect in return for billions spent on policing?

These questions have to be resolved prior to considering how to deal with the crime problem on the police level.

I. THE ENGLISH MODEL

Our criminal law system is modeled after England's Common Law System. Basically, police in the United States are also founded on the English Model of policing.

In 1822 Sir Robert Peel, founder of the British Police System, first enunciated the basic principles of law enforcement. Although these principles are over 150 years old they still apply today. Peel's first principle was that "The basic mission for which the police exist is to reduce crime and disorder:" The further any police activity is from this goal—the less justification for its existence. Peel sums up his basic principles with his final principle: "The test of police efficiency is the absence of crime and disorder, not the visible evidence of police action in dealing with them."

Police perform three basic functions in trying to achieve the absence of crime and disorder:

Prevention
Deterrence
Apprehension

These basic functions overlap and are very seldom "pure". For example, crime reporting is almost a "pure" prevention function, but the reporting of descriptions of wanted persons and stolen goods can be considered an apprehension function.

Community Relations Programs and Police Athletic Leagues are examples of "pure" prevention functions. Certainly they are noble endeavors, but their impact on achieving the "absence" of street crime is extremely hard to measure. The most important prevention function is in crime reporting. We have all heard much about how society is responsible for the "root causes of crime." That may very well be, but the policeman is confronted with the reality of dealing with the victims and offenders on the street. It is true that police are only one part of the criminal justice system, (see Chart #7.1) and the Criminal Justice System in only one part of American Society. (see Chart #7.2)

Unit 7   THE GOALS OF POLICE SERVICE   69

POLICE IN THE CRIMINAL JUSTICE SYSTEM (C.J.S.)

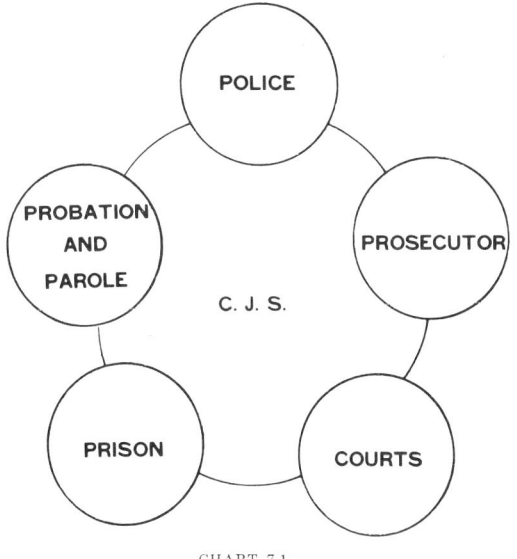

CHART 7.1

CRIMINAL JUSTICE SYSTEM IN SOCIETY

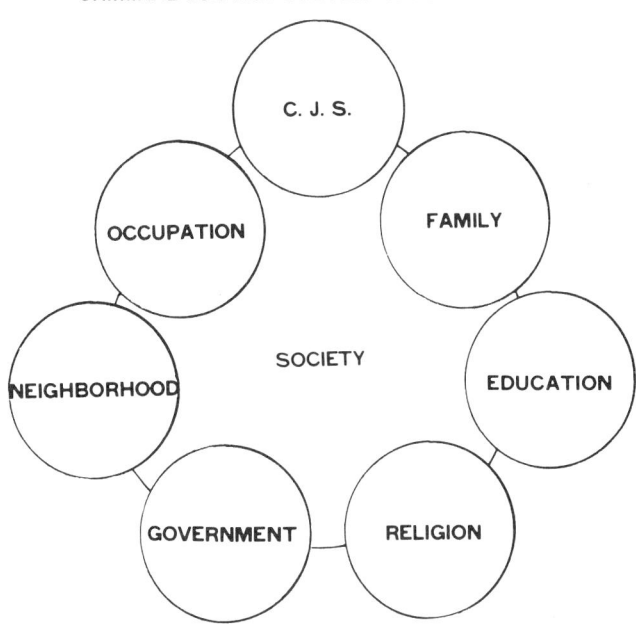

CHART 7.2

Parts of a system can be compared with the gears of a wristwatch; if one part breaks down, all parts are affected. Anyone with common sense knows what gear is defective in the Criminal Justice System today but you could get held in contempt of it if you mention its name. One of the main goals of this book is to develop legal crime fighting tactics that minimize the negative effects the courts have on our Criminal Justice System. (Refer to Unit 8 "Reactive vs Proactive Response To Crime" for details)

Meanwhile the police are confronted with an endless flow of victims. We have to deal with the lions and protect the lambs.

What can the police do under the Preventative Function? The answer is YELL! Crime reporting is analogous to the policeman playing the role of the Dutch boy with his finger in the dike—trying to save society from being swamped. The Uniform Crime Report reports in Unit I are the screams of that boy, trying to alert the rest of the criminal justice system and society to the danger. Again you can see the importance of accurate crime reporting. Maybe if we hold that dike and yell loud enough, we can give a society that got to the moon enough time to come up with solutions for the "root causes" of crime in our streets.

Prevention can come as a result of other functions. For example: the rehabilitation of an apprehended criminal in prison. Preventative measures by nature deal with the *Intent* element of crime.

Deterrence, on the other hand deals with the *opportunity to commit the act* element of crime. Deterrence is generally associated with police presence and visibility. This is usually achieved by regular patrol activities. Marked cars and uniformed patrolmen have been traditionally deployed as tools against crime. However, they may deflect crime more often than deter it.

Consider this circumstance—A young man is waiting at a deserted bus stop and he spots an attractive female. For reasons best known to him and perhaps his psychiatrist, he intends to rape her. No crime has been committed until he acts. Now he observes a patrolman making his rounds, so he does not commit the act. However, does he lose the intent? He may just go to

Unit 7   THE GOALS OF POLICE SERVICE   71

another area where the police are less prevalent and attack a different victim.

The effectiveness of patrol in being a crime deterrent is currently under question. Especially since the Kansas City study.

2. KANSAS CITY PATROL STUDY

The basic crime-fighting tactic of all American police departments—the regular patrol of the streets by uniformed men in marked cars—does not appear to prevent crime according to the preliminary findings of an elaborate year-long experiment.

This startling conclusion appears to challenge a fundamental tenet of most police officials and politicians that more policemen patrolling the streets is the answer to a city's crime problem.

Law enforcement experts estimate that half of the $4.5 billion a year spent for police protection by the cities, towns and counties of the United States is allocated to preventive patrol.

The experiment testing the effectiveness of preventive patrol was conducted in a 35 square-mile area of Kansas City from October 1, 1972 until September 20, 1973. It was designed by that city's police department, but monitored by an outside team of evaluators financed by a $461,244 grant from the Police Foundation, a nonprofit law enforcement research group.

The key finding to emerge is that in matched areas in Kansas City with no regular patrol cars, one patrol car and four or five patrol cars there were virtually no changes in levels of reported crime during the one-year test period.

To conduct the experiment, 15 patrol sectors with a total of 120,000 residents were divided into three groups with similar patterns of reported crime, income levels and population characteristics. The area included shopping centers, low-income apartment housing, hospitals and single-family dwellings.

On a random basis, the matched sectors were then given one of three levels of patrol. In each of the five sectors in the first group there was no regular patrol, and police cars entered them only when citizens made a specific request for service.

In each of the five sectors in the second group a single patrol roamed the streets, as had been done for many years.

Four or five cars provided a highly intensive level of continuous preventive patrol, in each of the five sectors in the third group.

The number of serious crimes reported in the five sectors with no regular patrol declined 0.7 percent during the experimental year from the previous year. For the five sectors with one patrol car, reported serious crime increased 12.5 percent. For the sector with four or five cars, serious crime increased 5.7 percent. The changes in the number of reported crimes in the three sets of patrol areas were so small that they were considered statistically insignificant.

Patrick V. Murphy, former Commissioner of the New York Police Department and recently appointed head of the Police Foundation, the organization that sponsored the experiment, said, "It is an article of faith in the police world that more patrol means less crime. If the experiment finally proves this is not the case, it will provide an invaluable guide to police departments and taxpayers trying to decide how to best allocate their resources." [1]

He further stated that "The preliminary findings of the experiment suggested that perhaps a great deal of money which is being poured into crime control is being spent on the wrong things. Perhaps patrolmen, instead of constantly driving around in their cars, should spend most of their time gathering intelligence, talking to people, advising businesses how to prevent crimes before they occur, investigating." [2] See Chart #7.3.

1. David Burnham, "A Police Study Challenges Value of Anti-Crime Patrols", The New York Times, (New York, N. Y.: November 11, 1973) p. 67.

2. Ibid. p. 67.

Unit 7 THE GOALS OF POLICE SERVICE 73

**IMPACT OF PREVENTIVE PATROL
ON REPORTED CRIME IN KANSAS CITY, MO.**

(HOMICIDE, RAPE, FELONIOUS ASSAULT, ROBBERY,
BURGLARY, GRAND LARCENY, AUTO THEFT)

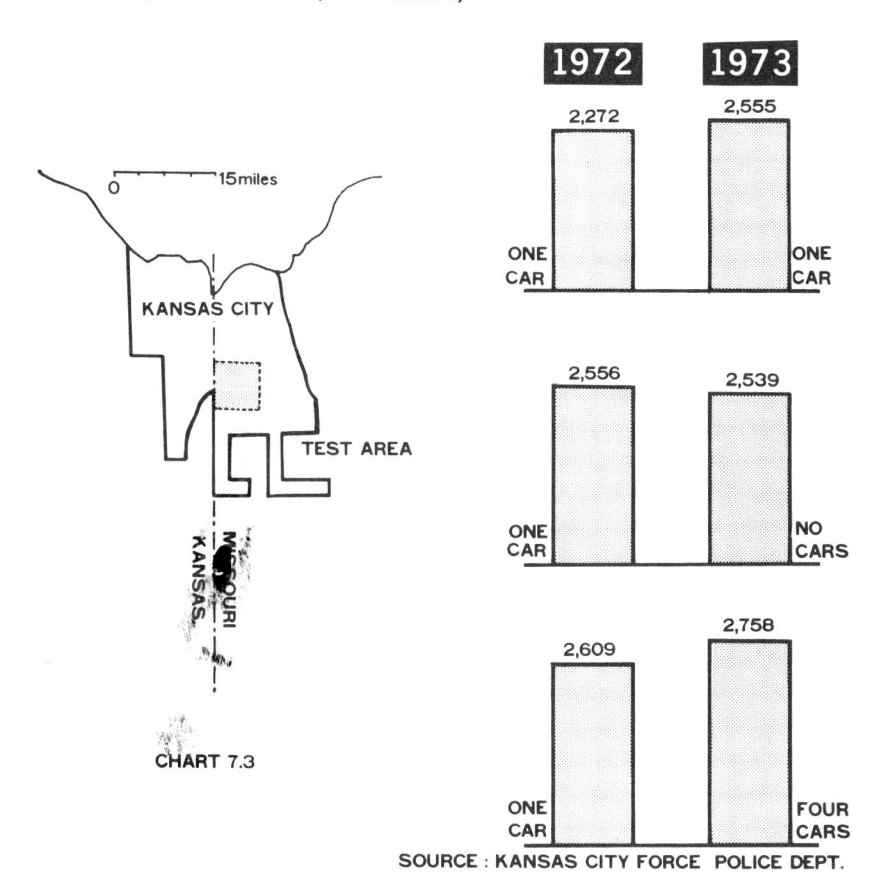

	1972	1973
ONE CAR / ONE CAR	2,272	2,555
ONE CAR / NO CARS	2,556	2,539
ONE CAR / FOUR CARS	2,609	2,758

CHART 7.3

SOURCE: KANSAS CITY FORCE POLICE DEPT.

This leads us to the third basic function—apprehension. This function is concerned with what the five-year-old boy mentioned, "Catching robbers." (or rapists or burglars, etc.) This function affects both *intent* and *opportunity*. Despite what some contemporary sociologists say about punishment being no deterrent to crime, experience of centuries of civilization has shown otherwise. There is a measure of prevention in potential rehabilitation while on parole or in jail. Also, who could dispute the deterrence effect of the apprehension function when you consider the—*opportunity to commit the act.* Robbers, 77 percent of whom are repeaters, have little opportunity to "do their thing" while in the slammer.

There is one other absolute and positive preventative measure under the apprehension function. As you know there are few lines of robbers queuing up at police headquarters waiting to surrender. More often than not they have to be taken by force and at times by deadly force. Those robbers killed probably account for some of the 23 percent that show up as non-repeaters—unless you believe in ghosts.

3. STYLES OF POLICING

Experts agree that there are three basic styles of policing in the United States. The Service Style is generally found in the more affluent suburbs and "bedroom communities". It is characterized by many services (such as ambulance service) being performed by police. Under the service style the accent is on community relations and the basic function of prevention is prevalent.

The Watchman Style is usually found in police organizations in older, established, eastern cities. It is best characterized by footbeats and marked patrols. The primary emphasis of the watchman style seems to be on deterrence.

The Legalistic Style prevails in more modern and progressive police departments. Organizations with a more favorable police image (e. g. State Police, County Police and the Los Angeles Police Department) seem to be legalistic in style. The basic police function of the legalistic style, as indicated by its name, is apprehension. This is the style recommended by the writer for best results against the crime problem.

No department known to this writer is essentially "pure" in style. Departments often reflect all three styles but a predominant style usually prevails. The best style for your area is the one that keeps crime low.

4. SUMMARY

The basic mission for which the police exist is to reduce crime and disorder. The further police activity strays from this goal the least justification for its existence.

Police engage in three basic functions to fight crime: Prevention, Deterrence, and Apprehension. Role confusion results when you try to do all three at once. For example, if a police stakeout team is inside a bank waiting for a holdup (apprehension function) and a K-9 man in uniform is on patrol outside the bank (deterrence function) a waste of police resources results. This kind of abuse of police tactics is widespread in most departments.

Also, some police programs are "window dressing". For example, if a police community relations program (prevention function) does not result in lower crime rates—it should be abandoned.

The basic police functions are related to styles of policing. A close examination of the theories will show a relationship between: Service style and prevention; Watchman style and deterrence; Legalistic style and apprehension. The latter style and function seems the best bet to reduce a crime problem.

Since many other elements of society: Religion, Education, Family, etc. have a prevention-type role concerning crime, it behooves police to find their proper role and perform it. The police are the only members of society charged with carrying out the apprehension function. The rest of the criminal justice system depends on police to initiate the action. Therefore in order to have a successful anti-crime program police must develop crime-specific goals on selected repressible crimes. (Robbery, Burglary and Auto Theft for starts). Since these crimes have high recidivism rates, apprehension and incarceration of criminal repeaters will result in lower crime rates, thus achieving the basic goal of police service.

Going back to the comparison of crime to disease,
What stage are we in?
How do we cure it?
—With "preventive" medicine? (Prevention)
—With treatment and possible infection of other areas? (Deterrence)
—Or by surgery? (Apprehension)

If you opt for the saw, join me in proceeding further, because at this stage, (crime epidemic) drastic action is needed. It is interesting to note here that many elements of society (church, school, family, etc.) are responsible for preventing and deterring crime. Only the police are charged with the responsibility of apprehension. If we accept this responsibility and do it well, we can give the other elements of society enough time to catch up with their deficiencies that too often contribute to the crime problem.

References
1. James Q. Wilson, Varieties of Police Behavior, (New York: Atheneum, 1972)

5. QUESTIONS FOR DISCUSSION

1. What is the basic goal of police service?
2. List the three basic police functions. What function do you feel will have the best chance of lowering crime in your community?
3. Identify what basic function applies to the given police tactics or task: K–9 patrol; Police Community Relations; Stakeout duty; Juvenile work; patrol in a marked police vehicle; patrol in an unmarked police vehicle; surveillance of known offenders; Police Athletic League duties; helicopters on patrol; responding to silent holdup alarm.
4. Draw a flow chart of the Criminal Justice System. Which element must initiate action against criminals? How are the

Unit 7   THE GOALS OF POLICE SERVICE   77

elements of the Criminal Justice System dependent upon each other?

5. What are the basic styles of policing in the United States? What style is predominant in your area? Which style do you recommend? Why?

6. Explain the findings of the Kansas City Patrol Study. What are its ramifications on marked police patrol?

UNIT 8

REACTIVE vs. PROACTIVE RESPONSE TO CRIME

There are two basic ways police perform the apprehension function:

—By criminal investigation of crimes already committed

—By responding to and intervening in a crime in progress

Traditionally police in the United States have engaged in criminal investigation in the apprehension stage. (Reactive Response) Consider recent court decisions against police activities:

Mapp v. Ohio, 367 U.S. 643 (1961).
  Exclusionary rule on search and seizure

Escobedo v. Illinois, 378 U.S. 478 (1964).
  Limits police ability to obtain criminal confessions

Miranda v. Arizona, 384 U.S. 436 (1966).
  Limits police ability to obtain criminal confessions

Chimel v. California, 395 U.S. 752 (1970).
  Restricts the area of a search incidental to an arrest

These rulings and many others have been directed toward the traditional reactive or criminal investigation method of apprehension. Since police cannot be present during the commission of most crimes to catch the doer in the act, it can be expected that we will continue to see emphasis on criminal investigation as the mainstay of apprehension. However, the other form of apprehension—responding to a crime in progress—offers a much more proactive opportunity to "catch-em-in-the-act." Name two court decisions that hamper police from apprehending the criminal while he is doing his thing. Tough-huh?

This is the way to go. There is a vast untapped potential for catching criminals in the act. These are the tactics and methods that will be the prime concern of "Tactical Approaches to Crimes in Progress." A prosecutor has a better case when he has a professional officer giving direct testimony of a crime he witnessed

Unit 8   REACTIVE vs. PROACTIVE RESPONSE   79

than depending on a weak-eyed, 80 year-old-lady to identify a pursesnatcher, mugger or a rapist. More convictions (eventually) mean more criminals denied the opportunity to commit their act.

1. DETECTIVE WORK

The Detective Bureau is the mainstay of the criminal investigation approach to apprehension. A good detective should be judged, not on his clearance rate, but by his physical arrest and multiple clearance rate.

Physical arrests by detectives are made by the detective identifying the doer and by going out and "collaring" the suspect. Multiple clearance is the solving of previously reported crimes by interrogation or other investigative techniques.

Since I spent several years as a detective, I appreciate the difficulty and glamour of the job. The true potential for success in the proactive approach lies in the ability of the detective to establish patterns (perhaps with the aid of a computer) and gather intelligence on crimes *about to be committed*. I cannot underestimate the value of this detective activity.

Woe to the criminals when an effective detective operation alerts a TAC squad of an impending robbery or burglary. Most good detectives would like a chance to be in on the arrest and when possible the apprehension should be a joint effort between the detective and TAC squad. Instead of sitting behind idle typewriters in Detective Headquarters watching "Kojak" and "Toma" on television they should be performing the roles themselves—on the street.

2. STUDY ON DETECTIVE vs. THE ROBBERS

A three-year, $200,000 study has found that the police detective, hero of countless books and films, is not very useful in catching robbers.

The recently completed study, "The Prevention and Control of Robbery" was undertaken by the Center on Administration of Criminal Justice at the University of California and financed in part by the Justice Department's Law Enforcement Assistance Administration.

The study, headed by Floyd Feeney and Adrianne Weir, members of President Johnson's Crime Commission, found that detectives made only 10 to 30 percent of robbery arrests in a number of cities. It suggested that major detective forces might not be required except in the largest cities.

The report said that "In no other area of police operations do there appear to be so many myths or so much resistance either to change or serious self-examination."

Partly because of "entrenched political power in many departments of the existing detective bureaus", the report said, "the service as a whole seems unwilling to confront the serious issues involved."

Noting that Oklahoma City allocated only 2 percent of its total force to detective units while Cincinnati assigned 18 percent, the report called for a careful analysis of:

—The effectiveness of detectives in apprehending various kinds of criminals.

—The division of responsibility between patrol and detective units.

—Whether robbery investigations were better handled by specialized or general detective units.

3. CRIMINAL INTELLIGENCE—ENHANCING THE PROACTIVE RESPONSE

Again, although I am advocating a proactive response to street crime, I am not recommending abandoning the old mainstay of criminal investigation. In fact, it should be reordered and intensified. Emphasis should be placed on getting detectives out of headquarters and onto the street. One measure of how much time

Unit 8   REACTIVE vs. PROACTIVE RESPONSE   81

your detectives spend on the street is mileage chalked up by detective fleets. If they are putting more mileage on their typewriters than on their cars and shoe leather, you have a problem.

There are several things that could be done to intensify the criminal investigation approach and enhance the proactive approach. One is in the area of informants, the other is trading "little fishes" for "bigger fishes."

Many departments sever vice work (gambling, prostitution, liquor enforcement, narcotics) from detective work. This is a mistake. Some of the best criminal informants can be found among the "street people" engaged in these activities. A detective is not going to find a good informant in a nursery school, church or synagogue. He has to cultivate them on the street where crime also flourishes. Every bookie, pimp, hustler, bartender, club owner and junkie is a potential "snitch." Now these people don't come up with the important info for the love of police. You have to have something to trade. One is money; the other is "slack."

Every detective should have an adequate monthly allowance for cultivating "street people" into good informants. Too often the paperwork involved with accounting for the money deters its use. The funds should be discretionary and the detective held accountable for results in the form of quality pinches and good intelligence information. In case of hiring an undercover operator or paying a substantial sum for needed information, the detective should have recourse to a large fund through proper channels.

When you consider the other informant motivator, "slack", I am not recommending that individuals be given a "license to steal", but I am taking cognizance of the time honored law enforcement tradition of trading little fishes (petty offenders) for bigger fishes (major offenders).

Although there is potential for abuse in this system as there is in the system of informant's fees, you cannot justify its exclusion from the police arsenal against crime. It is not too difficult for a commander to find out who is "wheeling and dealing" and who is producing quality pinches and information. Given the proper authority the detective will be able to do the job. In fact, most detectives will agree they would rather be more than a detective in name only.

4. SUMMARY

We have been considering the two ways that police perform the apprehension function and have found that the reactive and proactive responses are not mutually exclusive. In fact, one can complement the other. All it takes is policemen and detectives exchanging criminal information and functioning on the street. This leads us to the question, what if there were neither detectives nor policemen on the streets at all? What would be the result? Perhaps Unit 9—"A Day Without Police", will shed some light on what happens when there is absolutely no police protection in a large city.

5. QUESTIONS FOR DISCUSSION

1. What are the two basic ways police perform the apprehension function? What is the traditional response to the crime problem?
2. List several recent Supreme Court decisions that have affected police operations. What response to the crime problem do they concern? Why are there no decisions concerning the "proactive" response to crime?
3. Which response to the crime problem is likely to result in an almost 100% conviction rate? Why?
4. How can members of a tac squad and detective squad cooperate in fighting crime? Is this cooperation essential?
5. Who makes most of the arrests for the crime of robbery? (Uniform or Detectives) Why?

Unit 8 REACTIVE vs. PROACTIVE RESPONSE

6. Should the traditional "reactive" response to the crime problem be abandoned? Why? Why not?
7. How can both responses (proactive & reactive) to the crime problem be enhanced? Discuss the pros and cons on developing informants.

UNIT 9

A DAY WITHOUT POLICE

What if the police in your city went off duty for a day? What would happen? Would citizens obey the law even though they knew there were no police around to apprehend them for criminal acts?

Citizens in a large city had such questions answered for them recently when both their policemen and firemen went on strike. What occurred in that city could also happen elsewhere.

It was Montreal, Canada, that was left for a day without the police. Policemen there went on strike in an effort to obtain a wage increase that would bring their pay into line with what Toronto policemen were receiving. What occurred during that day was revealing.

The strike of Montreal's 3,700 policemen began at eight o'clock Wednesday morning, October 7, 1969. Most of the policemen assembled in Paul Sauve Arena for an all-day meeting. Some senior officers sought to keep a skeleton staff on duty, but militant young officers forced them to leave.

The Quebec Provincial Police, a much smaller force maintained by the provincial government, tried to provide limited protection for the city throughout the day. However, some of the striking municipal police also interfered with these law enforcement officers. The Montreal Star reported:

> Militant Montreal policemen at the Paul Sauve Arena, hearing the QPP were taking over their duties, decided to short circuit the plan.
>
> They began monitoring the QPP radio bands. Whenever a car was summoned to a specific address, a dozen city officers piled into a riot squad truck and drove off to meet the QPP cruiser.

Unit 9 A DAY WITHOUT POLICE

The cruisers were hijacked and driven, sirens wailing and lights flashing, back to the Paul Sauve Arena. Cheering Montreal police greeted each arrival.

Eight commandeered cruisers later, and with their radio frequencies jammed intermittently, the entire QPP force was summoned back to headquarters.

Thus, the city of Montreal was left almost entirely without police protection. What occurred that day has caused many persons to wonder if something similar would occur in their city under such circumstances.

Rioting, arson and looting broke out. In parts of Montreal there were piles of broken glass, blocks of looted stores and burned-out vehicles.

During the day there were twenty-three major holdups, including ten bank robberies. Armed men made off with $28,000 from the City and District Savings Bank on St. Denis Street. Four men with machine guns held up a finance company. Conditions became so bad that in a radio address Lucien Saulnier, Chairman of the Executive Committee of the City, advised citizens to stay home and protect their property. One householder who did, shot a burglar dead.

Around 8 p. m. scores of taxis pulled up at the Murray Hill Limousine Company garage. Taxi drivers had long held a grudge against the company. Molotov cocktails were thrown, and buses and cars were set afire. Employees opened fire on the mob with shotguns. A provincial policeman was shot dead; other persons were wounded by gunfire.

Passersby were caught up in the violence, and a mob, two to three hundred strong, left the Murray Hill garage and proceeded toward Montreal's main shopping and hotel district. With clubs, baseball bats and rocks the mob commenced an orgy of senseless destruction and looting.

They smashed the plate-glass windows of the Queen Elizabeth Hotel, looting the merchandise. The depredation of the lower floor of the beautiful IBM building followed. Next the Windsor Hotel and Mount Royal Hotel had the plate-glass broken and the shops looted.

The pillagers swept east on St. Catherine Street, smashing windows and looting stores as they went. Broken plate-glass was scattered along the street for two miles. So extensive was the damage that a glass expert estimated that it would cost $2,000,000 merely to replace the broken windows. The total damage from fires, destruction and theft has been placed at millions more.

Jewelry stores, clothing stores and windows full of electrical equipment were prime targets. Photographs appearing in the public press showed thieves helping themselves to merchandise.

When four officers of the Quebec Provincial Police tried at 11:30 p. m. to bring the mob under control they were literally trampled down by the surging rioters. A QPP cruiser that ventured along the street was seized by the mob and chopped into a total wreck while the officers sat inside.

With police restrictions removed, law and order had collapsed. Government leaders said the city was "threatened by anarchy." Leo Pearson, a member of the legislature, said: "Before we know it we could have a full scale revolution on our hands." The extent of the lawlessness was amazing. One man reported:

"I don't mean hoodlums and habitual lawbreakers, I mean just plain people committed offenses they would not dream of trying if there was a policeman standing on the corner. I saw cars driven through red lights. Drivers shot up the wrong side of the street because they realized no one would catch them. You wouldn't believe the number of car accidents I saw, because drivers took chances cutting corners and crossing traffic lanes against regulations. They knew there was no cop around to make a record of it."

As the situation grew more serious, the Quebec Provincial Government took steps to bring the lawlessness under control. At 4:30 p. m. all provincial police and the municipal police of fifty-six smaller municipalities were placed under the unified command of Maurice St. Pierre, Director of the Quebec Provincial Police.

Unit 9 A DAY WITHOUT POLICE 87

At 8:10 p. m. Provincial Attorney General Remi Paul called on the federal government to send in the army to restore order. Troops of the Royal 22nd Regiment were brought to Montreal from Valcartier near Quebec City.

Additionally, the provincial legislature moved rapidly to pass a special law. It became effective at 10 p. m. ordering the police to resume their duties at midnight, sixteen hours after the strike began. The law provided penalties of $25 to $100 per day for failure to comply, and fines of $5,000 to $50,000 per day for any union or union representative who encouraged violation of the statute.

When informed of the law, Sergeant Guy Marcil, President of the Police Brotherhood, spoke to the policemen still keeping vigil in the arena. He ordered them to return to their stations. As they did so, a surface calm was restored, but armed soldiers remained on guard.

A political demonstration scheduled for October 10 at City Hall was ordered canceled. To ensure the maintenance of order, more than 5,000 armed men of the Montreal Police, Quebec Provincial Police, and the Royal Canadian armed forces surrounded City Hall. It was the largest display of armed might in a Canadian city since World War II. The demonstration was stopped and the crowd dispersed without further outbreaks.

Many, stunned by the suddenness and savagery of the violence, pondered the significance of what occurred. What does it mean? Why such a destructive outbreak?

What occurred in Montreal, many persons undoubtedly will conclude, could occur in their city if it were left without police protection. Former Attorney General of Quebec, Claude Wagner, described the unhappy situation very bluntly, explaining: "When the police quit, we know we are on the brink of a revolution."

Prime Minister Pierre Elliott Trudeau also noted the widespread nature of the problem. He said that the walkout by Montreal policemen and firemen is simply "part of a total society running amok."

1. SUMMARY

It is interesting to compare this dreadful situation with the Kansas City study on the effect of Police Patrol on the Incidence of Crime. The difference in what happened in Montreal compared to Kansas City is that in the Canadian City the police were not available at all. You have often heard that crime prevention by police is hard to measure. For one long day Montreal had the scale and it measured "anarchy."

2. QUESTIONS FOR DISCUSSION

1. What do you think would happen if all the police in your city went on strike for a day?
2. Should police be permitted to strike? Discuss.
3. How do you explain the reaction of people to the Montreal Police strike?
4. Compare this situation with recent partial police "job actions" such as in New York and San Francisco.
5. How did the Montreal Police strike compare with the Kansas City Patrol Study?

UNIT 10

ROLE IMPLEMENTATION

According to the National Advisory Commission on Criminal Justice Standards and Goals, the police agency is a service arm of government and should develop policy consistent with the goals and objectives of the governing authority. When the police chief executive is silent, others in the police agency, even the basic policemen, may set policies or interpret local government policies on their own. Such interpretations are often wrong. Besides, it is the police chief executive who is directly responsible to the governing authority. Therefore, he has an irrevocable responsibility to insure that policy is formulated and is consistent with local government.

The purpose of this unit and the National Commission Standards it contains is to assist the police chief executive in establishing policy and implementing the role of the agency and the policemen in the community.

I. DEVELOPMENT OF GOALS AND OBJECTIVES

It is imperative that every police agency develop short- and long-range goals and objectives to guide agency functions. To assist in this development, every unit commander should review and reduce to writing the principal goals and objectives of his unit.

1. Every police agency and every unit within the agency should insure that its goals and objectives are:
    a. Consistent with the role of the police as defined by the agency's chief executive;
    b. Responsive to community needs;
    c. Reasonably attainable;
    d. Sufficiently flexible to permit change as needed; and
    e. Quantifiable and measurable where possible.

2. Every police agency should provide for maximum input both from within and without the agency in the development of its goals and objectives. It should:

   a. Create an atmosphere that encourages unrestricted submission of ideas by all employees regardless of rank; and

   b. Establish methods to obtain ideas from a variety of organizations and individuals outside the agency.

3. Every police agency and every unit within each agency should publish and disseminate its goals and objectives to provide uniform direction of employee efforts.

4. Every police chief executive should require every unit commander to make a periodic review of unit goals and objectives and submit a written evaluation of the progress made toward the attainment of these goals.

Annually, in conjunction with the budget preparation, every police chief executive should provide for review and evaluation of all agency goals and objectives and for revisions where appropriate.

A. NATIONAL ADVISORY COMMISSION COMMENTARY

One of the most pressing and challenging duties of the police chief executive is establishing goals and objectives toward which all personnel of the police agency should be directing their efforts. But to achieve goals, agencywide cooperation is necessary.

The establishment and achievement of goals and of objectives follow such similar paths that the words goal and objective are often interchanged. Definitions from the California Council on Criminal Justice's "A GUIDE FOR CRIMINAL JUSTICE PLANNING" will be used throughout this discussion:

Goal—a statement of broad direction, general purpose or intent. A goal is general and timeless and is not concerned with a particular achievement within a specified time period.

Objective—a desired accomplishment which can be measured within a given time frame and under specifiable conditions.

The attainment of the objective advances the system toward a corresponding goal.

Fundamental to the establishment of all goals and objectives is a perception of the problems encountered or anticipated by the agency. Clear definition and careful analysis of the factors generating the problem may clearly indicate possible solutions and suggest appropriate goals and objectives. On the other hand, the failure to perceive or to understand a problem may lead to the establishment of goals or objectives that could be nonproductive or even counterproductive.

B. WORKABLE GOALS AND OBJECTIVES

Every police agency requires both long- and short-range goals and objectives. Many problems which the police agency wishes to solve may require years of effort, while others lend themselves to a more rapid solution. The more time required for solution of a problem, the less reliable predictions will tend to be. Long-range goals must be more flexible and more adaptable to possible changing conditions than short-range goals, although the latter, too, must be sufficiently flexible to meet changing conditions.

In establishing goals and objectives, the police chief executive is bound, of course, by constitutional limitations and by the laws under which he serves. Additionally, he must insure that the goals and objectives of the agency are consistent with the role of the police he had defined for his agency. These goals and objectives, in turn, should provide constraints upon commanders of agency units in establishing unit goals and objectives.

Just as agency goals and objectives are necessary to coordinate and direct the efforts of agency personnel, so unit goals and objectives are essential to coordinate and direct efforts of unit personnel to fulfill the mission of the unit. Unit goals and objectives should be put into writing and should be reviewed by the chief executive. They should complement the agency's overall goals and objectives.

All goals and objectives, agencywide and unit, should be directly responsive to community needs. Normally, if problem definition and analysis have been adequate and alternative solutions carefully screened, responsiveness to community needs can be achieved.

Goals and objectives will be most effective if they are reasonably attainable. It is not necessary that they be easily attainable; often it is advantageous if they present a real challenge. But goals or objectives that are impossible to attain cause discouragement and reduced effort. The setting of impossible goals defeats one of the purposes; unifying effort. Goals or objectives that are unattainable immediately should be incorporated into agency plans for further development if they become more practical.

Where possible, goals and objectives should be quantifiable and measurable. This makes the standards and goals more specific, and usually requires more detailed analysis of the factors leading to their establishment. Quantification and measurability give a better understanding of exactly what is needed and what has been accomplished.

Unlike a public works agency that can set specific tangible objectives, police agencies perform many activities that have intangible results. The difficulty of quantification and measurability is no excuse for not making use of them where possible.

C. DEVELOPMENT OF GOALS AND OBJECTIVES

Neither the police chief executive nor the unit commander alone, can establish goals and objectives. All employees within the agency, particularly employees at the execution level, can contribute to the understanding of the problems. These employees have face-to-face contact with members of the community and are coping with problems in the field. They, in turn, will understand the problems to be met only through contact and discussion of the problems with members of the community.

Obtaining input from within the agency requires an atmosphere that encourages all employees, regardless of rank, to submit ideas. Such an atmosphere must be genuine; it must start at the top and permeate the entire agency. Employees should understand that their evaluation of the problem, their analysis of cause, and their suggestions of possible solutions are all needed. The Kansas City, Missouri, Police Department has formalized this process by establishing task forces composed of personnel of all ranks, with emphasis on the lower ranks, to work out solutions to problems in certain areas. The agency has succeeded in creating the desired atmosphere, but it is too soon to evaluate the contribution of these task forces.

Other agencies of government often are a good source of ideas and assistance, as are community and service organizations. In order to obtain a response that is representative of the community, the police agency should take care to solicit input from private as well as official sources. Additionally, and of utmost importance, is the requirement set out in the first standard of this unit that the goals and objectives of the police department must be directed by the policies of the governing body which provides formal authority for the police function.

Community meetings can be valuable for providing private input, although in some cases there is a disappointingly small number of people involved in community activity. Furthermore, those responding have not always been representative of the community, and in some cases response from community meetings does not always reach the top levels of the police agency. The last is always a risk if command personnel do not attend the community meetings.

D. INTERNAL PUBLICATION OF GOALS AND OBJECTIVES

No goal or objective, no matter how well founded or how well articulated, will be of value to the agency unless it is published and disseminated among the agency personnel who will be responsible for achieving it. Each employee must know what the goals and objectives are; he must understand them or be able to refer to them if in doubt. Only then can he work effectively with other employees and direct his efforts toward achieving those goals and objectives.

E. REVIEW AND REVISION OF GOALS AND OBJECTIVES

Commanders should use the goals and objectives of their units to measure unit progress and to indicate where additional direction might be needed. Requiring each unit commander to make a periodic review of all unit goals and objectives and to submit a written progress assures the chief executive of such attention. It also assures him that unit goals and objectives are being reviewed for continuing validity.

In conjunction with annual budget preparation and justification, the chief executive should require that all agency goals and objectives be reviewed, evaluated, and revised where appropriate. This permits re-evaluation of priorities in terms of available funding. If a goal or objective does not have sufficient priority to merit funding, it should be modified, postponed, or abandoned.

2. ESTABLISHING THE ROLE OF THE PATROL OFFICER (STANDARD 8.1)

Every police chief executive immediately should develop written policy that defines the role of the patrol officer, and should establish operational objectives and priorities that reflect the most effective use of the patrol officer in reducing crime.

1. Every police chief executive should acknowledge that the patrol officer is the agency's primary element for the deliverance of police services and prevention of criminal activity.

2. Every police chief executive should insure maximum efficiency in the deliverance of patrol services by setting out in written policy the objectives and priorities governing these services. This policy:

    a. Should insure that resources are concentrated on fundamental police duties;

b. Should insure that patrol officers are engaged in tasks that are related to the police function;

c. Should require immediate response to incidents where there is an immediate threat to the safety of an individual, a report of a crime in progress, or a crime committed and the apprehension of the suspected offender is likely. Urban area response time —from the time a call is dispatched to the arrival at the scene—under normal conditions should not exceed 3 minutes for emergency calls, and 20 minutes for non-emergency calls;

d. Should emphasize the need for preventive patrol to reduce the opportunity for criminal activity; and

e. Should provide a procedure for accepting reports of criminal incidents not requiring a field investigation.

3. Every police chief executive should insure that all elements of the agency, especially the patrol and communications elements, know the priority placed upon each request for police service.

4. Every police chief executive should implement a public information program to inform the community of the agency's policies regarding the deliverance of police service. This program should include provisions to involve citizens in crime prevention activities.

A. NATIONAL ADVISORY COMMISSION COMMENTARY

The patrol officer has two basic responsibilities, regardless of the size of the police agency in which he works; to prevent criminal activity and to provide day-to-day police services to the community. All the patrol officer's duties and responsibilities are encompassed in these two broad mandates.

The specific duties and responsibilities of the patrol officer are innumerable, as varied and complex as the society in which he works. In his multi-purpose role, the patrol officer serves as a protector of public safety, enforcer of law, controller of traffic, and investigator and interpreter of the law.

In his role as protector, he promotes and preserves order, defends persons from imminent physical harm, responds to requests for protective service, and resolves conflicts between individuals and groups. As law enforcer, his first duty is the protection of constitutional guarantees; his second, the enforcement of statutes. He should encourage voluntary compliance with the law and should seek to reduce the opportunity for criminal activity.

The patrol officer engages in a wide variety of traffic control activities. This function is particularly important in connection with traffic accidents, demonstrations, riots, and disasters.

As an investigator, the patrol officer conducts preliminary investigations of complaints of criminal acts, gathers physical evidence, and presents it with testimony at judicial proceedings and other formal hearings. In the course of his investigations, the patrol officer identifies and apprehends suspected offenders, recovers stolen and lost property, and frequently uncovers evidence of other crime. (It should be noted, however, that in some departments of 15 men or less, the patrol officer conducts the full investigation of many complaints, and a number of larger departments are experimenting with this procedure as part of team policing.)

The patrol officer is the first interpreter of the law and in effect performs a quasi-judicial function. He makes the first attempt to match the reality of human conflict with the law; he determines whether to take no action, to advise, to warn, or to arrest; he determines whether he must apply physical force, perhaps sufficient to cause death. It is he who must discern the fine distinction between a civil and a criminal conflict, between merely unorthodox behavior and a crime, between legitimate dissent and disturbance of the peace, between the truth and a lie. As interpreter of the law, he recognizes that a decision to arrest is only the first step in the determination of guilt or innocence. He is guided by, and guardian of, the Constitution.

The patrol officer in any city is the most visible representative of government. Usually in a motor vehicle, sometimes on foot, he patrols a specific area, responds to calls for service, and maintains order in the community. Unlike a specialist or a technician, a patrol officer must be proficient at a variety of tasks rather than skilled in a limited field. Although he is not a supervisor in the organizational sense, he is responsible for the safety and direction of hundreds of people each day.

John A. Webster's study of the patrol officer in a city of 400,000 revealed that only a small percentage of his time is spent actually fighting crime. Webster concludes that police chief executives should redirect the agency's emphasis to reflect the larger part of the patrol officer's function. This does not mean the patrol officer's effort to reduce crime should be reduced, but it does mean the agency should strive to improve the officer, his tools, and his tactics. Police chief executives must provide the patrol officer pay, recognition, equipment, and tactical direction commensurate with the complexity and diversity of his role.

3. PATROL SERVICE PRIORITIES

The primary goal of police agencies is to provide the best service at the lowest cost. Hiring additional personnel improves service but costs money; utilizing manpower more efficiently does not. The police chief executive should determine his agency's objectives and establish a priority on its services. Services provided by patrol officers should be measured against these objectives and priorities. When they are not essential, they should be eliminated. Unit 11 "Resource Allocation" lists non-emergency services and their possible delegation to other agencies.

Police agencies first must perform fundamental police duties. If police are burdened with non-enforcement duties or with low priority enforcement, officers are diverted from the tasks that directly reduce crime. The patrol officer's effort should be directed to combating crime, with the major emphasis on serious crimes.

A. RESPONSE TIME

Relieving patrol officers of minor tasks increases their capability to reduce crime. FBI studies indicate that the clearance rate of crime goes up as response time of patrol units is reduced. The figures show that police solve two-thirds of the crimes they respond to in less than 2 minutes, but only one out of five when response time is 5 minutes or longer. Therefore, unsolved crime is reduced when agencies insure that patrol officers are available and respond immediately to serious incidents.

Rapid response time also increases community confidence in the police. Police agencies should establish a reputation for swift apprehension of law violators. Patrol officers should be dispatched immediately where citizens are in danger, where a crime is in progress, and where the likelihood of apprehending the offender is great.

B. INFORMING PERSONNEL OF PRIORITIES

Every member of the agency should know the agency's objectives in order of priority. Above all, the patrol and communications elements must have coherent guidelines. The activities of the patrol force are governed for the most part by the radio dispatcher. Therefore, it is essential that communications personnel follow the order of priority in dispatching patrol officers. This practice will help insure that the patrol officer spends his time on the most significant crime problems.

In addition, the patrol officer is responsible for accomplishing the objectives of the agency on his own initiative and should be guided by priorities. If, for example, a patrol spends much of his time writing minor traffic citations in a district plagued by daylight residence burglaries, he is not contributing to the agency's effectiveness in reducing crime. Through specific policies and effective supervision, the patrol officer should be made aware of the activities demanding the greatest portion of his time, and should devote his efforts to these tasks.

4. ENHANCING THE ROLE OF THE PATROL OFFICER (STANDARD 8.2)

Every local government and police chief executive, recognizing that the patrol function is the most important element of the police agency, immediately should adopt policies that attract and retain highly qualified personnel in the patrol force.

1. Every local government should expand its classification and pay system to provide greater advancement opportunities within the patrol ranks.

The system should provide:

   a. Multiple pay grades within the basic rank;
   b. Opportunity for advancement within the basic rank to permit equality between patrol officers and investigators;
   c. Parity in top salary step between patrol officers and non-supervisory officers assigned to other operational functions;
   d. Proficiency pay for personnel who have demonstrated expertise in specific field activities that contribute to more efficient police service.

2. Every police chief executive should seek continually to enhance the role of the patrol officer by providing status and recognition from the community. The police chief executive should:

   a. Provide distinctive insignia indicating demonstrated expertise in specific field activities;
   b. Insure that all elements within the agency provide maximum assistance and cooperation to the patrol officer;

c. Implement a community information program emphasizing the importance of the patrol officer in the life of the community and encouraging community cooperation in providing police service;

d. Provide comprehensive initial and inservice training thoroughly to equip the patrol officer for his role;

e. Insure that field supervisory personnel possess the knowledge and skills necessary to guide the patrol officer;

f. Implement procedures to provide agencywide recognition of patrol officers who have consistently performed in an efficient and commendable manner;

g. Encourage suggestions on changes in policies, procedures, and other matters that affect the delivery of police services and reduction of crime;

h. Provide deployment flexibility to facilitate various approaches to individual community crime problems;

i. Adopt policies and procedures that allow the patrol officer to conduct the complete investigation of crimes which do not require extensive follow-up investigation, and allow them to close the investigation of those crimes; and

j. Insure that promotional oral examination boards recognize that patrol work provides valuable experience for men seeking promotion to supervisory positions.

A. NATIONAL ADVISORY COMMISSION COMMENTARY

There is no more important police function than the day to day job of the patrol officer. The success of the police agency depends on it and every effort should be made to attract and retain highly qualified patrolmen. But the policies of many police agencies encourage the best patrol officers to seek other assignments. These agencies make no provisions for officers who desire to ad-

Unit 10 ROLE IMPLEMENTATION 101

vance and earn more pay while remaining in the patrol function. As a result, qualified patrol officers often seek promotion to supervisor positions or transfer to other positions in order to obtain greater status and pay. An agency's policies should encourage highly qualified officers to remain on the patrol force to insure that it is truly the backbone of the police department.

In the vast majority of police agencies throughout the country, academy graduates are assigned to the patrol force. This initial assignment is viewed as an extension of recruit training; it is within the patrol environment that an officer serves his probationary period. After proving himself competent as a patrolman, the officer is considered for staff and specialized assignments. Consequently, patrol divisions experience continual manpower turnover as more and more recruits join patrol and talented patrol officers depart for other positions. This often results in a patrol force composed of the inexperienced and the mediocre.

B. CLASSIFICATION AND PAY SYSTEM

In most police agencies, no distinction is made between the duties and responsibilities of the patrol officer with 1 year of service and the officer with 15 years. As a result, a highly qualified, well motivated officer feels that he is not progressing unless he transfers from the patrol force. Even if he enjoys his work, he feels he should seek a position with more responsibility and status.

A system recently adopted in Los Angeles, Calif., provides multiple pay grades within the basic rank, granting well qualified patrol officers greater responsibilities and pay while they remain on the patrol force. When a patrol officer can advance to a salary equal to that of an investigator or supervisor, he is more likely to remain on the patrol force.

Such a classification and pay system permits an officer to choose the career path best suited to him. Adequate compensation encourages the competent officer who enjoys working in patrol to remain there and become even more proficient.

For example, proficiency pay can be given to officers who train recruits in patrol duty, who coordinate activities of a patrol team, or who have a special skill or experience that contributes to patrol efficiency. Special skills that may warrant proficiency pay include: evidence gathering and preservation; use of chemical agents and firearms; proficiency in a foreign language; operation of specialized vehicles such as motorcycles, aircraft, and boats; operation of specialized equipment such as radio, electronic surveillance devices, breathalyzer, and polygraph; photography; writing; accounting; and law.

Police agencies can benefit by training patrol officers to be part-time specialists. In smaller agencies that cannot afford fulltime specialized personnel, the patrol officer is adaptable to fill this need. In large urban agencies, the patrol officer can help relieve the burden on specialized officers.

Local government and police agencies should determine areas where specialization is needed, establish appropriate qualifications, schedule periodic examinations, and offer adequate proficiency pay.

C. STATUS AND RECOGNITION

Although important, salary alone will not make patrol service attractive to first-rate personnel. The patrol officer needs to feel that his role is important in accomplishing the agency's goals and objectives. Competent patrol officers should be granted greater responsibility and it should be indicated by a distinctive uniform insignia. Appropriate insignia also should be awarded to officers qualified as part-time specialists. Insignia enhances an officer's pride in his uniform and confidence in himself. It makes his status known to the public and to other officers.

Cooperation is essential in any organization. Quite often in police agencies, friction develops between the patrol officer and specialists. When the patrol officer is treated as relatively unimportant in the agency's operation, cooperation between the various supportive elements and the patrol officer can degenerate to petty rivalry and sometimes to hostility.

To preserve cooperation within a police agency, the chief executive should not permit such hostility to develop. There should be

Unit 10 ROLE IMPLEMENTATION 103

a general understanding throughout the agency that the patrol force is the primary element of the agency and that all specialized and supportive elements exist to supplement the work of the patrol officer.

The patrol officer also needs public understanding of his role in the community. Programs presented in schools, through the media, and at community meetings should emphasize the role of the patrol officer in satisfying day to day community needs. As citizens become aware of the patrol officer's job, they will be more willing to cooperate with him.

Police agencies should not limit their use of patrol officers to uniform patrol in marked police vehicles at fixed hours within artificial boundaries. For example, apprehension rates can be increased by using patrol officers in surveillance and undercover assignments and in plain clothes and unmarked cars in an area experiencing numerous burglaries or robberies. These and other unconventional approaches can reduce crime and raise morale among patrol officers.

By using regularly assigned patrol officers to cope with variations in criminal activity, the agency benefits from their experience and training and enhances their role.

D. INVESTIGATION

The patrol officer's investigative role also should be enlarged. Too often his involvement in a criminal investigation is limited to taking reports. He is expected to interview victims and witnesses, conduct a preliminary investigation, formulate a report, and return to service, all within 30 minutes. The result is usually a hastily prepared report, a cursory preliminary investigation, and an unsolved crime.

Allowing patrol officers to conduct follow-up investigations on some minor incidents relieves the burden on investigators, who usually have time only for major incidents. When no further investigation is possible, the patrol officer should close the case. When necessary, such closed cases can be reopened by the investigative branch of the agency.

As the action arm of the department, the patrol force can provide valuable insight into the operation of the entire agency. Worthwhile suggestions from frontline personnel too often are lost in the organizational structure. Channels of communication should always be open to receive and evaluate recommendations from officers in the field.

Some agencies allow patrol officers to contribute to administrative policy making. The Kansas City, Mo., Police Department appointed patrol officers on boards that evaluate police vehicle accidents and recommend disposition of the cases. Likewise, the patrol officer can contribute his first hand knowledge and experience in matters pertinent to uniform selection or vehicle design and accessory specifications.

E. INCENTIVES

Within every police agency certain patrol officers exhibit unusual initiative and dedication in their daily performance of duty. These men strive to upgrade their profession by consistently performing in the highest tradition of the police service. These officers should be formally commended by their agency and by the community. Too often, recognition is limited to officers who have captured a dangerous criminal or saved a life.

Officer of the Month awards and similar acknowledgements are used by several police agencies to commend outstanding officers. In some cities, such community organizations as Rotary International and Optimists International periodically honor distinguished police officers. On the national level, Parade Magazine, in cooperation with the International Association of Chiefs of Police, honors the Policeman of the Year. This award has given public recognition to the variety of superior police work that does more than apprehend criminals.

Police executives should consult regularly with patrol officers in developing means to reduce crime and increase police efficiency. No one is as close to the problems on the street as the field officer; he can be a rich source of crime reduction suggestions. Furthermore, he is acutely aware of the immediate effects of the methods he employs and can often suggest ways to improve them.

Just as the patrol force should be staffed by highly qualified, well trained patrol officers, it should also have competent, industrious leaders. They must be equal to the task of supervising officers assigned to a large geographical area. They must inspire the men they lead.

F. TRAINING

Providing comprehensive training for patrol officers is a necessary part of maintaining a competent patrol force. Athough patrol officers should be chosen for their sense and ability to react quickly, proper training reduces their need to improvise in difficult field situations.

Some police agencies require officers entering a specialized field to undergo preparatory training. Yet, despite the complexity of the patrol function, police agencies assign men to the patrol force who have only a general knowledge of police work obtained in recruit training. Intensive field training following police academy training should be provided, concentrating exclusively on the patrol function. Furthermore, just as technical positions require refresher and advanced training, the patrol officer's position demands that he receive regular inservice training in the proper techniques of performing his job.

Police chief executives should review the practices of promotion boards, many of which tend to overlook the officer who has remained in patrol for more than a few years. Career minded patrol officers sense this attitude and seek staff and specialized positions in an effort to increase their opportunity for advancement.

When policies are adopted to retain able officers in the patrol force, the quality of patrol personnel competing for promotions will be raised. This will help dispel the attitude that patrol officers do not possess the qualities required of good supervisors. This change of attitude should, in turn, discourage officers from transferring out of the patrol force merely to impress promotion boards. The result will enhance the role of the patrol officer.

5. SUMMARY

Goals and objectives are necessary in any business, particulary in police business. Unfortunately, some departments do not have clear goals and objectives. One reason is that if you don't have a goal—you can't fail. More often than not, police departments and units without goals and objectives have role confusion which usually results in failure.

Failure to perceive or to understand problems (crime and other problems) may lead to the establishment of goals or objectives that could be nonproductive or even counterproductive.

No goal or objective, no matter how well founded or how well articulated, will be of value to the agency unless it is published and disseminated among the agency personnel who will be responsible for achieving it.

The primary goal of police agencies is to provide the best service at the lowest cost. A priority of duties is necessary because if police are burdened with heavy non-enforcement duties or with low priority enforcement (perhaps prostitution), officers are diverted from the tasks that directly reduce crime. The patrol officer's effort should be directed to combatting serious crime.

Since most police resources are expended on patrol, the role of the patrol officer must be enhanced. A progressive classification and pay system, status and recognition, expanded investigatory duties and training can enhance the role of the patrol officer.

Later units will cover alternative units and tactics to the uniformed patrol officer.

6. QUESTIONS FOR DISCUSSION

1. What is the difference between a goal and objective?
2. Why must every police agency develop goals and objectives? Why don't some police agencies have goals and objectives?
3. What are the goals and objectives of your local department?
4. Why must goals and objectives be published and disseminated among agency personnel?
5. Compare the goals and objectives of a professional football coach with those of the police chief. What happens when either individual fails to achieve them?
6. How can the role of the uniformed patrol officer be enhanced?
7. What is the relationship between response time and crime clearance?
8. What are the enforcement—service priorities of your police department?
9. What possible crime-fighting alternatives do you see instead of uniformed police patrol? Explain.

*

SECTION 3
POLICE OPERATIONS

UNIT II

RESOURCE ALLOCATION

Manpower is the most important resource a police administrator can apply to the crime problem. If the war on crime is to be won it will be with policemen operating effectively where crime occurs. The crimes we considered earlier are commonly known as "street crimes" and they got their name from the locale in which they most frequently occur. In order to affect them we must take action that is directed towards the intent and opportunity to commit the act. This cannot be done by sworn policemen sitting behind a desk or performing some other task far removed from the basic police goal of reducing crime and disorder. It can only be accomplished by the police officer *on the street*.

Former New York Mayor John Lindsay, citing a study of a medium-sized city which showed that the local police allocated less than 17 percent of their working hours to crimes against persons and property, remarked that "even in the best police departments only one-tenth of the men are on the street at any hour, day or night". Where are the rest? Locked behind typewriters turning out the 15th copy of a report that may become just another testament to another unsolved crime. Being aware of the problem is not enough because several years after Mayor Lindsay's observation, a study revealed that some things just never change. Only 1,000 uniformed officers of the 31,000 strong NYPD force were found to be actually on duty in patrol cars at any time during a given day.

I. MANPOWER

Police manpower is generally divided by 4 to ensure 24-hour-a-day, 7-day-a-week coverage. (One shift days, one shift evenings, one shift nights, and one shift off.) This is a tremendous handicap because an 800 man department is reduced to 200 men and a 20,000 man department is reduced to 5,000 deployable patrolmen. You can grasp the magnitude of the problem when you consider the numbers of people an individual officer must police. In the eastern portion of the United States the police-public ratio runs to a high of about 5 officers per 1,000 citizens. (New York City-for example.) In the west the ratio is about 2 officers per 1,000 citizens. The national average for all cities is 2.4 police employees per 1,000 inhabitants. This ratio includes civilians and is counted before police manpower is divided by 4 to ensure round-the-clock coverage.

If there were no bureaucratic duties you would expect that 25 percent of police manpower would be available as crimefighters on the street. The difference between the optimum 25 percent and "the less than 10 percent" cited by Mayor Lindsay represents mostly "bureaucratic fat." This results from the nature of institutions, particularly tax-based ones, who create layers of paperwork and procedures that proliferate much for their own sake. Periodically, efficiency in operations is reacquired by tapping the only resource non-profit agencies have—the taxpayer. Today, however, the much talked about "taxpayer's revolt" against high taxes is becoming more of a reality each passing day. The taxpayer well is dry. No longer can departments add large numbers of people to their operations. They must become more efficient with their present resources. The day of accountability for the billions expended on the war against crime in America is approaching fast.

Now the policeman himself is not entirely responsible for the bureaucracy and non-essential positions and duties, but those involved in them usually tolerate it. More often than not these duties occur during "bankers hours". In the police community they are known as "sunshine jobs". Do not expect opposition to these jobs from those who hold them. Even though street crime may peak at 8 pm on Saturdays, who wants to give up a "sunshine job" with every Saturday and Sunday off?

As an example, I recall doing management consulting work in a medium sized city. There federally funded "Crime Prevention Unit" that was supposed to be fighting street crime in plainclothes, worked 9 am to 5 pm with Saturdays and Sundays off. Crime statistics showed that they should have been deployed from 6 pm to 2 am and off on Sundays and Mondays.

An ideal deployment program will ensure that the manpower matches the hours of the street crimes and that at least 12 percent of the total resources is on the street around the clock. During evening hours on critical days (usually Fridays or Saturdays) a 30-40 percent deployment would be quite reasonable. This brings up the question of where to get the manpower? The following section offers possible sources of police manpower for redeployment against street crime.

2. LIMITING NON-EMERGENCY SERVICES

The following list of police duties and possible delegations is a start in locating manpower to be deployed against crime:

NON-EMERGENCY SERVICES	DELEGATE TO
1. Licensing	Civilian Agencies
2. Embezzlement	Federal Agencies or private investigators
3. Inspections (Housing, vehicle, etc.)	Civilian Agencies
4. Communications Center Dispatchers	Injured and very senior policemen
5. Supervision of paroled convicts	State or Federal Parole Boards

NON-EMERGENCY SERVICES	DELEGATE TO
6. School crossings	Para Professionals or Police Cadets
7. Police Ambulance Service	Fire or Health Department
8. Examination and control of prostitutes	Health or Welfare Department
9. Daytime car washes	Midnight watch (after 3 am)
10. Gambling offenses	Federal and State Revenue Agencies
11. Registration of voters	Civilian Agencies
12. Census taking	Civilian Agencies
13. Auto safety inspections	Department of Motor Vehicles or Transportation
14. Parking enforcement	Para Professionals or Police Cadets
15. Community Relations Unit	Every police officer
16. Marine and Harbor Patrols	U.S. Coast Guard, Fire Department, or Port Authority
17. Relief for destitutes	Welfare Department
18. Auto gassing and maintenance	Civilian employees or credit card
19. Turnkey duties (jail attendant)	Civilian or limited duty police employees
20. Traffic Control	Para Professionals and Police Cadets
21. Weight Checkers	Civilian Agencies
22. Police Recruit Training	80% to colleges and universities
23. Tow Truck Operations	Civilians or private contractors
24. Bomb Squad Duties	U.S. Army Ordnance and/or Fire Department

Unit 11 RESOURCE ALLOCATION

	NON-EMERGENCY SERVICES	DELEGATE TO
25.	Youth Programs (Including athletics)	Department of Recreation (With Police Moral Support)
26.	Sanitation and Rat Control	Department of Health
27.	Dog pounds	S.P.C.A. or other private agency
28.	Court Attendance and Court Clerks	Civilians
29.	Serving Warrants (Non-violent crimes)	Judicial Process Servers
30.	Maintenance of order inside schools	Non-teaching professional and school disciplinarians
31.	Lost and Found Service	Civilian Agencies
32.	Turning off open fire hydrants	Water and/or Fire Department
33.	Non-criminal property damage reports	Private insurance companies
34.	Monitoring of anti-crime television screens	Fire Department (With direct communications link to police headquarters)
35.	Signing of store check logs	Eliminate completely
36.	Transportation of prisoners	Para Professionals or Prison Personnel
37.	Transporting civilians in police cars	Cab company
38.	Money escorts	Private common carriers
39.	Convoys (Non-dangerous material)	AAA or private agency
40.	Intoxicated persons	Health Department

NON-EMERGENCY SERVICES	DELEGATE TO
41. Missing adults (without suspicion)	Welfare Department
42. Vagrancy	Welfare Department
43. Runaway children (Over 16 without suspicion)	Welfare Department
44. Counterfiet money	Federal Authorities
45. Security of hospitals	Private guard agencies
46. Police Auto Pounds	Para Professionals or civilian watchmen
47. Transporting police vehicles to garage	Civilian personnel
48. Police headquarters desk and operations duty	50% to civilian clerks
49. Feeding and care of mounted and K-9 animals	Civilian handlers and hostlers
50. Recruit background investigations	Very senior or limited duty detectives
51. Investigation of minor automobile accidents	Para Professionals or Police Cadets

The practice of assigning sworn personnel to most of these duties is expensive and inefficient. It removes officers from police work to perform tasks that could be handled by less expert personnel.

Taking reports occupies a significant portion of the patrol officer's time. In most urban police agencies, the patrol officer is required to take reports on incidents ranging from minor vandalism to homicide. Obviously, priorities should be set. In agencies where there are not enough patrol officers to respond to minor incidents, a procedure should be established permitting the agency to accept reports by telephone.

Some cities have assigned many non-enforcement tasks to other government agencies. Detroit, Mich., for example, has transferred licensing dogs from the police to the health department. Kansas City, Mo., relieved the police from towing vehicles and assigned the task to the transportation department.

Civilian personnel can be used to free patrol officers from routine non-enforcement and limited enforcement tasks. The Los Angeles, Calif., Police Department uses civilians to direct traffic, enforce parking ordinances, and conduct staff studies. Ft. Lauderdale, Fla., and Lancaster, Penna., utilize para professionals for minor auto accident investigation.

3. RDO VOLUNTEERS

Another source of manpower is in a Regular Day Off (RDO) volunteer program. Under this program police volunteers are permitted to work extra-duty at no cost to the department. Their pay is subsidized by the user. For example the traffic detail at a race track could be manned by a dozen or so supervisors and men who have previously volunteered for such duty. They are paid by the race track either directly or through the department. This has the effect of two extra men for each volunteer. This is a result of having a man who would normally be off perform a duty that would take another on-duty man away from anti-crime patrol. Naturally, the RDO volunteer policeman (usually in uniform) has full powers of arrest and can take police action if necessary.

This technique can pay dividends in deflecting crime from business areas and shopping centers whose management desires (enough to pay for) extra police coverage. The RDO volunteer should be supervised by the regular patrol supervisor in the area. He should not perform duties which are in conflict with his position as a law enforcement officer. Examples of restricted duties would be: Sweeping up, parking cars, collecting money, bouncing customers from liquor establishments, or wearing any insignia of the host agency. This system has the added advantage of providing career-minded officers with a legitimate means of supplementing their income. It is very discouraging to see an off-duty officer stacking shelves in a supermarket when he could be outside protecting society.

There is only one fly-in-the-ointment. It comes from those "idea-killers" who say this will never work, mainly because of the financial problem arising out of injury to the officer while performing duties as an RDO volunteer. Who pays? Well, in most jurisdictions a policeman is a policeman 24-hours-a-day and when he is injured taking police action he is covered by his department. This is as it should be and RDO volunteers should be treated accordingly.

4. STACK CARS

Many non-emergency services, including some of the 51 listed in the beginning of this unit, can be performed by limited-duty or very senior policeman working 9 am to 5 pm, five days a week. Under this system a call of an abandoned vehicle coming in at 8 pm could be "stacked" for follow-up by the patrolman working the "stack car". This frees the regular patrol for emergency calls and anti-crime patrol.

5. DEPLOYMENT OF PATROL OFFICERS

According to the National Advisory Commission on Criminal Justice Standards and Goals every police agency immediately should develop a patrol deployment system that is responsive to the demands for police services and consistent with the effective use of the agency's patrol personnel. The deployment system should include collecting a workload study, and allocating personnel to patrol assignments within the agency.

1. Every police agency should establish a system for the collection and analysis of patrol deployment data according to area and time.

    a. A census tract, reporting area, or permanent grid system should be developed to determine geographical distribution of data; and

b. Seasonal, daily, and hourly variations should be considered in determining chronological distribution of data.

2. Every police agency should conduct a comprehensive workload study to determine the nature and volume of the demands for police service and the time expended on all activities performed by patrol personnel. The workload study should be the first step in developing a deployment data base and should be conducted at least annually thereafter. Information obtained from the workload study should be used:

   a. To develop operational objectives for patrol personnel;

   b. To establish priorities on the types of activities to be performed by patrol personnel; and

   c. To measure the efficiency and effectiveness of the patrol operation in achieving agency goals.

3. Every police agency should implement an allocation system for the geographical and chronological proportionate need distribution of patrol personnel. The allocation system should emphasize agency efforts to reduce crime, increase criminal apprehensions, minimize response time to calls for services, and equalize patrol personnel workload. This system should provide for the allocation of personnel to:

   a. Division or precincts in those agencies which are geographically decentralized;

   b. Shifts;

   c. Days of the week;

   d. Beats; and

   e. Fixed-post and relief assignments.

4. Every police agency should establish procedures for the implementation, operation and periodic evaluation and revision of the agency's deployment system. These pro-

cedures should include provisions to insure the active participation and willing cooperation of all agency personnel.

A. NATIONAL ADVISORY COMMISSION COMMENTARY

Most police activities are separated into line, staff and auxiliary service operations. Patrol, traffic, and detective line operations account for the largest part of the work of any police agency. Accordingly, the largest portion of police manpower resources traditionally are allocated to them. The staff and auxiliary service operations are designed to support the line operations directly or indirectly.

In recent years the pressure on police agencies to make changes and implement new programs, particularly in community relations, has caused a disproportionate increase in the number of personnel assigned to administrative and staff support functions. The practice in many agencies is to expand administrative and staff support activities by drawing personnel from other units within the agency. Because of their relatively large personnel strength, line operations usually provide a convenient source of manpower for administrative assignments. Even when the personnel are drawn from other sources, the ripple effect ultimately produces a vacancy in the line operations, often in the patrol force. One promising solution to this problem is the assignment of civilian police personnel to certain staff and adminstrative positions.

In addition, many agencies now require the line officer to devote at least a portion (and in some cases a considerable portion) of his time to community relations activities. The need for effective police-community inter-action is clear, and the expenditure of a reasonable amount of manpower resources in this endeavor is certainly justified as long as the primary objective is to reduce crime. The secondary objectives of these programs, such as increased mutual understanding or improvement of the police image, are admittedly desirable. However, these considerations cannot be allowed to diminish the agency's responsibilities to reduce crime, maintain public order, apprehend criminals, and respond effectively to other legitimate demands for police service. A reasonable balance between primary and secondary objectives must be maintained in the use of patrol personnel resources.

The resources expended on community relations should have a demonstrated effect on crime. If they do not, they should be redirected to achieve such an effect.

There is no universally accepted scientific methodology for determining the number of police personnel needed in a given jurisdiction or the percentage distribution of personnel within an agency's organizational structure. Officer to population ratios are often used to indicate total manpower needs. There have been no compelling arguments in support of police to people ratios; and these ratios differ widely from one jurisdiction to another.

Formulas to determine the percentage distribution of personnel functions within police agencies are similarly lacking in rules or guidelines. The typical agency deploys approximately 80 percent of its total sworn strength in patrol, traffic, and detective assignments. The remaining 20 percent are divided among the staff and auxiliary service functions. Within the line operations, patrol accounts for approximately 70 to 80 percent of available line personnel. The remaining 20 to 30 percent are in traffic and investigative assignments.

Existing patrol allocation systems distribute available manpower in proportion to predetermined criteria. Most of these systems are based on hazard or workload formulas. Certain factors which present a greater police problem, or are more time consuming, usually are weighted accordingly.

No better total patrol allocation system is available. The only existing alternatives to proportional distribution systems are systems which attempt to optimize specific aspects of patrol activities such as response to requests for services; these, however, are not total patrol allocation systems.

Proper deployment of patrol personnel begins with the collection and analysis of data that reflects the community's need for various police services and the types of activities performed by patrol officers. In some police agencies, deployment data collection is non-existent or inadequate. In others the systems lack provisions for evaluating and improving their deployment system or testing the efficiency of new deployment techniques.

It is essential that a deployment data collection and analysis system determine the proportional distribution of pertinent data by area and time. Spatial and temporal variations are critically important when evaluating crime, calls for services, and other vital patrol deployment factors.

Geographic distribution of deployment data is necessary in developing area assignments. The process is made easier by using a permanent grid, census tract, or reporting district system. Standard United States census tracts provide a convenient base; however, jurisdiction may require subdivision of census tracts into sectors or reporting districts. Permanent grid systems have been developed and used to advantage by agencies in Tampa, Florida, Tucson, Arizona and St. Louis, Missouri.

Chronological distribution of the demands for services, and the resulting workload on patrol officers, will vary on a seasonal, daily, and hourly basis. Deployment data must reflect these variations so that shift and day of week assignment are founded on real need.

An agency will have difficulty justifying equal time and area assignment of patrol personnel unless it can demonstrate that the problems affecting patrol deployment are distributed in the same manner. Regardless of the size of an agency, deployment data can be collected and analyzed, manually or by computer. The system must be tailored to the agency's needs and objectives.

B. WORKLOAD STUDY

The first step in developing a deployment data base is to determine the distribution of patrol personnel workload. The workload study must include a comprehensive assessment of the demands for patrol services in the community, and the types of

Unit 11   RESOURCE ALLOCATION   121

activities, services, and duties routinely performed by patrol personnel. Three fundamental patrol operation responsibilities must be considered in determining workload distribution; crime, calls for services, and arrests.

Reported crimes and calls for service should be analyzed by type, date, time, and location of occurrence. The time spent by patrol officers in both cases should be analyzed by assigned area, date, shift, and average time expended. An analysis should also be made of delay time in dispatching calls and response time to calls for services.

Arrests by patrol personnel also should be analyzed by type, date, time, location, and average time expended. Comparisons of apprehensions to reported crimes should be made by assigned area and type.

Data on crime, calls for services, and arrests, however, will not provide a complete picture of patrol supply and demand. It is necessary to determine what percentage of total patrol time is expended on non-emergency and non-criminal matters not directly connected with the primary duties of crime repression, criminal apprehension, and handling calls for services. A workload study should include an analysis of factors influencing field unit availability such as time spent on community interaction meetings, vehicle maintenance, court appearances, and all other public service and administrative activities.

C. COLLECTION AND ANALYSIS

The collection and analysis of workload data need not be a continuous process, but a workload study should be conducted at least annually. The extent of analysis required should be consistent with the volume and nature of local demands for patrol services and the size and resources of the agency. The information obtained from the workload study should form the basis for establishing patrol operation objectives and priorities and for measuring control function effectiveness. Crime workload data may indicate the advisability of implementing special crime repression techniques or deploying a crime tactical force.

Workload data on calls for service may identify the need for response priorities on calls and specialized response units for certain types of calls such as family disputes. Arrest data, combined with data on calls for service, may be used in adjusting personnel assignments and developing innovative patrol patterns and techniques to expedite the arrival of field units to crimes in progress, and to reduce travel time to calls in general.

An examination of miscellaneous activities engaged in by patrol personnel may reveal the need for priorities on the types of services rendered by patrol and to eliminate certain non-enforcement and non-emergency services from the patrol responsibility.

D. PERSONNEL ALLOCATION SYSTEM

Effective deployment of patrol personnel must begin with distribution of personnel on a proportionate need basis. Through careful study of crime occurrences, calls for services, and other selected factors, available manpower can be systematically distributed geographically and chronologically according to the relative needs for police service throughout the community. This process in itself will not guarantee the best use of patrol personnel, but it is the foundation for developing the most effective deployment strategy.

There are two key factors in the selective distribution of patrol officers. First, in dealing with crime repression and other assigned activities, the police chief executive must deploy his patrol officers in the districts where and when the problem exists. Second, each officer or team of officers should have approximately the same workload.

In determining the proportionate need distribution of patrol personnel, the police chief executive must decide what factors to include in an allocation system. For the purpose of illustration, three basic factors will be used: selected repressible crimes, calls for services, and arrests.

An analysis of reported crimes is essential to the decision making process of any police agency. Most allocation systems, how-

Unit 11 RESOURCE ALLOCATION 123

ever, tend to emphasize crimes that are believed to be more susceptible to repression by the presence of uniformed patrol personnel, or which indicate a serious need for police service, or both.

There are differing opinions and a lack of empirical research on the extent to which patrol deters crime. As mentioned in Unit 6 there is evidence that some so called crimes of passion are not deterred by police presence. However, even if a particular crime is considered non-repressible, its repetition indicates a police problem. Aggravated assaults are to a certain extent repressible, especially those occurring in public places. Murders and rapes indicate the need for patrol personnel in those areas with a higher proportion of crimes of violence. Additionally, the location and time of non-repressible crimes are to a certain extent predictable when considered in bulk. These crimes can be reduced by special crime control techniques, particularly community interaction programs that encourage citizen involvement in neighborhood anti-crime campaigns.

Calls for services are included in an allocation system index because they represent a recognizable and readily measurable demand for police services. Apprehending suspected offenders and processing arrestees are also included.

Experience shows that using the number of calls for service and the number of arrests without regard for time expended is of little or no value in determining workload. For example, the same number of service calls and arrests may occur on two different shifts. All the activities on one shift, however, may take twice as long as on the other shift. Therefore, using only the number of incidents would indicate falsely that the workload was the same on both watches.

Service calls and arrests should be weighted on the basis of the average elapsed time by watch for each of the activities. Selected repressible crimes should not be so weighted, because they involve no expenditure of field time.

Another factor in establishing an allocation system is the frequency of tabulation of the various factors. In most agencies, a quarterly tabulation provides the information required, with reports issued in January, April, July and October. The factors are calculated by category for these 4 months and then totaled. In agencies with more than one precinct or division, a percentage allocation should be determined for each geographic division and applied to the allotted patrol personnel. A certain number of fixed posts must be manned in each patrol division regardless of the number of officers on patrol duty in the field. That is the overhead or basic operating manpower for the division. It includes jailers, desk officers, and other fixed posts and specialty assignments. These positions are deducted from the total number of personnel to determine the final number available for field patrol deployment.

E. DETERMINING SHIFT HOURS

The first step in the distribution of personnel—at the divisional level in decentralized agencies—is to determine the shift hours. Because of the variables involved, neither arrests nor elapsed time should be used in determining watch hours.

The number of calls for services and the number of selected crimes should be compiled by hour of day for each of the two factors. After computing the percentage for each hour a graph can be plotted to indicate the hourly distribution of the problem.

Shift hours should begin at the periods when the incidence of crime is greatest. When the times have been selected, the average percentage of the problem during each 8-hour period should be plotted on the chart. The chart is used only as a guide—there are several considerations in determining shift hours. For example, establishing certain shift hours may require changing from two-man cars to one-man cars, or the reverse on a specific watch. Another possibility is that a correct choice of shift hours may eliminate the necessity for a midwatch (a fourth overlapping shift). A midwatch should be considered only when the incidence of crime from the average line within one or two shifts is serious enough that the carry over of the problem would require additional personnel for the last part of one watch and first part of an-

Unit 11 RESOURCE ALLOCATION 125

other. The human element must also be considered. People do not like to go to work at 3 or 4 a. m.

Once the choice of shift hours has been made, the shift hours of adjoining divisions should be determined to insure that both divisions have not selected the same times. If the hourly fluctuation of the problem indicates that a major change is not feasible, each division can remedy the problem by moving the watch hours forward or backward 15 minutes.

When shift hours have been established, consideration must be given to the fact that the amount of time required in proper disposal of a call or an arrest will vary from watch to watch. A one month tabulation of elapsed time can be used to obtain a weight factor for calls and arrests. The number of calls and arrests and the time involved handling them on each shift can be determined and a weight factor obtained for each shift.

F. DISTRIBUTION OF PERSONNEL BY SHIFTS

The distribution of policemen by shift is accomplished first by determining the percentage of the total problem on each shift and then distributing a proportionate percentage of field policemen to each shift.

To determine the percentage of the problem, each of the three factors (selected repressible crimes, calls for services, and arrests) is totaled by hour of day for the 4 topic months and the hourly totals for calls for services and arrests, multiplied by their respective weight factors. Again, the selected crimes are not given a weight factor. Finally, respective percentages of the problem should be computed on a shiftwide basis.

After the percentage of the workload for each shift is determined, the total number of available field policemen should be computed. This is done by subtracting the fixed post positions from the total number of available patrol officers. Available field policemen should then be distributed to the three shifts according to the distribution of the problem.

G. DISTRIBUTION OF FIELD POLICEMEN BY DAY OF WEEK

Once the number of policemen assigned to each shift is determined, the appropriate day of week distribution of field policemen on each shift can be determined. The first step is to analyze the distribution of the police problem by day of the week within each of the three shifts. Such an analysis may show a marked increase in workload on Saturday but not on Thursday nights, for example. Under these circumstances, if the watch commander has the same number of officers working each night of the week, officers working Saturday nights would carry a much heavier workload than officers working Thursday nights.

H. DISTRIBUTION OF FIELD POLICEMEN BY BEATS

The size of each beat should be based upon the percentage of the police problem in that area. The assignment of comparable workloads for each beat on a given shift on a given day can be accomplished by assembling the cenus tract grids or reporting districts in such a way that the combined percentage of the problem is approximately equal in each patrol district or beat.

In distributing field policemen by day of week and by beat, the workload must be measured separately for each of the three selected 8-hour shift periods. Using the same deployment plan for all three shifts would result in a 24-hour measurement of the workload governing the distribution of radio cars manned by policemen working only 8 of those 24 hours. Measuring the workload during each of the three 8-hour shifts precludes the possibility of overdeployment in certain districts and provides more equitable distribution of the workload among the officers assigned to the various shifts.

The selected crimes, arrests, and calls for services should be separated by hour of day and day of week within each reporting district, grid map, or census tract. The reporting district totals for each shift should then be weighted by the average number of minutes required to handle each of those activities on the various shifts.

In a separate reporting district or grid map for each shift, the percentage of the workload should be entered in each reporting district. With the geographic distribution of the police problem depicted in this manner, a separate set of car plans can be prepared for each shift, taking into consideration not only workload but also geographic traffic flow, and other features that might affect access to certain areas. Adding the workload percentages shown in each reporting district of each unit's beat, or area of assignment, will show the workload of the assigned personnel. If there is a discrepancy, reporting districts may have to be added or subtracted from the area to equalize the workload.

I. FIXED POSTS, AVAILABILITY AND RELIEF

Fixed-post assignments, may be divided into two groups; assigned positions and specialized positions. An assigned position is manned by a constant number of personnel. If they are not available, no one will normally be assigned in their stead.

Because the number of men required for an assigned position may fluctuate daily due to workload but rarely will fluctuate an appreciable amount weekly, it is sufficient to compute the need for a week. The number of officers assigned to fixed posts should be reviewed periodically to insure that such assignments are minimal and in keeping with agency police.

Most patrol assignments must be manned 7 days a week. Therefore, a formula should be devised to determine availability and relief factors for any given patrol assignment. The most commonly accepted formula is a statistical model of the average policeman's working year that can be applied with an acceptable degree of reliability to any position or assignment.

The factors which comprise the formula are: regular days off per man per year; average sick days per man per year; and average injured-on-duty (IOD) days per man per year.

The following is an example of the method used to obtain the availability and relief factors:

A. Regular days off per man per year, including holidays
   115 days
B. Vacation days off per man per year.
   14 days
C. Average sick days per man per year.
   3.8 days
D. Average injury days per man per year.
   2.2 days

Availability Factor

$$\frac{365 - A(115) + B(14) + C(3.8) + D(2.2)}{365} = \frac{365 - 135}{365} = \frac{230}{365} = .63 \text{ Availability Factor}$$

$1.00 - .63 = .37$

$\frac{.37}{.63} = .5873$ or .6 Relief Factor

The availability factor is the average percentage of time a policeman can be expected to be available for duty per year. If a position must be manned 100 percent of the time, then more than one man must be assigned to that position. This relief factor is a mathematical function of the availability factor.

With an availability factor of 63 percent, as in this example, 37 percent must be made up by another man. However, the other man is also available only 63 percent of the time. As the formula for relief factor shows, this translates to 37 percent of man's 63 percent available time or 60 percent of his total working time.

Continuing with the example, a position that must be manned constantly on a given shift and that requires one man present at all times will require one man plus .6 man for the position. This formula will work for any number of positions. For example, 3 positions require 3 + (3 × .6) or 4.8 men.

The average agency will find that a relief factor computed in tenths is sufficiently accurate for its needs. Large agencies may determine that a relief factor computed in hundredths will be needed for greater statistical accuracy.

J. DEPLOYMENT SYSTEM PROCEDURES

The success of a patrol deployment system depends directly upon the support afforded by all personnel involved in the program. The active participation and willing cooperation of all personnel is greatly enhanced if representatives of all levels within the agency are included in the planning and implementation of the system.

Procedures for the implementation and on going operation of the system should be established and distributed in the form of agency directives from the police chief executive. These directives should provide procedural guidelines and detailed information on the need for an adequate and accurate deployment data base, the purpose of proportional need distribution of patrol personnel, and the objectives and goals of the deployment system.

Procedures should include periodic deployment system evaluation based on timely information derived from an analysis of current patrol deployment data. Personnel allocations to geographic divisions or precincts in decentralized agencies should be evaluated and appropriately revised at least yearly. Shift, day of week, beat configurations, and personnel complements should be evaluated and appropriately revised at least quarterly.

Appropriate training programs should be established for all personnel involved in the system. The training should be tailored to the needs of personnel responsible for the various facets of the system, including the reporting, collection, and analysis of deployment data, and the use, evaluation, and revision of the deployment system.

Provisions to insure the adequacy of deployment data and to facilitate the use of the data in allocating personnel should include the development of new forms and source documents or the revision of existing reports to accommodate the required information. Data source documents should be subject to supervisory review and approval to enhance the accuracy of the data base.

6. SUMMARY

The only way the crime problem is going to be solved is by applying police resources where the crime is happening—on the street.

Manpower is the most important resource a police administrator can apply to the crime problem. One way to increase the amount of available police manpower against the crime problem is to limit non-emergency services performed by police. Many of these duties can be performed by other governmental agencies or eliminated altogether.

A system of RDO volunteers, stack cars and proper deployment of officers can be helpful in providing extra manpower for the war on crime.

7. QUESTIONS FOR DISCUSSION

1. What is the most important resource a police administrator can apply to the crime problem? Why?
2. How can extra police manpower be placed on-the-street against crime?
3. In your own department, explain what non-emergency police jobs you could eliminate or delegate to other agencies.
4. What is the RDO volunteer program?
5. How does the "stack car" program add extra police manpower when needed?
6. How should patrol officers be deployed?
7. What is the first step in developing a deployment data base?

UNIT 12

COMMUNICATIONS

Communications is the lifeline of police operations, particularly those involving emergency calls, undercover details, and crowd control operations. Refer to Unit 18 (Use of Decoys) for details on communications and tactical undercover operations.

1. RADIO

Radio is the primary police method of transmitting information between headquarters and men in the field. Every police vehicle should be radio-equipped. Unmarked patrol and surveillance vehicles should have their radios hidden under the dash or in the glove comparment. As a rule, car radios are generally more powerful and more reliable than walkie-talkies. Although there are less battery problems with car radios, walkie-talkies have improved tremendously in the past decade. No beatman should be without a two-way radio, both for his safety and enhancing his ability to apprehend criminals.

2. DISPATCHERS

The radio dispatchers are among the most important individuals responsible for success in apprehending criminals. Although there are many fine civilian dispatchers in police service, it is an area where the presence of trained, sworn personnel is an absolute necessity. The radio room, communication center, or dispatching office is the literal nerve center of the police department. When allocating resources it is wise to assign injured, limited duty, or very senior officers to dispatching duties.

This is one of the few areas in police administration where I do not recommend wholesale delegation of duties to civilians, cadets, or paraprofessionals. Experience has shown that the presence of "street-seasoned" officers in the radio room can prove invaluable during emergencies.

3. TELEPHONES

Telephones are used by police departments to a much greater extent than is commonly realized. They are used to transmit lengthy and detailed information in the interest of conserving air time. They are used for calls between field officers and headquarters personnel for conversations which should not be carried on over the radio. Of course, they are also the principal means of communication with headquarters for foot patrol officers who have no radio equipment available.

Both public and private telephones can be used, so the patrol officer should be familiar with the location of all convenient telephones on his beat. Police telephone systems, however, are more commonly used. These are wired directly to police headquarters and are placed at strategic locations throughout the patrol area, usually on power, light or telephone poles. In some communities they are also connected to tape recorders, thus permitting patrol officers to dictate reports during or following a tour of duty.

The use of call boxes may be diminishing as radio systems are improving and multiple frequencies become available. It is likely, however, that they will continue in use in many communities for years to come. They are also finding increasing usefulness as a means of permitting citizens to call for police assistance.

The patrol officer should not obstruct his vision when using the call box by putting his face in the box, but should stand away. In addition, he should exercise extreme caution when he has a prisoner in custody, for officers have been injured when call box doors have been slammed against the side of their heads or hands in escape attempts. At night he should conceal his flashlight beam so that his presence at the call box will not be obvious. Courtesy requires that he not speak unnecessarily loud and he not slam the call box door shut upon completing his message.

Unit 12 COMMUNICATIONS 133

POLICE RADIO DISPATCHERS

4. SIGNAL LIGHTS

Some communities use a system of signal lights—usually red or blue in color—as a means of communication. This is a rather old technique, but still useful.

The lights are generally mounted on power, light, or telephone poles on top of call boxes; or they may be suspended above intersections. They can be lit by headquarters, with certain flashing or steady lights indicating certain messages to field personnel who cannot be reached by police radio. Field personnel must know locations from which these signals can be seen and must, of course, be familiar with the code system. Recall systems have been utilized to summon footbeat men back to a patrol car with remotely activated flashing lights. Also, some jurisdictions use signal lights in conjunction with helicopter patrols as an anti-robbery and/or burglary program.

5. ALARM SYSTEMS

Every working police officer knows that the overwhelming majority of holdup and burglar alarms are false. However, this is no reason to treat them lightly. Each one should be treated as if a real crime was going down. Everything should be done to improve the alarm systems in cooperation with the private sector. Audible alarms should be discouraged because they only scare robbers away. Bank security personnel usually are most cooperative and open to suggestion. Don't despair—as long as you have alarm systems you are going to be plagued with false calls. A 90% false rate is not unreasonable. Remember at this rate you have at least one chance in ten of catching a criminal.

Just how efficient are the typical silent holdup alarms? I recall an incident where stakeout officers *using their own tactical anti-holdup alarm system,* responded to a bank robbery occurring less than 100 yards from their post. They put the arm on the offenders, hailed a passing police wagon and placed the prisoners in the back. Approximately four minutes after they had the "baddies" in tow, the police wagon's radio blurted out: "Broad and Erie, Community Federal Savings and Loan; silent holdup alarm". The standard alarm had to go through the private company who in turn summoned police. How far do you think the robbers could have traveled in those four precious minutes?

I am not suggesting we put the private alarm companies out of business, but I am suggesting that we can improve on existing alarms and supplement them by use of tactical police alarms. I know of two basic systems: One designed against burglary; the other against robbery. This unit will cover the anti-burglary alarm system used by the Cedar Rapids Police Department. Later (in Unit 19) we will consider tactical anti-holdup alarm systems.

A. A BETTER CRIMINAL MOUSETRAP

The Cedar Rapids Police Department has a "better mousetrap". Most law enforcement officials agree that, indeed, a "better mousetrap" is needed to combat the rising incidence of burglaries.

Thanks to their "mousetrap," a low-cost silent alarm system, they are catching burglars as they never have before, and are showing the business community that it can be of valuable assistance in reducing crime.

Cedar Rapids is a city of about 115,000 population, and the department has a complement of 131 officers.

During 1970, the department gathered data on low-cost silent burglar alarms placed in 350 business establishments with direct lines to the department's communication center. This particular project—the alarm system and study—is the "first of its kind" in the country.

(I) PURPOSE OF STUDY

The purpose of the study was to compare the 350 "alarmed" businesses with a group of "nonalarmed" similar businesses. Only businesses which had previously been burglarized were included in both groups for the tests. It was anticipated from the outset that for various reasons, i. e., firms going out of business, moving, remodeling, etc., that the department would be unable to conduct the study on a full complement of each group for the entire period. As it developed, complete matches were possible in only 142 locations of each group.

In the experimental alarmed group there were 23 burglaries and 11 captures during the test period while the group with no alarms had 44 burglaries and only six captures.

As these figures show, there were captures in 48 percent of the burglaries in the alarmed group and 14 percent in the nonalarmed group. The apprehension figures represent the number of cases in which captures were made, not the number of burglars captured.

Businesses without alarms have a greater chance of being burglarized because, apparently, most burglars inspect premises beforehand and avoid locations where they spot or suspect alarm systems. It is difficult to completely hide alarm systems in buildings already constructed and occupied.

Contracts for the project, entitled "Installation, Test and Evaluation of a Large-Scale Burglar Alarm System for a Municipal Police Department," were awarded to a national company. Each installation cost $185.60, and all costs were paid through December 31, 1970, by a project grant from the Law Enforcement Assistance Administration.

Only the lowest cost detection devices were specified and used. These include magnetic switches which activate the alarm system when a magnet in a door or window is moved away from a switch, plunger switches similar to the type that light a refrigerator, vibration switches that detect pounding or major movement, and pull-apart cords for overhead doors or similar locations where the other devices are not practical.

(2) HIDDEN KEY

The alarm systems at all business sites are activated by turning a hidden security key outside after the building has been closed for the day. Each alarm is connected to a control box which serves two functions. First, it allows each business to check the system before activating it to insure that all protected openings are closed so a false alarm will not result. Secondly, the control box indicates through the signal at the police station whether a break in the system has occurred on the premises where the alarms are installed or in the leased telephone lines running to the station.

Holdup buttons were installed at no extra cost in all locations. They not only serve the purpose of rapid notification of a robbery, but also are another convenient means of checking the system. The buttons are wired to be active whether the burglar alarm is activated or not. A key is needed to reset the button after it has been pushed.

There was one unanticipated benefit from the installation of the holdup buttons. During the experiment, an alarm was received from a tavern after closing hours and a burglar was captured inside. Investigating officers discovered the intruder, who had obviously hidden inside before closing, had unknowingly pushed the button while rummaging around the bar.

A number of small businesses were studied to see if there is a relationship between the type of business and the apparent spotting of the alarm system. In the case of service stations, there were five burglaries at alarmed locations and 11 at locations with no alarms.

In schools, four alarmed locations were burglarized. Ten were burglarized where there were no alarms. In restaurants, the ratio was 2 to 8. These are the types of locations easily "cased" and, thus, potential burglars frequently spot the alarm.

The results for burglarized taverns were less favorable. There were six burglaries at alarmed locations and seven at locations with no alarms. However, although the data has not been completely analyzed, a number of tavern burglars were believed to be juveniles who would not ordinarily be familiar with the tavern layout.

Installation of the alarm systems has beneficially affected two groups in the community. One group, business operators, has benefited through either prevention of burglaries or quick apprehension of the burglars. The other group is juvenile burglars. Present data show a high percentage of burglars are juveniles, and many of their violations are "impulse" crimes. While results with this group are less tangible and direct, the alarm system has reduced the juvenile offender's attempts. Further, the high capture rate often identifies a juvenile in his first criminal offense. This provides his family and juvenile authorities an earlier chance to work with the youth and hopefully deter him from a criminal career before he becomes a "seasoned" lawbreaker.

(3) CLEARANCES

There are approximately 3,000 nonresidential or business locations in Cedar Rapids, and during 1970 the department recorded 304 break-ins in these establishments. In 238 burglaries of locations without alarms, 36 cases were cleared by capture and four by admission or discovery of stolen property. This is a clearance rate of 17 percent. In 66 burglaries of locations with alarms, there were 19 instances of breaking and entering cleared by capture and two by admission or discovery of stolen property, or a 32 percent clearance rate.

There is one factor which may have had some effect on the clearance rate for cases where alarm systems were active. Since schools are often burglarized, alarms were installed in a number of school buildings. However, because of the size of these institutions, it was impractical and too expensive to protect but a few key positions in the buildings involved. Consequently, a school could be burglarized and, unless the intruders violated the protected area, the alarm would not activate.

Of the 2,650 locations without alarms under the experiment, 9 percent had burglaries while in the 350 alarmed locations, 19 percent had burglaries. This supports the premise for installing alarms in locations with previous burglary experience. From the burglar's point of view conditions conducive to the first violation usually lead to subsequent break-ins at the same location.

Burglary is usually defined as any breaking and entering with intent to commit a crime. For the purpose of the study, any breaking, even if there was no evidence of entry or theft, was classified as a burglary unless there was definite evidence to show the violation was only vandalism. There was a reason for this broad definition.

They were aware that many burglars, usually the more experienced ones, break in a building and then secret themselves nearby to see if police show up to investigate. If officers arrive shortly, the burglars know, of course, the building is protected by an alarm and flee from the area. If officers do not arrive within a reasonable time, the thieves proceed with the burglary.

To offset this tactic, many times officers did not drive directly to the scene, but rather to a location nearby and cautiously watch the area for a few minutes before moving in to determine if any suspicious activity occurs.

(4) FALSE ALARM RATE

The rate for false alarms for establishments participating in the experiment was 79 percent for the first 3 months, but dropped to 52 percent for the last 3 months. The higher rate for the first 3 months was caused primarily by employees' and owners' unfamiliarity with the equipment. As the personnel became more familiar with the systems, the rate dropped and showed signs of leveling off. No strong effort was made to reduce this rate. However, officers explained proper operation of the systems and procedures to follow to reduce false alarms each time they responded to a false report.

With proper training and procedures, false alarms can be reduced. However, officers involved in the project felt the 52 percent rate is tolerable inasmuch as burglars are being caught.

Like many other criminals, burglars are cautious. They look for alarms before attempting to burglarize a business. This is shown by the number of burglaries in the unalarmed control group compared to those in the group of establishments with alarms. This cautiousness is also indicated by the high rate of entry at unprotected points. Only three cases were recorded where burglaries occurred and were undetected because alarms were disconnected or not activated by business owners or managers. In spite of this, the clearance rate resulting from alarms was 32 percent, well above the national rate of 18.9 percent.

There are not now, and it is doubtful there ever will be, enough police officers to hold crime rates at present levels or to reduce crime without assistance from technical systems.

One major way of increasing efficiency in any sort of operation, police or otherwise, is to improve the speed and accuracy of communications.

Physical protection through the use of window bars, locks, and similar items has limited value in that such devices can be penetrated, given enough time and skill.

Cost for a high degree of physical protection can be excessive. Sufficient police patrol to detect a high percentage of burglaries would be excessive, for usually a burglar looks like a burglar only for the short period of time it takes to break in.

The major impact of the project has been that the volume of nonresidential burglaries has been contained even though the number of businesses has increased and population of the city has grown. This means a proportional savings through the reduction of loss by theft, vandalism, or destruction to gain entry. Thus, there are additional savings in police, prosecution, and court time corresponding to the reduction in the number of burglaries. Further, the less the officers have to respond to actual burglaries and false alarms, the more time they will have to devote to other police activity, such as investigation of other street crime.

The silent alarm system has one other thing going for it. The conviction rate has been a solid 100 percent.

6. ROADBLOCK NETWORKS

One of the most progressive things a police department can do in its war on crime is to initiate a plan for dealing with criminals who make their getaway by motor vehicle. It can be argued that only large departments have the amount of vehicles to implement a large scale roadblock network. However, any department can be successful in this area. Remember the smaller the town—the smaller the number of ingress and egress routes to cover. If you have only a few vehicles to seal off an area, make arrangements with surrounding departments to take up posts along bridges, main routes, etc. Generally the smaller the plan, the more chance for success. A good example of a successful roadblock network is the Philadelphia Police Department's Operation F.I.N.D.

A. OPERATION F.I.N.D.

"FILL THE BAG AND MAKE IT QUICK"

The above laconic demand is frequently the initial action in brief and frightening criminal dramas recurring at alarming rates in communities throughout the country. Add to this startling phrase a menacing gun, a frightened teller or employee, and a drawer of money, and you have the essentials for an episode which usually climaxes when the armed gunman and the bag of money vanish through the front door. The frantic victim screams, the manager calls police, and the communications officer dispatches police cars to the scene.

In Philadelphia, one additional act takes place. Operation F.I.N.D. is activated.

F.I.N.D. is the acronym for Fugitive Interception Network Design, a plan set up to prevent the escape of felons from scenes of major crimes.

(1) ORGANIZATION

Operation F.I.N.D. was organized and instituted under the direction of former Police Commissioner of Philadelphia, Frank

L. Rizzo. He had always required and received quick response by patrol cars to armed robberies; but too often the criminals had already escaped in getaway cars. Occasionally, there was difficulty in quickly relaying the description and facts to the police radio for further broadcast. Time lapses gave the robbers an additional advantage over police.

As a result, the problem was reviewed and a workable plan devised, using fixed posts for patrol cars along the streets and highways leading from and adjacent to major crime incidence areas. Every important crime during a specific period was analyzed both from written reports and "on the spot" observation by staff officers. Then a study was made of the entire city. The sizes and boundaries of 50 designated sectors were determined through a review of statistical data. The study also revealed crime hazards and identified business areas, topography of each sector, and the police vehicles available in each area.

(2) PLAN OF ACTION

The followup included an individual plan of action for each sector. This plan, when activated, dispatched patrol cars to predetermined fixed posts which encircled the site of the crime. The posts were selected to form a net, making it difficult for escaping vehicles to penetrate. Additional training of the men was initiated, and a special information sheet was devised. This form, using the small block and checkoff technique, helped to secure and dispatch holdup information more quickly and efficiently. The department's police radio system could immediately relay "flash information" to all cars, cutting delays to a minimum.

Operation F.I.N.D., as the name indicates, involves every available policeman in a given area in a probing, far-reaching alert to immediately locate one or more dangerous suspects who are fleeing from the scene of a major crime. The plan is flexible, and if the suspects are not observed or apprehended within a few minutes of the crime, the periphery can be expanded to broaden the area of coverage.

Police orders for the plan state: "To activate the plan, a serious crime must have been committed and an adequate description of the escape vehicle and occupants must be obtained. A time lapse of not more than 5 minutes between the commission of the crime and the reception of the information is the established standard. The person reporting the crime must be quickly and thoroughly questioned by personnel of the radio room to ascertain if these essential factors are present."

(3) OPERATIONS

When Operation F.I.N.D. is activated, the command center in the Philadelphia police radio room quickly identifies the sector involved and pinpoints the exact location of the crime scene.

The fixed posts for patrol vehicles are already charted on the pertinent sector map in order to facilitate to the entire operation. Patrol vehicles are immediately radio-dispatched to their pre-designated locations which cordon the target area. Flash information concerning the offense, the escape direction taken by the suspects, the license number and type of vehicle, and the descriptions of occupants is repeatedly broadcasted to all police vehicles within the entire geographical division.

Patrol cars proceed rapidly to their assigned posts. They switch their radios to a special emergency frequency reserved exclusively for major crime investigations such as Operation F.I.N.D. This enables all cars in the operation to receive instructions and information and to communicate with each other without interruptions by radio communications not connected with the case.

(4) APPREHENSION

Other patrol vehicles in the area which are not assigned fixed posts then conduct a block-by-block search, checking licenses and cars. If the wanted car is not located or crime perpetrators are not apprehended within a reasonable period of time, consideration is given to expanding the time operation. The decision is at the discretion and judgment of the ranking officer of the command center. He must evaluate many variables, including how far an escaping car could travel in the elapsed time. His intimate knowledge of the terrain and the traffic conditions of the search area helps in reaching this decision.

Operation F.I.N.D. is completed when the automobile has been located and the occupants apprehended or when the police are completely convinced the vehicle is not within the net formed by the cordon of cars.

(5) PROGRAM PROVES SUCCESSFUL

The test of any plan is the results attained. During the first three years since the inception of F.I.N.D., it has been activated by the Philadelphia police 279 times. The success of the program far exceeded original expectations; 139 apprehensions of one or more persons have been made, posting a 50 percent apprehension average. Over a quarter million dollars in property has been recovered. A total of 194 persons have been arrested for serious crimes—the type of violations that led to the adoption of the plan.

In evaluating Operative F.I.N.D. the following statistical breakdown of the crimes was made, indicating crime clearance:

Bank robberies	12
Other armed robberies	59
Rape and kidnap	1
Homicide	3
Assault with intent to kill	9
Burglaries	11
Auto thefts	2
Vehicles recovered without occupants	42

In the final analysis, Operation F.I.N.D. is a basic, fundamental, and even elementary plan in today's sophisticated world of computers. Its success depends on speed, common sense, efficiency, and cooperation. These factors have been blended together to make Operation F.I.N.D. workable. The police radio system, the sector cars, the command center, and the individual officer all perform their part of the plan with skill and dedication. The result is that the Philadelphia police through Operation F.I.N.D. do a better job of capturing bandits and recovering stolen property and give more protection to law-abiding citizens.

7. SUMMARY

Good communications is the key to reduced response time. A reduced response time is the key to apprehension. More apprehension is the key to lower crime rates.

Police radio dispatchers are among the few "desk" assigned police personnel that can truly be considered "street-cops". The radio cord from their mike is the "umbilical cord" that connects them with the street. This is one administrative area where the assignment of sworn officers is recommended.

Alarm systems can be a tremendous aid in apprehending criminals. The best alarm systems are police tactical alarms as evidenced by Cedar Rapid's "mousetrap".

Roadblock networks such as "Operation FIND" aid police in apprehending criminals making a getaway in a motor vehicle. No matter what the size the department, police tactical alarms and preplanned roadblock networks are effective tools against the criminal.

8. QUESTIONS FOR DISCUSSION

1. How does good communications aid apprehension?
2. Who should staff your radio room? Why?
3. What is the major problem with private alarm systems? What can be done about it?

4. Explain how a police anti-burglary alarm system such as Cedar Rapid's "mousetrap" can be used in your jurisdiction.
5. Explain how you could improve police radio communications in your own department.
6. Describe the "Operation FIND" roadblock system. What are the essential details of such a system?
7. Plan an "Operation FIND" type roadblock system for your own department. What are its chances for success in apprehending criminals?

UNIT 13

HOLDUP INFORMATION SYSTEMS

1. RESPONSE TIME

Response time is the key to apprehension and a holdup information system is the key to good response time.

During many classroom experiments concerning holdup information systems, a hypothetical bank robbery was developed and analyzed. Groups of enforcement officers including state, county and local police from many jurisdictions participated in the development of the "response time" schematic. (Refer to illustration #13-1.) In the average bank robbery you have between two and six minutes to engage the holdup man in-the-act. This is where stakeouts and tactical alarm systems can be of great value. (Refer to Units 17 and 19)

On occasion, conventional silent holdup alarms are activated during or shortly before the holdup. More often than not, the alarm is activated as the robbers leave. The alarm is generally relayed to police in one of two ways:

> silent alarm   (1–4 minute delay)
> phone   (2–5 minute delay)

Once the police dispatchers have the information it takes ½ to 1 minute to get the "flash" information out to radio patrol cars. If the alarm came in by phone the dispatcher should immediately add the basic description of the perpetrators to the broadcast. At this stage the physical description of the holdup men is even more important than their names.

Example of flash broadcast:

> "Attention all cars . . . report of a holdup XYZ bank, 6th and Main . . . committed by two white males, early twenties, wearing dungaree jackets. Escaped on foot north on 6th from Main."

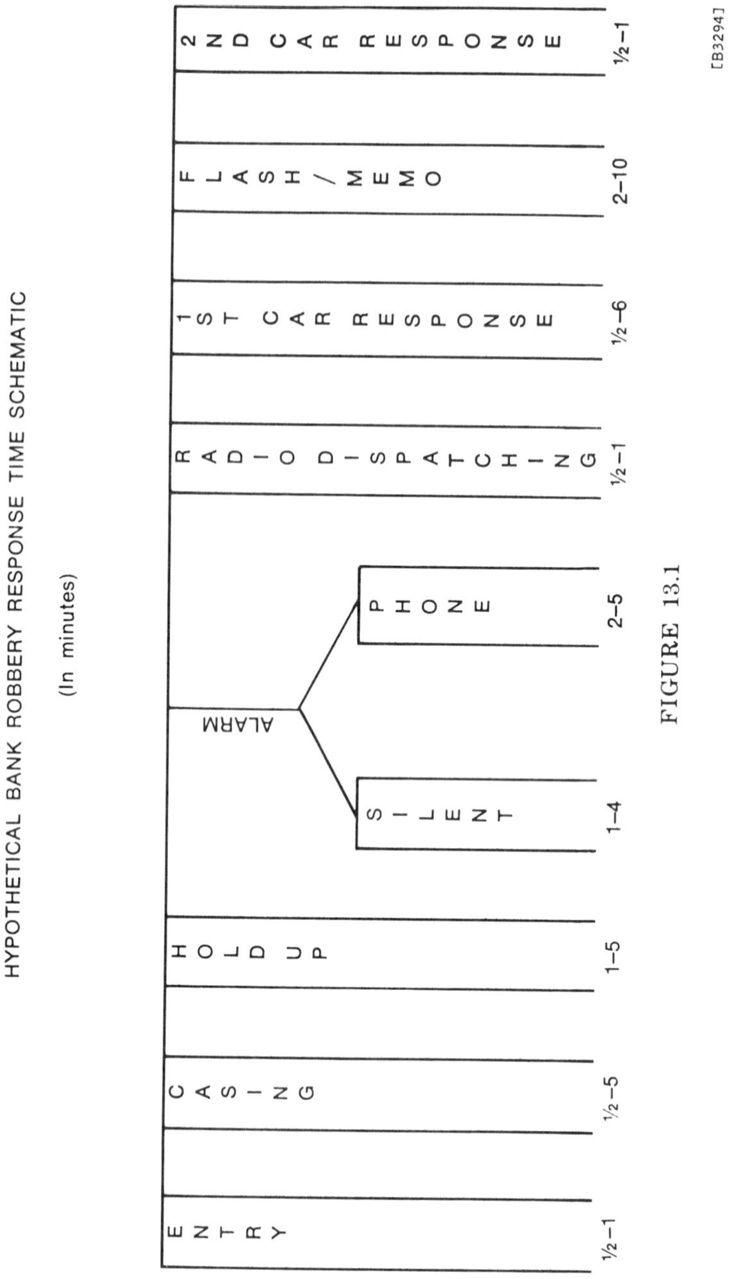

148   POLICE OPERATIONS   Sec. 3

HYPOTHETICAL BANK ROBBERY RESPONSE TIME SCHEMATIC

(In minutes)

ENTRY	CASING	HOLDUP	ALARM		RADIO DISPATCHING	1ST CAR RESPONSE	FLASH/MEMO	2ND CAR RESPONSE
			SILENT	PHONE				
½–1	½–5	1–5	1–4	2–5	½–1	½–6	2–10	½–1

FIGURE 13.1

[B3294]

Unit 13 HOLDUP INFORMATION SYSTEMS

Also at this stage it would be beneficial to have a holdup information system as illustrated in figure 13-2. This flyer is distributed to businesses that are high potential holdup targets. Incidentally, this is the most genuine form of police community relations. It lets the businessman know that the police are truly concerned with his plight in trying to make a living during a "crime epidemic". Prior to the arrival of the first patrol car the victim could fill in the more complete description of the offenders. One point to remember is that one, possibly two cars, should respond to a call of a "report of a holdup". This type of call must be distinguished from the "holdup in progress" where all available patrol vehicles in the area respond directly to the scene. Silent holdup alarms should be treated as a "holdup in progress" until the first car on the scene confirms the call. Refer to Unit 22 for additional details on the tactical response to robbery.

A knowledgeable police dispatcher will keep an "open" telephone line to the holdup scene. If the call comes in by phone he instructs the victim not to hang up. If the call comes in by silent alarm he should phone the target *after* broadcasting the alarm. Note: Planning and caution should be used as not to alert the holdup men that the police are responding. Passwords can be developed to confirm or cancel a holdup call.

Upon his arrival at the scene the officer, using all the precautions as recommended in Unit 22 (Tactical Approaches to Robbery) should either confirm or cancel the call by radio. Any additional flash information on the description or escape should be immediately relayed to the dispatcher (and incoming patrol vehicles) by radio.

Example of additional flash information:

> "Additional flash information on the bank robbery 6th and Main. Those two men are wearing white tennis shoes and were last seen running east on Elm from 6th Street with the manager of the bank in pursuit."

At this time the first officer on the scene should take the flyer (with sample radio holdup memorandum) from the victim/witness and complete it. If the witness and/or victim does not have one available as is likely during the stressful situation, the police

150   POLICE OPERATIONS   Sec. 3

HOLDUP!!

WHAT TO DO?

DON'T HESITATE
1. CALL POLICE
2. FILL IN ALL BLOCKS OF MEMORANDUM

DIAL 9-1-1

RADIO HOLDUP MEMORANDUM — Philadelphia Police Department

WEAPON	ROBBERY / ATTEMPT	ANY INJURED YES / NO	TIME	TYPE OF BUSINESS
LOCATION			COMMITTED BY	

DESCR. NO. 1	COLOR	AGE	HEIGHT	WEIGHT	HAIR
HAT (Color and Type)			JACKET (Color and Type)		
PANTS (Color)	SHOES (Color)		SHIRT	GLASSES	MUSTACHE
OTHER			HOW ESCAPED ☐ FOOT ☐ AUTO		
IF AUTO, DESCRIBE (Include License No.)			DIRECTION TAKEN		

75-130 (Rev. 12/64)   (Over)

Hand this information to Police

The first police officer responding will broadcast your information over Police Radio. Every police car in Philadelphia will be seeking suspects.

POLICE NEED YOUR HELP
           TO APPREHEND CRIMINALS

FIGURE 13.2
(Front)

Unit 13   HOLDUP INFORMATION SYSTEMS

HERE IS HOW YOU CAN HELP YOUR POLICE

1. Don't panic. Remain calm if a holdup takes place. DO NOT RESIST.

2. Observe. Be indentification conscious. Look for unusual features.

3. Call police first— **DIAL 9-1-1** and sound alarm as soon as possible.

4. Protect the crime scene. Stop others from disturbing articles of evidence.

5. Don't trust your memory. Jot down all information immediately.

6. Do not discuss holdup with anyone until police questioning is completed.

7. Supply all facts. Be willing to make positive identification.

8. Prosecute arrested criminals.

PHILADELPHIA POLICE DEPARTMENT

| FRANK L. RIZZO | HILLEL S. LEVINSON | JOSEPH F. O'NEILL |
| MAYOR | MANAGING DIRECTOR | COMMISSIONER |

FIGURE 13.2

(Rear)

officer should produce his own blank holdup information card (same as in figure 13.2) and complete it as quickly and accurately as possible. Then, using a phone if possible, he should call the complete description in to the dispatcher. The dispatcher has his own blank copy of the holdup memorandum. It is not necessary under the system to read off every descriptive category. Since the dispatcher has the same card only the information actually penciled in should be relayed. Where there is no information in a category the reporting officer simply says "blank". Thus a conversation referring to the second and third lines of the holdup memorandum will be reported to the dispatcher like this:

"None, blue dungaree with eagle patch on back, dark, white tennis, none, blue sun, blank. . ."

Translated on the dispatcher's copy of the holdup memorandum it would read and mean suspect had:

—no hat

—a blue dungaree jacket with an eagle patch on the back

—dark pants

—white tennis shoes

—barechested

—blue sunglasses

—unknown whether mustache or not

This system has been demonstrated and tested in the classroom by people who were not familiar with it and it reduced the response time in getting the information out and increased the accuracy of the descriptions.

Any department can develop its own holdup information system. The key elements are that blank copies of the report should be available at all times to:

—potential victims

—responding police officers

—police dispatchers

Unit 13   HOLDUP INFORMATION SYSTEMS   153

2. OBSERVATION AND DESCRIPTION

The ability to observe critically and describe accurately is essential to the success of any police officer. Like most skills, this ability is rarely a natural gift but one which must be developed. Once a police officer has developed his own skills in observation and description he will be better prepared to obtain good descriptions on criminal offenders.

A. OBSERVATION

Observation is complete awareness by an individual of his surroundings, achieved through maximum employment of the senses. Expert observation enables him to recognize and recall any object or situation accurately, fully, and clearly.

Our ability to perceive depends upon our innate ability, experience, and training in relation to our environment, for perceive means to see and understand.

Accurate observation requires the mental effort necessary to recognize, analyze, and relate the constituent parts of our surroundings, and to interpret the patterns and relationships present. However, we usually perceive or comprehend only that which interests us or is capable of being understood with minimum effort. An extensive vocabulary is usually built upon knowledge of and a clear conception of the object to which a term is applied. The person with a wealth of descriptive terms comprehends more thoroughly than the person with an inadequate vocabulary. A woman's interest in color, based on its importance to her personal appearance, endues her with knowledge of the various shades of colors and the vocabulary necessary to describe them. Conversely, a man may observe only basic colors. An Eskimo suddenly transplanted to Times Square would be able to comprehend or describe few of the sights and sounds around him, as he would lack the necessary vocabulary. The person untrained in observation usually perceives another person as a whole, and not as a grouping of particular physical characteristics. We meet people every day but these meetings do not enlarge our ability to describe the features of those persons. The techniques of observation and description are acquired only by continual mental effort. An understanding of the techniques involved in accurate observation are important to police investigators.

To train himself to make accurate observations the officer must:

(1) Practice continual and complete awareness and alertness so that he can observe and understand persons, situations, objects, or incidents.

(2) Replace casual observation of generalities with study and observation of detail.

(3) Train himself to estimate as accurately as possible the passage of time, the speed of moving objects, directions, and distances.

(4) Be familiar with colors, shades of colors, and distinctions among varying degrees of intensity of light.

(5) Be able to visualize that which takes place in his presence.

(6) Acquire ability to observe objects and incidents in terms of potential evidence and in relation to the investigation.

The officer who is aware of the fallibility of the senses will understand why different persons put different interpretations on the same facts. He will realize that variation in the testimony of two or more persons, each of whom has witnessed the same occurrence, does not necessarily mean that one of them is trying to deceive him or that those with the minority version are mistaken. Because he realizes that it is unusual for two or more persons to agree on the facts of an incident or to describe it in identical terms, he will not overlook the possibility of collusion when there is agreement and identical description by witnesses.

To be observant requires training. The officer should learn to fix in his mind the peculiar details of a face and the characteristics of an object or scent. He must bear in mind that observation

Unit 13   HOLDUP INFORMATION SYSTEMS

implies a careful distinction between facts observed and interpretation of those facts. Substitution of an individual interpretation of a fact for the fact itself is a common error.

When an officer questions a witness to an incident, his questioning should appeal only to the memory and not influence the answers of the witness through suggestion. Many of the observation reports made by untrained laymen are the result of guesswork wherein the imagination builds on, and frequently reworks, the few details actually seen. In this process the mind rationalizes the resultant compound into a logical but not necessarily accurate or factual picture. Suggestive or leading questions merely encourage this human weakness; the skilled interrogator avoids them.

Proper training in visual observation does not require that the officer attempt to observe and remember every face and every scene. Rather, he should concentrate on retention of details with which he will probably be concerned in his operations.

B. DESCRIPTION OF PERSONS

Description is the technique of factually reporting one's own observations or the sensory experiences recounted by another person. Since the purpose of description is to present an accurate word picture, the use of standard terms in describing persons contributes importantly to the value of reports prepared by police officers.

A cornerstone of the investigator's system of describing persons is the complete Portrait Parle. This is the modern version of the original Portrait Parle, a complicated and lengthy system devised late in the nineteenth century by Alphonse Bertillion, a clerk in the French Surete. "Portrait Parle" means, in effect, "a spoken picture." While the Portrait Parle is usually obtained when the individual is in custody or under close observation, it is also a standard method of describing individuals under observation in other circumstances. It is used in describing, for future investigative reference, unidentified individuals to other officers so that they may form an accurate mental picture of them; and in identifying individuals from photographs. The Portrait Parle contains the standard terminology used to describe particular identifying physical characteristics. It is flexible, permitting additions and omissions as required by the situation.

The goal of the police officer should be to train himself so that he can obtain a complete physical description of an individual in a matter of seconds. This ability may be acquired in the following manner.

(1) By learning the meaning of the numerous words used in describing various features.

(2) By studying and practicing the description of one or two features, such as eyes or nose, as they appear on several different persons and continuing this practice until all features have been covered.

(3) By learning a definite order of proceeding from one feature to another. A good example is from the top to the bottom in the following manner: hair, forehead, eyebrows, eyes, etc.

An accurate but incomplete description is much better than a complete but inaccurate description. The descriptive details an officer obtains should be capable of creating in the mind of another a definite and accurate picture. While descriptions should be as complete as possible so that they can be used by other police officers who are responding to the crime.

Almost every person possesses some distinguishing or outstanding physical characteristic. Hence, this is the most important part of a person's description. If this distinguishing characteristic is not initially apparent, the officer must look for it. Such a characteristic may be extraordinarily large ears, scars, a club foot, a peculiar gait, or an unconscious nervous habit. Thus, where time for observation is short or conditions impede observation, the officer should concentrate on observing the following physical characteristics:

1. Outstanding or distinguishing characteristic
2. Height

Unit 13 HOLDUP INFORMATION SYSTEMS

3. Build
4. Weight
5. Age
6. Race
7. Sex
8. Nose
9. Eyes
10. Ears

C. DESCRIPTION OF VEHICLES

Although teenage boys are the best witnesses for describing vehicles, the responding officer is not always lucky enough to have them available. However there are some facts that almost *anyone* can relay to the officer:

—Was it an old or late model car?

—Was it unusually clean or dirty?

—What shade of color was it?

—What was unusual about the car?

Too often precise descriptions of vehicles are given out in good faith, but result in failure. A victim may state the holdup men escaped in a 64/chevy painted blue. First you must establish if the victim is sure of the year. If he is guessing and an officer who *knows* a 64 chevy when he sees one passes the holdup men in a 66 chevy—he might drive right by. An older model chevy will suffice until you are sure or qualify the description with an "about 1964 model". Then there is the problem of the color. As you know there are many shades of blue running from pale blue to navy blue. The shade of the color is very important to responding officers and is frequently omitted. Another important factor is what color is over what color in the case of two-tone vehicles. An old model chevy with a white vinyl top over turquoise is a lot easier to observe fleeing from a holdup than a blue and white 64 chevy Cal. license number XYZ123. Of course the license number should be broadcasted if known, but there are more important characteristics to the police responding to a holdup.

Unusual characteristics such as damage, broken windows or lights, primer or off color fenders, racing stripes, decals or lettering, etc. are very valuable identifiers of escaping and wanted vehicles.

3. SUMMARY

Holdup information systems are a valuable police tool in combatting robberies and similar type crimes against the person. The system must be prepared in advance and distributed to the principal "actors" (victim, patrol officer and radio dispatcher).

The principal advantages in having a holdup information system are faster and more accurate wanted messages (AKA "Lookouts" and "Bolos").

Police officers should be trained to develop the ability to observe critically and describe accurately. This aids not only in apprehension, but in obtaining of better descriptions from victims.

Unusual characteristics about persons or autos are extremely important in the apprehension of criminals. It is more important to the responding officers to know, for example, that an escaping bank robbery suspect's left hand is in a cast that the teller recognizing him as Mr. Johnson, a former customer. The same applies to autos. The fact that it is a light green chevy with a red primer left front fender can be more important than a partial license number.

A good working knowledge of observation and description is essential for the next unit—"Surveillance".

4. QUESTIONS FOR DISCUSSION

1. How can you use a holdup information system to reduce response time and increase apprehensions?

Unit 13   HOLDUP INFORMATION SYSTEMS   159

2. How much time does the average bank robbery take? During which phases of a bank robbery do police have a chance of apprehending the doers?

3. Who are the major participants in a holdup information system?

4. Who is responsible for confirming the call and getting the "flash" information on the suspects out?

5. Discuss the importance of good observation and description techniques. How can police officers enhance their ability to observe and describe?

6. Explain why it could be more important for officers responding to a crime in progress to have information on unusual characteristics about the perpetrators than, say, the name of the perpetrator.

7. List unusual characteristics about wanted persons that would be helpful in apprehending criminals. Which are the most important ones?

8. List unusual characteristics about wanted autos that would be helpful in apprehending criminals. Which are the most important ones?

UNIT 14

SURVEILLANCES

In many criminal cases a point is reached where little or no advantage can be obtained by further questioning of the complainant or the friendly witnesses. It is time, then, for the investigator to go into the field to locate the criminal or, if he is known, to study his habits. At this point, the investigator must resign himself to the tedious, but essential task of observing the activities of witnesses or principals in the case. In other words, he must employ a technique of observation, known as surveillance.

I. SURVEILLANCE DEFINITIONS

1. Surveillance — The secretive and continuous watching of persons, vehicles, places or objectives to obtain information concerning the activities and identities of individuals.

2. Surveillant — The person who maintains the surveillance or performs the observation.

3. Convoy — A person employed by a subject to detect a surveillance. The convoy usually follows the subject trying to ascertain if anyone is following him.

4. Decoy — A person who attempts to divert the surveillant's attention from the subject. Many times a look-alike or dress-alike.

5. Plant — A person who watches a particular location, usually inside the operation.

6. Shadow — Synonymous with surveillant.

7. Subject — The person, place or thing under surveillance.

8.	Tail	Synonymous with surveillant.
9.	Made Burned Blown	Terms used to denote that the surveillance on surveillant's identity has been discovered by the subject.
10.	Stakeout	A fixed surveillance.

2. USES OF SURVEILLANCE

Some of the uses of a surveillance are:

1. To verify the reliability of an informant and his information.
2. To protect a dignitary who needs, but refuses security.
3. To obtain sufficient evidence to make a physical arrest or to secure an arrest or search warrant.
4. To locate and apprehend suspects and wanted persons.
5. To locate residences, hangouts, or other places frequented by the subject.
6. To identify relationships between known or suspected criminals, their accomplices, friends, relatives and associates.
7. To attempt to prevent a person from committing a crime.
8. To determine the most feasible method of conducting a raid or approach for an apprehension or rescue.
9. To prepare schedules and timetables of movements of persons for analysis in conducting further investigation.
10. To safeguard places and things, or protect a witness.

3. PREPARATION FOR A SURVEILLANCE

The surveillant should:

—Be average in size, build and general appearance.

—Have no noticeable peculiarities in appearance or mannerism.

—Wear no conspicious jewelry or clothing.

—Have the perserverance and capacity to wait for hours at a time without showing signs of impatience or irritation.

—Have the appearance of attending strictly to his own business and of not being interested in what others may be doing.

—Be resourceful, versatile and quick-witted so that he can readily conceive reasons or excuses for being in any given place.

—Be a good talker, able to talk his was out of embarrassing situations without arousing suspicion.

—Develop a good memory, as he cannot make on the spot notes during the surveillance.

—Conduct a briefing with all members of the surveillance team and the superiors to discuss the action to be taken in every contingency, the equipment that will be used, signals between the officers and type of surveillance used with alternate methods.

—Become thoroughly familiar with the case and the objective of the surveillance.

—Obtain as much information as possible about the subject, especially the things he can't change or disguise.

4. INFORMATION REGARDING THE LOCALITY OF THE SURVEILLANCE

The officer should make a reconnaissance of the area to determine:

1. Suitable vantage points
2. Traffic conditions
3. Name and location of streets
4. Alleys and driveways
5. Entrances and exits of buildings
6. Transportation facilities

7. Avenues of escape
8. Public buildings and places
9. Inhabitants of the neighborhood.

5. EQUIPMENT NEEDED

1. Money
   The surveillant should carry sufficient money to allow him to remain with the subject.
   In this area, sufficient and correct change for transportation.
   Money for theaters, amusements and pay telephones.
   For all types of restaurants and diners.
   Correct change for tolls on bridges and highways.
   Marked money for buys.
2. Transportation
   Number of vehicles
   Types of vehicles—van, auto, motorcycle
   Numerous license plates
   Food and drink
   Bumper stickers and other items to alter the appearance of the vehicle
   Reserve can of gasoline
   Bottle for urination
3. Personal Identification
   Fictitious credentials or identification
      Uniform
      Family history
      Employment
4. Personal Effects—Conservation is the Keynote
   Woman's hat and scarf
   Reversible jacket or coat
   Small hat or cap
   Eyeglasses—clear lenses and sunglasses
   Change of clothing—old to dressy

5. Recording Equipment
   Small tape recorder
   Binoculars
   Camera—telephoto lens
   Star scope for night viewing
6. Radio Equipment
   Regular police radio in car
   Police walkie-talkie
   Extra earphones and extension microphones
7. Miscellaneous Equipment
   Road and city maps for auto surveillance

The basic idea in surveillance is to have the surveillant become invisible. Since this is impossible, the next best thing is to blend into the environment so well that he becomes indistinguishable. The surveillant takes on the dress and demeanor of the neighborhood in which he happens to be working. He will frequently alter his appearance not wearing the same clothing all day or everyday. He will not make abrupt or unnatural movements that will call attention to him. It may be better to lose sight of the subject than arouse suspicion by abrupt movements.

6. MOVING SURVEILLANCE

The general types of moving surveillance are:

Close   Keeping the subject under observation at all times without becoming aware that he is being followed.

Loose   Spot checks on the subject, also known as intermittent surveillance. The surveillant observes the subject a little each day, following him on a particular leg of the journey until all stops are identified. (Useful for a cautious subject such as numbers banker or runner where they go to the same place each day and their operations become routine.)

Rough	A variation of the close surveillance but no attempt is made to conceal the surveillants actions. The object is to stay with the subject at all times whether he likes it or not. It is used to harass, and restrict his movements and generally upset the operation. (Used on known racketeers, narcotic dealers, etc., when it is very difficult to obtain evidence against them.)
Check tail	Also called convoys. The subject has someone following him to see if he is being watched. Wives of subjects are sometimes used for this purpose.

7. FIXED SURVEILLANCE

If the subject's home, place of business, or location of operation is to be kept under surveillance, it requires the selection of an observation point which will effectively conceal the surveillant while at the same time permitting him to observe the individual under surveillance. On occasion, an adjacent or nearby room or building will serve this purpose well. The interior of a parked car, camper, truck, or other vehicle is also often used.

Where indoor or interior facilities are not available or acceptable and an outdoor position must be used, the surveillant must take on a role that will allow him to remain in the neighborhood without arousing suspicion.

The surveillant could set up a newspaper or shoeshine stand or similar arrangement, or disguise himself as a painter, laborer, street cleaner, utility repairman, window washer, or some other person who appears to belong to the area.

Whatever position the surveillant uses he should have a position that offers maximum observation of all entrances and exits to the area under surveillance.

Rooftops are excellent vantage points but the surveillant must select an area far enough away to avoid detection.

8. FOOT SURVEILLANCE

One Man Tail

The one man tail is a difficult one, in all cases it must be a close one or the person being followed will be lost. It is readily noted by anyone by just turning the corner, stopping, and watching for the surveillant to follow him. Unless a loose tail is sufficient coverage a one man tail is almost useless. When observation has disclosed a regular routine on the part of the subject, then the one man loose tail can be used.

Two or More Surveillance

In surveillance using two or more men there are two basic operations. One is the group method where all surveillants are observing the subject at the same time and the other is the leap frog method where one or two men observe the subject and the other members of the team observe the surveillants with the team members changing places.

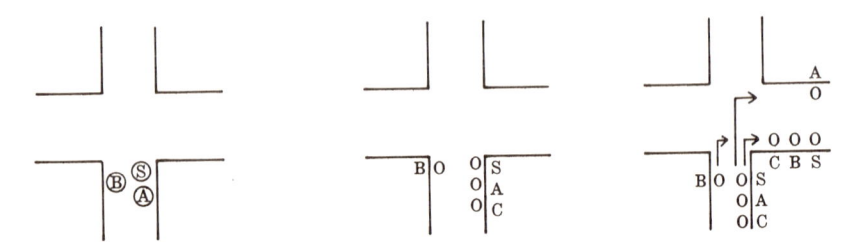

2 man group surveillance   leap frog method

9. SPECIFIC SITUATIONS

If tailing and the subject places you in a compromising situation, do some natural act such as: Buy a newspaper, window shop, light a cigarette or start a conversation with a passerby.

A. RESTAURANT

If the subject enters a restaurant, at least one tail follows him. The tail should order something that can be prepared and served rapidly. The surveillant must finish his meal and be ready to leave before the subject. If possible, sit near the subject to overhear the conversation that takes place. When the surveillant returns to the street take up a position away from the subject and let the other surveillants move up in following position.

B. PUBLIC CONVEYANCE

If the subject should use a public conveyance, board the same car or bus and sit to rear of subject. Check with your supervisor in advance to determine if you should remain with the subject on long trips. (e. g. plane, boat or train)

The surveillant may be able to obtain information by listening when he purchases the ticket, by questioning the ticket agent, by observing the flight number or advertised destination on the boat, bus or train.

On leaving such conveyance the investigator must stall for time until the suspect moves off. Pausing to light a cigarette, to look at street signs, to consult a notebook or piece of paper are a few devices to gain time.

(Don't overlook the possibility of checking the exterior of the suspect's luggage on these trips when it is out of his presence.)

C. ELEVATOR

If he goes in and pushes a button, just follow with him. If he doesn't push the button and waits for you to do so, push the top floor button and observe on what floor he gets off.

D. TAXI

Try to get another taxi—use the backup car—make note of time, location, name of cab company, number of cab, license number. If you lose him, check cab company later and get his destination from the office file.

E. TELEPHONE BOOTH

Try to overhear the conversation. Act inconspicuously by faking a call in an adjacent booth or look up a phone number in the directory.

F. HOTEL

If he registers, get the manager to find out the room number. If necessary, attempt to obtain the adjoining room.

NOTE: All outgoing calls made by the subject will normally be recorded by the hotel switchboard operator.

If necessary, check with maids, room service, etc., for information.

Don't overlook the trash removed from his room.

G. CONTACT

If the subject makes a contact, get the time, place, length and manner of contact. Obtain a description of the contact—if possible photograph the contact. Try to overhear conversation. Observe attitude of subject toward contact. Obtain list of out of town telephone numbers called by the subject.

H. TRICKS USED BY SUBJECT

A subject who feels that he is being followed may use one of the following:

1. Stop abruptly and look at the people behind him.
2. Casually look around.
3. Reverse the course and retrace his steps.
4. Board a bus, trolley or subway and get off just before they start to move.
5. Ride a short distance on public conveyance and get off watching who also gets off.
6. Circle the block in a taxi.
7. Stop abruptly after turning a corner.
8. Enter a building and leave by another exit immediately.
9. Use a convoy to detect surveillant.
10. Watch reflections in shop windows.

11. Walk at alternate pace. (slowly and rapidly)
12. Stop to tie his shoe, looking around for a surveillant.
13. Drop an object or piece of paper to see if anyone retrieves it.
14. Arrange with a friend to wait in a shop, tavern or other place to see if anyone is following him.
15. In a fixed location observe from a window or roof across the street to see if equipment or suspicious persons are visible.
16. In hotel lobbies or similar places watch for persons who act unusually observant.
17. Leave lobby, restaurant, etc., quickly, then suddenly turn around to see if anyone has suddenly jumped up without apparent reason or objective.

I. TESTING FOR A MAKE

It is difficult to know when the subject *makes* the surveillant. Some subjects act naturally since they don't want to trade a known surveillant for one they do not know.

Never conclude that you have been discovered. You have to overcome the natural tendency to believe you are discovered just because the subject glances in your direction a few times.

If the subject obviously discovers the surveillant, the latter should normally drop the tail and, if possible, be replaced by another surveillant. In some critical cases the surveillance should be stopped as soon as the subject is known to suspect the surveillance. This determination should be made at the initial briefing session before the start of the surveillance.

If the subject eludes the surveillant, every effort should be made to reestablish the surveillance as promptly as possible. This can best be accomplished by checking known hangouts or addresses frequented by the subject.

10. AUTOMOBILE SURVEILLANCE

When the automobile surveillance is necessary it requires careful preparation. The automobile used should be of common nondescript appearance, but not the typical "un-marked" police car. The license plates should not be traceable and not distinctive as the typical series supplied to the city vehicles. Disconnect the interior lights by removing the fuse or unscrewing the bulb. The latter will permit you to restore light for consulting maps or writing notes, etc.

If the surveillance entails going from one state to another it may be advantageous to have license plates from that state available and a method developed to rapidly change the plates from state to state. Magnets or spring clips could be used. If necessary, the inspection stickers could be changed by obtaining an out of state inspection sticker, encasing it in thin clear plastic and fastening it to the window with transparent adhesive tape.

The automobile surveillance can be quite difficult when the subject auto is non-descript. One technique to make the subject's vehicle readily identifiable is to spray liquid glass from an aerosol can on the rear bumper. The reflective material can be seen from a perpendicular position to the rear but is practically invisible from any other angle.

Reflective tape can be fastened to the rear of the vehicle for identification, also the use of advertising type bumper stickers.

In extremely serious cases where it is imperative not to lose the subject and the surveillant must have additional assistance, the subject's automobile can be disabled to delay his departure. This can be accomplished by:

1. Changing the setting on the carburetor air valves to give too much gasoline to the engine.
2. The choke mechanism can be readjusted to prevent starting.

3. Close the points on the distributor with an allen wrench.
4. Short out the battery.
5. Arrange for a convenient flat tire.

A. ONE SURVEILLANCE VEHICLE

This is not advisable, but if necessary, the surveillant should position himself directly behind the subject's car. The distance will vary with the type of area and the volume of traffic.

In congested areas no more than two vehicles should be permitted to come between the subjects car and the surveillant.

On the highway allow a few cars to stay between the subject and you. If it is a limited access highway and you know the area, you can allow the subject to get out of sight once in a while.

An alternative is to be parallel to the subject's car. The surveillant will operate his vehicle on a street parallel to the street used by the subject. The surveillant will drive rapidly from one intersection to the next and look for the subject's vehicle. When he observes the vehicle continuing straight he goes to the next intersection. If the vehicle does not appear, he presumes the subject parked or stopped in that block. If the subject's car makes a turn, the surveillant drives behind him until he can get to another parallel street. This may be necessary to use in night time and suburban areas when the surveillant must remain behind the subject for too long a period of time.

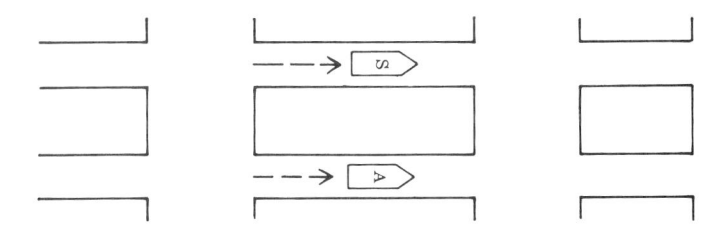

B. TWO SURVEILLANCE VEHICLES

Normally both cars will follow directly behind the subject's car. The first vehicle will observe the subject and the second vehicle will observe the surveillant's car.

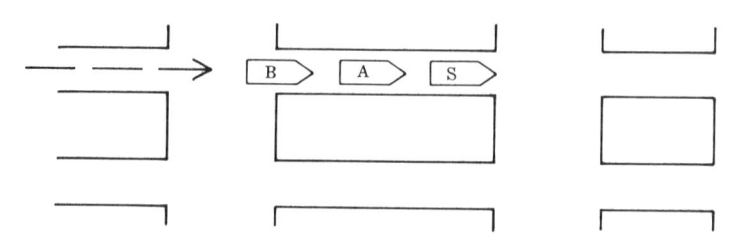

The cars will change positions periodically to keep the same car from being behind the subject for too long a period of time.

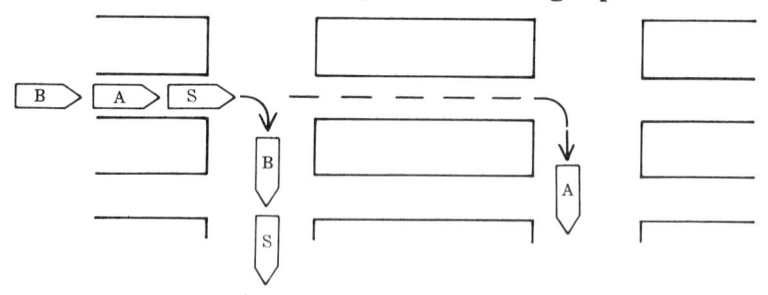

A variation of this is to have one vehicle follow the subject and the second vehicle to parallel the subject on an adjacent street, again changing positions when necessary.

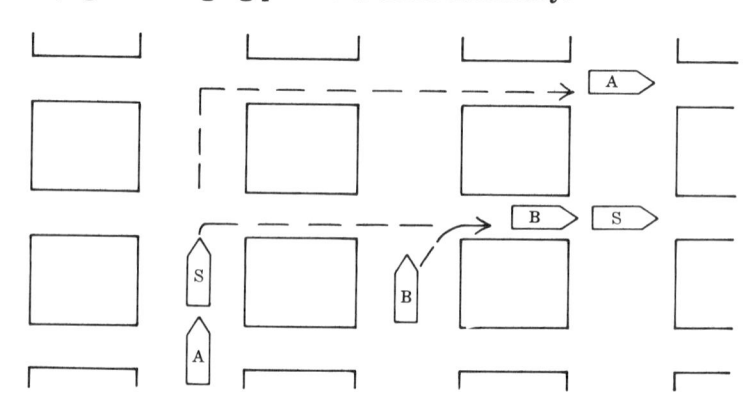

C. THREE SURVEILLANCE VEHICLES

It is obvious that three or more vehicles will ensure a greater ability to follow the subject without being made or losing him.

The surveillant can use parallel routes, rotate the position of the vehicles more often, and one can lead the subject's car on occasion.

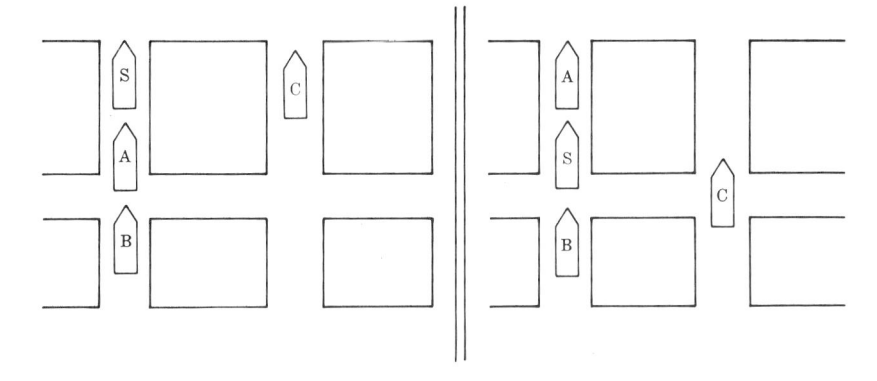

If the subject is extremely conscious of the possibility of a tail and it is not imperative to follow him closely every day, a leapfrog method can be used. The surveillant can follow the subject for a certain period of time or geographic distance, break off the tail and resume the tail the following day from the point where he left off the day before.

In vehicle surveillance, a minimum two men per vehicle is required. One to drive and the other to operate the radio and record the events that take place. Also the passenger can get out and initiate a foot surveillance if the subject unexpectedly parks his vehicle and travels on foot.

The vehicle behind the subject's vehicle will be the radio command car. He will issue directions and instructions, as each surveillance car changes position so also will the term 'command car' be changed to the vehicle behind the subject's car.

If it is necessary to park in an area for a period of time and the officers want to keep the subject's vehicle under observation, one surveillant can remain with the vehicle and the other can tail on foot. The surveillant in the vehicle can change positions in the vehicle, sitting on the passenger side as if he is waiting for the driver to return.

The surveillant can move the vehicle from one location to another occasionally. He can park the vehicle a block away from the subject's vehicle, either behind the vehicle or in the block beyond the vehicle. Normally, the subject expects the surveillant to remain behind him. By parking past him he may be deceived. The surveillant in the parked vehicle can put on a woman's hat, scarf, eyeglasses or wig to change his identity.

In a two man surveillance the passenger may lay down in the vehicle to make the auto appear to have one occupant. Also, do not mix races in the surveillance vehicle. This is a give-a-way. The surveillants should be of the same race as the subject.

D. TEST FOR AUTO SURVEILLANCE

Drive at a high rate of speed until he reaches the crest of a hill, or a curve, or turning a corner, then reduce speed rapidly or stop and wait for the surveillant to pass.

Make a u-turn in an unlikely place and observe if another vehicle makes a similar move.

Drive—park—drive—park—for short periods remaining in the automobile. Drive into a dead-end street.

II. DO'S AND DON'TS OF SURVEILLANCE

The following lists of do's and don'ts apply to various kinds of surveillance and different types of situations.

A surveillant should:
1. Watch at all times to be sure that he is not also being shadowed.
2. Always have a likely story ready to justify his presence at any time or place.
3. Always try to do something that would naturally be done at that time and place. For example, if he is in a cafe, he should order something to eat.

4. Take great care, if baggage or rooms are searched to leave everything in the same condition in which it was found. Each object examined should be restored to its original position and condition as soon as possible after being disturbed.
5. Use subterfuges whenever possible. For example, if the subject stops to talk to a friend, the officer can stop someone on the street and ask questions.
6. Walk close to buildings in business areas, so that the subject will not see the shadower's reflection in a store window.
7. When appropriate, estimate a subject's destination by checking his speedometer immediately before and after he takes a trip.
8. Use decoy communications, such as fake telegrams or telephone calls made under a pretext, to determine occupancy of premises.
9. Carry glasses, a cap, and any other small items that can be used to effect a change in appearance.
10. Arrange for garbage and trash examination. (Many valuable leads and much information may be found in papers and correspondence found in a subject's trash or garbage.)
11. Develop sources of information or of local fixed surveillance, such as storekeepers or janitors.
12. Make use of the fact that on Sundays and Holidays, violators are less likely to suspect surveillance and may become careless.

The surveillant should remember that the most useful equipment he can apply to surveillance is his imagination.

A surveillant should not:
1. Meet the gaze of the subject.
2. Slink from place to place; he should act naturally.
3. Arouse suspicion of other police.

4. Allow himself to be guided by any unsubstantiated feeling of being hot.
5. Immediately go home or to his office after being "uncovered", as the subject may follow to confirm his suspicions.
6. Peek from doorways, from behind poles, or from other similar places.
7. Ask hotel clerks, bellboys, or anyone else who has contact with the subject for information about the subject until it has been determined that he is not a friend of the subject and that he can be trusted.

12. SUMMARY

Surveillance is usually thought of as a "reactive approach" to crime—the surveillance of persons suspected of committing a past crime.

The main reason surveillance is dealt with here is that it is one of the mainstays of the "proactive approach" to the crime problem. Both crime targets and crime perpetrators could be surveilled under this approach. Since there are many more crime targets than criminals, it would seem logical that known active robbers, for example, should be tailed until they "do their thing". The New Orleans Police Department is the only major department known to this writer that has an anti-crime surveillance program for know offenders.

Officers need the proper equipment and training for effective surveillance.

Good communications are a must and practice surveillance in the field is highly recommended.

It is also helpful to know anit-surveillance tricks and tests used by subjects of surveillance. Later, in Units 22, 23 and 24 you will see use of surveillances against robbers, burglars and auto thieves. Also, the same fundamentals apply in backing-up a police decoy (see Unit 18, "Use of Decoys").

13. QUESTIONS FOR DISCUSSION

1. List the uses of a police surveillance. How could this technique be used to combat crimes in progress?
2. What preparations should be taken prior to surveillance?
3. What information on the locality of the surveillance is necessary? How can it be obtained?
4. What equipment is needed for an effective surveillance? Why?
5. How would you go about setting up a fixed surveillance? A foot surveillance? A moving surveillance?
6. What anti-surveillance could be used by a subject?
7. What should be done if the subject "makes" the officer on a covert surveillance?
8. List the major "do's" and "don'ts" concerning surveillance.

UNIT 15

SEARCHES

The two basic qualities of successful police search operations are organization and tenacity on part of the search team. This unit is primarily concerned with search for bodies (suspects) rather than for evidence. However, the basic principles for both searches are similar.

I. GENERAL GUIDELINES FOR ALL SEARCHES

Even though no two searches are the same, a pattern of actions that must be taken for all types of searches can be observed. There are several basic steps in police procedure that can be applied in these situations. The most urgent actions to be taken are to request assistance, to surround the building, and to seal off all exits. The following points should also be considered:

A. OBJECTIVE

Request supervisory assistance and establish search objectives. When a police officer arrives at the scene and determines that a search of the building is necessary, he should obtain the necessary assistance to seal off the building and establish communications. At this point, consideration should be given to the following when initiating a building search:

1. What is to be accomplished?
2. Is the search to be conducted for evidence, service of a body warrant, or apprehension of an armed and hostile adversary?

B. PLANNING

Planning is a very important step for any efficient and sucussful operation. Keep the plan as simple as the occasion permits. Some points to consider are:

1. What cars will cover the exits, and at what position of the building will they be located?

2. How should vehicles deploy lights?
3. Determine whether the district policemen will search the building, or if additional specialized assistance is required.
4. Obtain a floor plan of the building if time permits, from the owner, occupant, landlord, security officer or private protective agent at the scene.
5. Determine the best point of entry to the building, and where the search will begin once inside the building. The element of surprise should be utilized to the officer's best advantage when conducting a search or making a physical arrest.

C. ORGANIZING

Usually a supervisor will be at the scene and will determine who is to participate in the search. The supervisor must insure that every man at the scene knows his specific duties, whether it is guarding the rear of the building or being a member of the search team. It is necessary to set up a communications car to receive and transmit calls to Police Radio. Organize a small search party and inform each member as to his responsibilities upon entering, searching and leaving the building.

1. The search party should be kept to a minimum number of men; large teams lead to confusion and the men get in each others way.
2. Ensure that the police officers outside of the building know that there is a search team inside the building, and the points at which the team is to enter and leave. This should eliminate the possibility of an accident, whereby the officers outside mistake the officers inside for suspects.

D. COMMUNICATIONS

Communications during a building search, in most cases, is a necessity. There are three methods generally employed.

1. Radio communications via police radio in a designated communications vehicle on scene.

2. Employing a telephone conveniently located in the area of the search. This telephone communication is maintained via direct open line with the radio room to facilitate exchange of relevant information. Two (2) police officers should be utilized, one to stay on the open line, keeping same operating, and one officer to transmit information to and from scene commander.
3. If the equipment is available, and time allows, the search party should have a hand-held portable radio to maintain communications while inside the buildings with personnel outside.

E. CONTROL

All members of the search party must work as a team, each man supporting the others. The leader of the search must coordinate and control the situation. In all searches of buildings; i. e. *doors found open,* responding to a *burglary alarm* or *barricaded persons,* a supervisor should be present before the building is entered.

If the building is to be searched to apprehend a trapped suspect or a barricaded person, the exits should be covered and a supervisor summoned to the scene before entry is made, unless there is an immediate danger to life.

2. MECHANICS OF THE SEARCH OF BUILDINGS

The search of buildings is most effective if it is methodical. Haphazard seaching tends to result in some locations being searched more than once and others being overlooked entirely. A systematic procedure is particularly important if a large number of officers are involved in the search.

There may be times when the search of a building involves special danger for the searching officers. For example, the search may be for a wanted person, or it may involve occupants who will resort to violence when evidence of their wrongdoing is discovered.

Rules for such searches will depend on many things—the reason for the search, the time of day or night, the number of officers involved, the type of building being searched, etc. There are, however, some rules which are good police practice in most cases. A list of these rules follow:

1. At no time is a one man search justified. If you are the only man on duty in your area, summon another officer from a neighboring jurisdiction.
2. The building to be searched should be approached carefully if there is any reason to anticipate danger or resistance. In order that hidden suspects or possessors of contraband not be warned that a search is about to take place, sirens and flashing lights should not be used and the patrol car should be parked some distance from the building.
3. Search officers should be divided into groups. Each group should be assigned to a particular area or search responsibility, depending upon the area, the type of building, and the nature of the search.
4. Doors, windows, stairs and elevators should be kept under surveillance during the search to assure that persons or articles being sought do not leave the premises or move to locations already searched.
5. One room should be searched at a time.
6. Officers should exercise caution in entering a room or a new floor level. Suspects being sought or persons hiding contraband commonly attack at that time. Doors which open inward should be slammed to the wall in the event that someone is hiding behind them. Officers should not remain silhouetted in an open doorway.
7. The flashlight should be held out and away from the body of the officer.
8. The service revolver should be drawn but not cocked during the search if there is any reason to suspect danger or resistance.

9. A citizen who is accompanying a searching officer should follow, not precede, him.
10. Badges should worn in plain view.
11. Searches should not be discontinued after the apprehension of one suspect—others may also be on the premises.
12. Keep K-9 dogs on leash when searching rooftops or other areas dangerous to the animal.

3. BUILDING SEARCHES

Types of building searches:
1. service of body warrant
2. for suspects known to be inside of building
3. open properties—possible burglary suspects inside
4. for evidence

Type #3—open properties will be dealt with under Unit 23 "Tactical Approaches to Burglary".

Type #4—building search for evidence is more related to criminal investigation and will not be dealt with here.

4. SEARCHING A BUILDING WITH A WARRANT OF ARREST

Many times policemen and detectives must serve body warrants for the arrest of persons on various charges. Most of these warrants are served inside buildings. Sometimes police must search these buildings to find suspects. Even though every search or warrant service is not identical, there are certain basic principles that, if followed, will help accomplish this task with some degree of efficiency and safety. Plan to make the arrest at a location that offers maximum advantages to you and a minimum to the suspect. Action in a crowded area should be avoided since this may afford many avenues of escape for the suspect, and may inhibit the actions of the police.

In addition, the suspects may have supporters in the vicinity who may come to their aid. If possible, it is preferable to serve body warrants in the early morning hours, 5 to 6 a. m. This is after the bars and clubs have closed and the person most likely will be at home, and perhaps, even sleeping. If so, this will put the suspect at a disadvantage as he will be effected by sleep and not functioning at full mental capacity. Further, service at such an early morning hour reduces the possibility of arousing the neighbors and family, as most people are usually asleep at this hour. In many instances it is important to locate and arrest the suspect on the first attempt to serve the warrant otherwise the suspect will possibly be alerted to the fact that the police are looking for him. If the suspect is not located on the first attempt he may go into hiding or flee the jurisdiction altogether.

Before serving the warrant check the record of the suspect to learn something about his background. You may be asked to serve a warrant for a minor offense and the suspect will be free on bail or on parole for a more serious crime and think you are going to arrest him for this crime. His record also may show arrests for crimes that indicate he is prone to violence, such as numerous arrests for assault and battery on an officer. If a detective or plainclothesman is going to serve the warrant, bring a uniformed officer to the point of entry with you to repudiate the suspect's charges at a later date that he did not know who was there, and/or thought that the plainclothes officers were burglars or holdup men. Always have an additional officer cover the rear of the property before going to the point of entry.

Knock on the door as lightly as possible as to attract the attention of someone inside, but not awaken the whole household. Usually one of the parents or a female member of the family will answer the door (they seem to be light sleepers) especially if there are young children in the household. Identify yourself to this person and if time and conditions allow, show them the warrant. Ensure that the person answering the door does not cause a commotion and wake the suspect. Ascertain from the responding party the location of the suspect and whether he is asleep or awake. If in the building, try to ascertain the suspect's condition; i. e., sleep, intoxicated, sick.

Quietly proceed to the room occupied by the suspect, bringing along with you the person who answered the door. Enter the room quietly, and if the suspect is in bed and asleep, try to approach the bed from behind the head of the suspect. This places the officer in a position which is advantageous to his safety. If this is not possible, have one of the officers at the foot of the bed and another at the side of the bed near the suspect's head. The officer at the foot of the bed will shine his flashlight into the eyes of the suspect temporarily blinding him, and if he is sleeping with a weapon concealed under the covers or pillow, he will not be in a good position to assault the officers and will be unable to ascertain the number of policemen in the room. If the suspect attempts to assault the officer at the foot of the bed the officer standing next to the head of the bed can surprise and subdue the suspect.

If the background of the suspect or the charges on the warrant necessitate it, the officers should have their guns drawn and be prepared to use them. If the suspect surrenders without any resistance he should be told by the officer at the foot of the bed, that they are policemen and have a warrant for him, and instruct the suspect to slowly place one hand at a time over his head. The officer at the head of the bed should not give his position away by moving or talking. Remember, any request made by the suspect should be denied until he has been taken into physical custody, is securely confined and searched. At this point, the suspect should be directed to get out of the bed, move slowly, and keep his hands above his head at all times. Place the suspect in a position for a wall search against the nearest available wall. The suspect should be instructed to get out of the bed on the side away from the door if possible. The officer at the foot of the bed will keep the suspect under surveillance while the other officer searches the bed after first turning on the room lights.

Then search the suspect and the immediate vicinity of the arrest in the presence of the arrested person, for any articles he may have discarded or for evidence of his criminal activity. If the suspect is undressed, have him tell you where his clothing is located, and one of the officers will get the clothes for him. Search the clothing before giving same to the suspect. When the suspect has dressed, handcuff him in the proper manner and remove him from the building. Police must be reasonably certain that the individual to be arrested is actually the person wanted or named on the warrant. It the offender is not known to the officers, he should be pointed out by someone who knows him and he must produce proper identification. The officers should obtain a description and photograph of the suspect before service of the warrant is attempted. If the family and/or friends want information in regard to the suspect, the officer should furnish this information *AFTER* the suspect has been securely confined inside the Police van. Do not allow members of the family and/or other interested people to come near the prisoner or have physical contact with him during his arrest and removal from the building.

5. SEARCHING A BUILDING FOR SUSPECTS KNOWN TO BE INSIDE

There are instances where policemen know that someone is inside a property or are called to a scene where a person has *barricaded* himself inside a building. The initial procedure is basically the same as in a building search when a door has been found open, or an alarm has been set off. The most important point is to call for assistance and surround the building to prevent the escape of the suspects and ensure the safety of innocent bystanders. This must be accomplished as quickly and safely as possible. After the building has been sealed off there is usually no need for haste.

The first officer on the scene should take the following steps:

1. Obtain all available information and notify Police Radio of all conditions as they develop.

2. Attempt to learn the name, age, race, sex, mental condition, etc. of the person barricaded.
3. Set up a radio patrol car as temporary command and communications post and inform Police Radio of the exact location of this car.
4. Restrict pedestrian and vehicular traffic at the scene if the person is barricaded, or if the traffic will interfere with police operations.
5. Place yourself in a position where you can observe the building, but where the barricaded person cannot see you.
6. Relate all available information to the first supervisor on the scene.

The first supervisor on the scene should:
1. Evacuate the area if necessary.
2. Establish security of the evacuated area.
3. Establish a perimeter around the scene.
4. Set up an extra manpower pool at the perimeter or at the command car, if necessary.
5. Consider the need for fire apparatus; ladders, etc.

The responsibilities of the overall commander at the scene:

Obtain all related information concerning the situation, such as:
1. Number of persons involved.
2. Identification of the persons inside.
3. Police Radio can ascertain the prior record of the suspect which can be used to indicate the basic personality of the suspect; i. e., past experience and attitude of the suspect towards violence, police, etc. Will he possibly surrender peacefully? Will an overwhelming show of force suffice, or must he be taken into custody by force, personal appeal from parents, wife, priest, etc.
4. Is the suspect ARMED, if so, with what type of equipment and weapon?

5. Physical information on the building; i. e., what type of heating system—hot air, etc. How many floors—basement—storage rooms? Where are the doors and windows located? What is the interior plan of the building? Is tear gas necessary? If used, will it set the building on fire due to the type of construction of contents? Will it be effective should suspect utilize hot air vent system/air conditioning vent system to acquire fresh air?
6. Have fire apparatus respond to the scene to supply ladders and/or related equipment needed to conduct search of roof and adjacent elevations. Ladders can also be used to place Tac Unit personnel into positions to return sniper fire. One maxim in sniper cases is to secure the "highground". Fire fighting equipment on the scene could also be utilized in case of fire.
7. At night, obtain sufficient lighting equipment. The fire department has available a light wagon with a mounted bank of lights and portable floodlights.
8. Have K-9 respond to the scene.
9. Obtain supporting weapons from the Tactical Unit.

(I) PREPARATION FOR ENTRY INTO THE BUILDING

If it has been determined that the police must enter the building, follow the general entry guidelines aforementioned. The overall commander should determine the size of the search party needed and assign its members ensuring that they are aware of their duties. He should also determine the point of entry and method of entry, use of fire power, tear gas, smoke screen, to be utilized. The element of surprise is used whenever possible in effecting an arrest or entering a building. Prior planning will indicate where surprise is feasible. A word of caution—In vice or narcotics raids, it is advisable to enter the building from several points simultaneousuly, however when the suspects are armed and there is a chance of gunplay, only one point should be entered to avoid having officers caught in their own crossfire.

188	POLICE OPERATIONS	Sec. 3

All officers at the scene will be informed of police entry into the building and directed to discontinue immediately any fire power directed toward the building.

POLICE COMBAT TEAM

Unit 15 SEARCHES 189

"SNIPER" AIMS RIFLE FROM SECOND STORY WINDOW

POLICE COMBAT TEAM PREPARES FOR ASSAULT ON "SNIPER'S" POSITION

COMBAT TEAM LAYS DOWN SUPPRESSING FIRE

POLICE COMBAT TEAM APPLIES TEAR GAS TO INSIDE OF
BUILDING AND SMOKE COVER OUTSIDE

Unit 15 SEARCHES 193

NOTE THE INITIAL EFFECTS OF GAS AND SMOKE

194 POLICE OPERATIONS Sec. 3

THE SMOKE AND GAS TAKE EFFECT

Unit 15 SEARCHES 195

THE "SNIPER" IS "BLINDED" BY SMOKE AND GAS

196　　　　　　POLICE OPERATIONS　　　　　　Sec. 3

2 MEMBERS OF COMBAT TEAM ENTER "SNIPER'S" LOCATION WHILE OTHERS COVER

All utilities should be turned off at their source into the building before the search team moves through the building. This will deny the person barricaded the use of electricity, gas or water.

Unit 15　　　　　　　SEARCHES　　　　　　　197

Our primary concern as police officers is the protection of life and property. We should first attempt to vocally persuade the *armed* suspect or barricaded person from the building, then use

COMBAT TEAM IN REAL LIFE ACTION—2 ARMED ROBBERS CAPTURED IN FIREFIGHT

Photo by Philadelphia Daily News

other methods such as gas, smoke or K-9 to remove him. If the situation warrants removing the suspect by force we must ensure, by every means possible, that no innocent persons or policemen become needless casualties.

(2) ENTRY INTO THE BUILDING

Actual entry into a building in search of an armed suspect should be done only by the Tac Unit personnel or Police Combat team. All members of the search party should know their individual and collective duties, the point and method entry, which member will be in charge, and who will replace him if need be. The members should also ensure that they have all their equipment with them. Vests, helmets, gas masks, additional gas cannisters, lights, weapons, extra ammo and handcuffs.

The overall commander should have someone attempt to persuade the suspect to give up; even if he does not give up, his response may give away his position inside the building and may also distract the suspect while entry is being made. While advancing to the point of entry make use of all available cover; i. e. trees, walls, alleys, automobiles, etc. Enter the building by having two (2) members of the stakeout team open the door and enter diagonally, using speed and surprise.

Once inside the building, stop and listen, then check the room for suspects. If the room is clear of suspects bring in the rest of the team. If necessary, when entry to building is being undertaken, shut off the telephone service. When moving from room to room or floor to floor, utilizing hallways, corridors or stairs, stay close to the walls. In old buildings with squeaky floors, walk flatfooted to avoid giving away your position. While opening a door, lift the door by the handle to take the pressure off the hinges and prevent squeaking.

The members of the team should stay apart and refrain from grouping together which would make them an easy target. When walking through a darkened room, stay in the middle to avoid bumping into or tripping over furniture. If you make a noise, stop and ascertain suspect's reaction if any, drop to a prone position for safety, and make the suspect come to you.

Members of the combat team must have patience. The tension of the situation will put a heavy psychological strain on the suspect, making him less fit to engage the officers. This may cause him to change his position, giving away his exact location and making him more vulnerable.

When the suspect has been located in a particular room, decide whether to try to persuade him to give up, to use gas or to take him by surprise by forcing the door and entering the room. If persuasion is to be used *do not stand in front or near the door* if the walls are constructed of thin materials such as wall board. The suspect can shoot through walls and doors injuring and/or killing the officers. If the suspect does shoot through the door, attempt to ascertain the location of the source of fire by the direction of the bullets (angle of projectile after passing through wall/door, where they pass, or from the noise of the weapon). If the suspect does not have a hostage with him, return fire through the doors and walls into the room. If it is necessary to enter the room, ensure that the hallway or room you are in is darkened.

Try the door and ascertain if it is locked. If not, swing it open, staying away from the front of the door. If the door is locked, determine whether to kick it open or use a pry axe. When the door has been opened, pause for a few minutes in silence to increase the psychological strain on the suspect.

(3) ENTERING THE ROOM

One man wearing protective gear should enter the room. If possible, the policeman entering the room should be armed with a shotgun in addition to his service revolver. Both he and his backup man should be trained and prepared to neutralize opposition, if encountered.

Apprehended persons should be removed from the building as soon as possible, and the search of the building should be continued as there may be more than one suspect in the building.

6. SUMMARY

The important points to remember in any type of search, are to surround the building, to seal off exits and to keep in mind the basic duties of the police. These duties are: Protection of life and property, prevention of crime and the apprehension of suspects who violate the laws. Never enter a building alone. Always consider the feasibility of obtaining assistance from supporting units in building searches, such as K-9.

7. QUESTIONS FOR DISCUSSION

1. What are the two basic qualities of successful police search operations? Explain.
2. Is a one man search of a building justified? Why or why not?
3. What preparations should be made prior to a search of a building for suspects? What equipment is necessary?
4. What are the duties of the first officer on the scene of a "barricaded man"?
5. What are the duties of the first supervisor at the scene of a "barricaded man"?
6. What are the duties of the overall police commander at the scene of a "barricaded man"?
7. Are police ever justified in making multiple entrances to a building in searches for suspects? What about when the suspects are armed?
8. What recent searches of buildings for suspects occurred in your jurisdiction? What did police do right?; or wrong?

SECTION 4

PROACTIVE CRIME FIGHTING TACTICS

UNIT 16

SPECIAL CRIME TACTICAL FORCES

According to the National Advisory Commission on Criminal Justice, Standards and Goals (Standard 9.8), every police agency employing more than 75 personnel should have immediately available, consistent with an analysis of its need, a flexible and highly mobile tactical force for rapid deployment against special crime problems.

1. Every chief executive should establish written policies and procedures that govern deployment of the tactical force against any problem. These policies and procedures should stipulate at least:

    a. That the tactical force will be deployed on the basis of current crime pattern analyses or validated current information on expected crime activity;

    b. That the tactical force will be deployed against a problem only when the regularly assigned patrol force is not adequate to be effective against that problem; and

    c. That tactical force deployment strategy will be based on an objective analysis of the problem; overt saturation as a low visibility detection and apprehension operation.

2. Every police agency employing more than 400 personnel should consider maintaining a full-time tactical force, and every agency employing more than 75 but fewer than 400 should con-

sider maintaining a full- or part-time tactical force, depending on local problems.

    a. The numerical strength of the tactical force should depend on agency needs and local problems.

    b. A full-time tactical force should include an analytical staff element.

    c. A part-time tactical force should use qualified personnel from anywhere within the agency.

    d. Every tactical force should have a central headquarters and should operate from that headquarters when deployed against a problem.

    e. Field commanders should be informed of tactical force activities within their area of responsibility. Tactical force activities should be consistent with the policies of the field commander of the area in which they are working.

    f. Every tactical force should be equipped with necessary specialized equipment, vehicles, radios, vision devices, and weapons.

I. NATIONAL ADVISORY COMMISSION COMMENTARY

Every police administrator is often troubled by an apparent inability to deploy his patrol strength for maximum effect against particular problems. Limited personnel and the many problems of regular patrol service frequently preclude the attaining of proper selective enforcement, or selective pressure, against special crime problems. To achieve proper emphasis and pressure against particular crime situations, crime tactical forces are often deployed to serve as compact, flexible operational task forces in given locations at times when a concentrated effort is needed.

The tactical unit is normally comprised of a small force of selected men from within the agency's own personnel pool. The numbers and ranks of its supervisors are determined by the numerical strength of the unit. Special tactical crime forces may

Unit 16　SPECIAL CRIME TACTICAL FORCES

vary from a few men on a small force to 200 or more on large forces. New York City's Police Department has 690 carefully chosen and well-trained personnel in its tactical unit; the special squads of the District of Columbia and Los Angeles number over 200 men. Tactical units are used extensively in many other agencies, including Honolulu, Hawaii; Kalamazoo, Mich.; Syracuse, N. Y.; Amarillo, Tex.; Savannah, Ga.; and Chicago, Ill.

Ordinarily these units are motorized and assigned to areas where research has determined that problems are occurring. According to Municipal Police Administration, "flexibility should be the tactical force's hallmark."

For example, the unit may work in plainclothes on a daylight burglary problem. Then, abruptly, they may be assigned to work in uniform on the night watch on a drunk driver problem, and the next night on a skylight burglar. If there is no specific problem, the unit members may be deployed over an extensive geographic area, then, if needed, quickly pulled together as a cohesive and coordinated unit to search for a particularly dangerous robbery suspect.

The tactical unit should be functionally responsible to the patrol commander under whom it is operating. The tactical force is present to augment the regular patrol force and to serve as a catalyst in making the line units effective in achieving their common ends. Tactical units who use greater force, or who show less respect for the public than the patrol units in the area, may achieve their immediate goal while alienating the community. Tactical unit personnel should be made aware of the problems, policies, and sensitive areas of the locations in which they work.

2. DEPLOYMENT

Written policies and procedures should specify that the deployment of tactical forces is limited to current crime pattern analyses or validated intelligence that indicates a crime problem has developed or is growing in a given location.

The San Francisco Police Department, after carefully studying rising rates of robberies, burglaries, and auto thefts (up 3, 5, and 21 percent, respectively), decided in 1969 to supplement the entire department's efforts in reducing car thefts by placing a task force of 20 motorcycle officers in the field to concentrate on checking suspects' vehicles. With the knowledge that many criminals use stolen cars in the commission of other criminal acts, the tactical force members concentrated on areas of high auto theft incidence in the city's nine police districts. During peak hours of activity throughout the initial 5 months of the tactical force's deployment, auto thefts decreased 21 percent while the national rate increased 14 percent. During the same period, robberies decreased 17 percent and burglaries 1 percent, compared with a national increase of 10 and 13 percent.

Policy should also indicate that the tactical force be deployed only when the special crime problem cannot be effectively combatted by the regularly assigned patrol force. Patrol members who must concentrate their efforts in a specific area create an imbalance in other geographic areas. While daily arrests, investigations, and requests for police service can be forecast with some degree of accuracy, there will always be exceptions. Supplemental patrol units, in the form of special crime tactical personnel, may be deployed to saturate high crime areas during periods where there is justification for such measures. Special tactical forces should not be assigned to areas where statistics disclose that greater numbers of patrolmen are not really necessary or where the presence of more men would be likely to aggravate a condition already under control.

When it has been decided that, based upon current crime pattern and patrol manpower shortages, a tactical crime force is needed, deployment strategy must be based on an objective analysis of the problem. If what is needed is a deterrent in the form of additional police presence, then the tactical force should be employed in uniform and in marked police vehicles. Overt saturation discourages such crime problems as juvenile gang activity and gives the local public a sense of security that otherwise might be absent.

On the other hand, covert saturation, or inconspicuous officer presence, should be the tactic employed when criminal offenders are not significantly deterred by the presence of uniformed officers.

Continuing analysis should be made of the effects of the various deployment patterns of the tactical squad. Deployment procedures should be modified if the tactical squad is not meeting its objectives.

3. TAC FORCE ORGANIZATION, STAFF AND COMMAND

To reduce crime, the police agency must make the criminal element aware of the probability of apprehension. Saturation patrol, as a tactic of special crime task forces, has proved to be one of the effective methods of crime prevention. Every city police administrator and every concerned suburban police chief executive should implement special crime tactical forces to supplement his agency's normal patrol activity, preferably on a full-time basis.

Close coordination between the tactical force and the patrol and investigative operation is of paramount importance. Because tactical units supplement and assist the patrol force, their activities should be consistent with those of the patrol officers. Field commanders must be informed of tactical force activities within their area of responsibility to insure coordinated efforts and preclude any possible friction or misunderstandings that might otherwise occur.

The Los Angeles Police Department's Metropolitan Division is an example of a full-time multifaceted tactical force. The members of Metropolitan Division are used daily in many assignments throughout the city. The division may deploy its 200 members in any strength necessary to augment concerned geographical patrol divisions in policing situations requiring additional policemen. One of the division's most important functions is maintaining selective enforcement details in high frequency crime areas. Particular emphasis is directed to the suppression of burglary, robbery, auto theft, and burglary-theft of motor vehicles. The Metropolitan Division is a good example of a centrally located police tactical unit able to operate and respond from central headquarters when deployed against a problem. Additionally, it illustrates the value of including a complete analytical staff within this type of task force organization. In virtually all cases, deployment is based upon careful quantitative analysis of special crime areas. Data are examined to ascertain the impact and effectiveness of the division's employment. Refer to Unit 17 for additional details on LAPD's Metropolitan Division.

The Special Operations Group is a select unit operating within the Chicago Police Department to combat special street crime problems. When the task force was created in 1956, it had two platoons with approximately 40 officers whose objective was saturation patrol to reduce crime in certain parts of the city. In 1961 the Special Operations Group was expanded and divided into four tactical units assigned to different areas of the city. A fifth, recently organized special operating unit includes the following sub units; transit authority police, a special events detail, a canine unit, a helicopter unit, and a water patrol unit. The Special Operations Group, as a part of the patrol bureau, answers directly to the chief of that bureau.

The Detroit Police Department has two distinct types of tactical forces. One is the Tactical Mobile Unit, which serves as a crime prevention unit. It was designed to provide a highly visible deterrent operation using distinctly marked vehicles to saturate any high crime area at any time. The officers are trained to handle both planned and spontaneous disorders, riots, and demonstrations. The second tactical operation is the Stop The Robberies, Enjoy Safe Streets (STRESS). It is a low visibility plan that is designed to reduce street robbery and other violent street crimes, principally through the use of decoy techniques.

4. PART-TIME UNITS

Agencies unable to provide a full-time tactical force should assemble a part-time tactical unit, readily responsive to the severity of the local crime situation. Varying conditions within each community will indicate the need for a tactical operation and the number of officers required. Ideally, each member of the tactical force should be a volunteer selected on the basis of special skills useful to the unit. Officers of the unit should be regularly assigned members of the agency.

While a tactical force does not have to be an organizational entity, particularly when the need for such a force is only intermittent, it is vital that such a capability be available at least on an interagency cooperative basis.

The Kansas City, Mo., Police Department uses a tactical force on an intermittent basis, principally as an investigative supplement. Referred to as the Metro Squad, its membership comprises law enforcement agencies in both Missouri and Kansas. Each participating agency can request, through the squad's board of directors, that the squad provide investigative support. The Metro Squad has successfully operated unhindered by county or States lines.

The Law Enforcement Assistance Administration funded the Michigan Intelligence Network Gangs Squad (MINGS), a cooperative effort of the Michigan State Police, The Michigan Association of Chiefs of Police, and the Michigan Sheriffs Association. The State was divided into regions, and a coordinator was named for each region. Officers from the participating agencies were trained, and equipment was purchased for operations. Upon a request from a police agency, the respective regional coordinator of the MINGS project group decides if the problem requires a tactical operation. If so, participating agencies, including the requesting agency, provides manpower and equipment.

Other area wide investigation and tactical forces exist in the St. Louis, Mo., and Altanta, Ga., areas. These and similar cooperative efforts have proved highly effective to agencies lacking full-time tactical force strength.

Without appropriate specialized equipment, police response to special crime problems is almost universally unsatisfactory. The equipment needed is dependent upon the functions of the tactical force and will vary from operation to operation.

5. EXPERIMENTAL ARM OF THE POLICE DEPARTMENT

The innovative police administrator will use his tac unit as the experimental arm of the police department. The deterrent effect of police could be tested by saturation of high crime areas with uniformed tactical forces. On the other hand, decoys, surveillances, and stakeouts could be used to measure the impact of apprehension oriented patrol on street crime. The tactic offering the greatest potential is a combination of the above approaches. Regular patrol could saturate given areas while adjacent areas are left uncovered except for decoys and stakeouts.

Different tours of duty can also be an experiment for the Tac Unit. If you are considering the 4-10 plan, (4 days, 10 hours-a-day) the TAC Unit is the ideal place to start.

6. ANSWER TO CORRUPTION AND BRUTALITY

There are two perennial bugaboos that plague police service: Police Corruption and Police Brutality. These charges can be kept to an absolute minimum by utilization of a legalistic-style, apprehension-oriented approach to the crime problem. Since Tac squads personify this approach you could reduce complaints of corruption and brutality by their extensive use.

For example, in two years as Commander of the Stakeout Unit of the Philadelphia Police Department, I did not receive one complaint questioning the integrity of members of my command. Holdupmen and rapists don't offer bribes and who in their right mind would accept one if they did. On the other hand, I don't

Unit 16 SPECIAL CRIME TACTICAL FORCES

recall one vice pinch among the 1800 Part I and gun arrests made by the unit each year. Now, I am not advocating abandonment of vice enforcement, only treating it as a revenue problem. The best method of vice enforcement would be by detectives (see Unit 8) and hand-picked officers utilizing court authorized wire taps to get the big-time operators. Close cooperation with the IRS and the State revenue people can be a great asset in breaking the back of organized crime. Legalized gambling will have the same effect. As long as police administrators depend on department wide vice enforcement, you will have the perennial charges of corruption. Remove the task and you remove the threat of contamination.

As far as brutality goes, studies of brutality complaints in Philadelphia and Chicago have revealed that the overwhelming majority of brutality complaints occur during police-invoked, order-maintenance situations.

In Philadelphia a federal suit on alleged police brutality was filed by COPPAR (Coalition of Organizations on Police Accountability and Responsibility). How many cases resulted from police apprehending felons?

> "Of 33 incidents of alleged brutality or related police misconduct raised by Goode-COPPAR, in only one case were the police attempting to apprehend a suspect in a felony."

In November 1973 the Chicago Tribune published an eight-part study of alleged police brutality. The Tribune analyzed 34 cases and in just three were the police investigating a felony.

By having a large TAC Unit working against holdupmen and burglars you can reduce complaints of police brutality. Of course you have to limit the rules to apprehending felons. Each officer should know the goals of the unit, one of which is not to give the unit a bad name by poor police practices and discourtesy to the public. The fact that courtesy does not mean weakness must be stressed by supervisors and commanders. Analysis of complaints against police involving the Philadelphia Police Stakeout Unit revealed only 9 complaints in a year during 27,000 police contacts with the public. (Part I and gun arrests, occupied vehicle investigations, and suspicious pedestrian investigations). This totals up to about one complaint for each 3,000 contacts. I doubt that a shoemaker could maintain as good a record in public relations.

The secret in keeping the complaints low is by the officers having full knowledge of their role which involved no police-invoked order maintenance duties and by police advising the persons they were investigating of the reason for the investigation.

7. TAC UNIT ACTIVITY

Individual members of the TAC Unit should be rated on their production in the following categories:

Primary Goals

—Part One arrests.

—Gun violation arrests.

Secondary Goals

—Quality occupied vehicular investigations.

—Quality suspicious person investigations.

—Computer inquiries.

—Curfew violation arrests (if applicable).

—Truancy arrests.

You can readily see why the primary goals are measured. The secondary goals can be considered the primary *means* of achieving crime reduction. Units 23 and 24 will discuss the positive effects of truancy and curfew enforcement on selected crimes.

I recall how one department's TAC Unit justified their existence in a federally funded Anti-Crime program. During one summer month they did not arrest one robber or burglar but they nearly devastated the local "gay" population by conducting a stakeout and making more than a dozen arrests in an amusement park toilet. What a misuse of police resources!

8. LOCATION OF TAC UNIT HEADQUARTERS

I know of one TAC Unit that is located within city limits but far from the high-crime areas. About two hours patrol time per day is wasted by men who travel long distances to their beats. If at all possible locate your TAC Unit Headquarters as close to the crime problem as possible.

If your TAC Unit involves K-9 it is best for members to kennel the dog at home. In one department up to three hours patrol time a day is wasted by men reporting to a central kennel to pick up their dog before proceeding to their beats. Incentives such as extra pay or mileage allowance could be provided to K-9 personnel to compensate for the care and transportation of their animal charges. In any case, it is imperative that they spend eight hours a day on the street.

9. TAC UNIT OPERATIONS ROOM

In some larger departments each TAC Unit has its own operations room (administrative office). The ideal arrangement would be for the centrally located TAC Unit Headquarters to have one operations room with a common operations room supervisor and a separate desk for each Tactical Unit sharing the headquarters. This will enable commanders to place more manpower where it is needed—on the street.

10. TAC UNIT WEAPONS

Weapons and ammunition used by members of a TAC Unit should be of sufficient calibre and design to ensure that the police are not "outgunned" by the criminals they are expected to challenge. There has been a great controversy in police circles over the proper weapons (revolver vs automatic) and ammo (conventional vs hollowpoint) practical for police use and it is not the purpose of this section to resolve it. However, it is important that the officer working the street have some input into the weapons and ammo necessary to keep the tactical advantage over criminals. Uniformity is desirable but effectiveness is critical. The key to the weaponry question is not how lethal or non-lethal a weapon or ammo is, but how effective it is in incapacitating the felon so that he may not harm the officers or bystanders.

11. SUMMARY

Although the National Advisory Commission on Criminal Justice, Standards and Goals recommends a TAC Unit for every department employing 75 or more sworn personnel. I recommend that every department of 20 or more personnel initiate an anti-crime TAC Unit. In fact at least 20% of available patrol manpower should be assigned to the task.

The deployment of TAC Unit personnel should be based upon the crime problem. Day of the week patterns, time of day patterns, geographical and intelligence crime data are helpful in deployment of TAC Units.

Some departments with seasonal or varying crime patterns find part time TAC Units helpful.

If used wisely the TAC Unit could be the experimental arm of the police department. It is a natural organization for federally funded anti-crime programs.

Members of TAC Units should be used against specific crimes such as, robbery, burglary and auto theft. The TAC Unit personnel need to be properly selected, trained, motivated, and equipped to do the job. Other units of instruction will cover these aspects and Unit 17 will cover Model TAC Units in Los Angeles, New York and Philadelphia.

12. QUESTIONS FOR DISCUSSION

1. What size police departments need special anti-crime TAC Units? Why?
2. Design a TAC Unit for your local department. How many men would it have? What days and hours would they work? What crimes would be their target?

Unit 16   SPECIAL CRIME TACTICAL FORCES

3. Discuss the benefits of part-time TAC Units and mutual aid pacts between smaller departments.
4. What experiments could your TAC Unit undertake?
5. How could your TAC Unit lower charges of corruption and brutality by police?
6. What are the primary and secondary goals of a TAC Unit?
7. Discuss what selection process training is necessary for an effective TAC Unit.
8. What kinds of weapons and ammunition do you recommend for a TAC Unit? Why?

UNIT 17

MODEL TACTICAL UNITS

1. PHILADELPHIA P. D. STAKEOUT UNIT

Plagued with a rash of bank holdups in February, 1964, the Philadelphia Police Department formed a stakeout unit comprised of sixty men working in two-man teams. The unit was successful in effecting many outstanding arrests and the robbery rate decline. In 1967, the Police Commissioner, then Frank L. Rizzo, expanded the unit to its present strength of 110 men under the supervision of a Captain, 2 Lieutenants, 4 Sergeants, and 4 Corporals. Their mission was to provide on site coverage of financial institutions and businesses considered prime holdup targets.

The robbery rate for the first five years of the stakeout operations was held to an increase of less than 1% at a time when other cities had robberies skyrocketing.

Due to an increase in gun related crimes and attacks on police the mission of the Stakeout Unit has been expanded. In addition to normal stakeout duties of covering banks and commercial houses, the unit has been mobilized. Each of the nine divisions throughout the city has a stakeout car on an around-the-clock basis. Their mission now includes support for the regular patrol forces on all felonies and radio calls involving weapons, handling of barricaded persons, protection of dignitaries, escorts for violent escape prone prisoners and anti-sniper duties.

Candidates for the unit undergo a thorough and intensive screening prior to their acceptance. After qualifying with a score of at least eighty-five on the Practical Pistol Course, the applicant is tested on a moving picture course to determine his judgment. If the candidate is acceptable, he undergoes extensive training in the use of all equipment used by the units.

Unit 17 MODEL TACTICAL UNITS 215

Members of the squad average 36 Part I arrests per two-man team per year. The highest producing team made 65 Part I arrests in 12 months.

A. EQUIPMENT RECOMMENDED FOR TAC UNITS

QUANTITY	DESCRIPTION
1	WINCHESTER MODEL 1200 SHOTGUN
1	WINCHESTER MODEL 12 SHOTGUN (For launching gas and smoke grenades)
1	WINCHESTER MODEL 70 30–06
1	WINCHESTER MODEL 70 22–250
1	UZZI MACHINE GUN 9 MM
1	M–1 CARBINE .30 CALIBER
1	LAKE ERIE TEAR GAS GUN—1½"
2	SCOTT AIR—PAKS
2	CERAMIC VESTS
1	RESUSITATOR
1	MEGAPHONE
1	HALF–MILE LIGHT
1	HIGH INTENSITY LIGHT
1	PAIR OF BINOCULARS 10 × 50
2	RIOT HELMETS WITH SHIELDS
2	BLUE NYLON VESTS
30	LAKE ERIE GAS MASKS
50	FLEXIBLE CUFF TIES
1	BUCKET AND ROPE
1	FIRE EXTINGUISHER
2	PLASTIC SHIELDS
2	THERMOS JUGS
1	PRY BAR
1	BOMB BLANKET
1	GRENADE LAUNCHER
1	AEROSOL GAS DISPENSER
100 Rds.	30–06 RIFLE AMMUNITION
100 Rds.	22–250 RIFLE AMMUNITION

QUANTITY	DESCRIPTION
500 Rds.	.38 SPECIAL AMMUNITION
250 Rds.	.12 GAUGE RIFLED SLUGS
250 Rds.	.12 GAUGE 00 BUCK
1000 Rds.	.30 CARBINE AMMUNITION
2000 Rds.	0 MM MACHINE
1 BANDOLIER	10–12 GAUGE RIFLE SLUGS AND 10–12 GAUGE 00 BUCK
50 Rds.	.30 CARBINE IN 2 POUCH CLIPS
10	GAS GRENADES
6	POCKET GAS GRENADES #109
10	SMOKE GRENADES
10	FLITE RITE GAS PROJECTILES
20	SHORT RANGE GAS SHELLS
25	.12 GAUGE BARRICADE GAS SHELLS
25	.12 GAUGE LONG RANGE GAS SHELLS
25	.12 GAUGE TWIN SHOT SHELLS
18	.12 GAUGE BLANK LAUNCHING SHELLS

SIX OF TEN PHILA.P.D. TACTICAL SUPPORT VANS
(SAM TRUCKS)

218 PROACTIVE CRIME FIGHTING TACTICS Sec. 4

PART OF EQUIPMENT CARRIED IN SAM TRUCKS

MORE EQUIPMENT CARRIED BY SAM TRUCKS

OFFICER IS "SUITED-UP" FOR WARRANT SERVICE ON ARMED FELON OR BARRICADED MAN

2. LOS ANGELES P. D. METROPOLITAN DIVISION

The Metropolitan Division of the Los Angeles Police Department was originally organized in 1930. In November, 1967, the Division was increased from 70 officers to 200 officers and appropriate supervisors to form a Crime Task Force.

A. ORGANIZATION

Metropolitan Division is commanded by a Police Captain. There are three platoons, each commanded by a Lieutenant. The platoons are divided into 10-man squads which are supervised by a Sergeant.

The platoons are assigned to general geographical segments of the city and are manned by those officers whose residences are most compatible with the same area of the city.

One platoon is a part of the Department's Special Weapons and Tactics (SWAT) Section. In addition to its crime suppression assignments, this platoon provides the Department with the 24-hour coverage necessary for immediate response to barricaded suspects, snipers, and other high risk incidents.

B. PURPOSE

Metropolitan Division has the primary responsibility of maintaining a manpower pool that can be quickly deployed through the city to handle assignments ranging from directing traffic to the suppression of riots.

C. FUNCTIONS

Simply stated, the personnel of Metropolitan Division are used daily, city-wide, in a myriad of assignments. The Division may be deployed in any number to augment concerned divisions in policing events which may require additional personnel.

However, one of the Division's most active functions is maintaining selective enforcement details in high frequency crime areas. Particular efforts are directed to the suppression of burglary, robbery, auto theft, and burglary/theft from motor vehicles.

D. PERSONNEL SELECTION

The personnel of Metropolitan Division are particularly selected. They must have attained a proficiency rating indicating they are among the upper 25% of the officers in the Department. They must have a minimum of three years field experience and be in excellent physical condition. Supervisory personnel in Metropolitan Division thoroughly investigate each applicant. He is then critiqued by the officers of the Division. If the applicant is approved, he is placed on a list and transferred in when an opening exists.

E. EQUIPMENT

Metropolitan Division is able to perform its functions due greatly to the vehicle fleet available to it. Ninety six vehicles, unmarked, equipped with two 4-channel radios, PA device, portable dash mounted red light, under hood electronic siren, hand spot light, two CC unit handie-talkie radios, binoculars, two shotguns, and portable magnetic door panels that describe the vehicle as a police unit when used by the officers in uniform.

The vehicles are garaged at an assigned officer's residence. Often, the officers report directly to the scene of a problem, rather than assembling in a central location first. This immediate response capability is especially beneficial in a riotous or major disaster condition.

F. UNIFORM

The particular uniform or mode of dress is dictated by the detail or assignment. The officers work plain clothes details. Recently, a two-piece coverall utility uniform was adopted for use during fires, floods, or other unusual occurrences. Officers maintain one regular uniform at their homes and another at Georgia Street Station.

G. TRAINING

The personnel assigned to Metropolitan Division receive special training in numerous police functions. Considerable time is devoted to crowd control techniques. Each officer is given the opportunity to function as a team leader during this phase of training.

Patrol maneuvers, investigative techniques, and stakeout tactics are other areas that are constantly re-explored in the Division's training program.

H. LOS ANGELES POLICE DEPARTMENT SPECIAL WEAPONS AND TACTICS SECTION

(1) PURPOSE

The Special Weapons and Tactics (SWAT) Section provides a pool of highly trained personnel to be used in those instances where marksmanship or other skills required to cope with guerrilla tactics is particularly crucial. Specifically, SWAT teams are deployed to protect policemen from sniper attack when officers are engaged in riotous-crowd control or other activities where there exists the threat of potential sniper activity. SWAT teams provide high ground and perimeter security for visiting dignitaries, perform rescue missions when officers or citizens are isolated by sniper fire, rescue hostages, and deploy at incidents where armed suspects have barricaded themselves.

(2) ORGANIZATION

Each SWAT team is composed of five members. Each team is a permanent self-sufficient unit which trains together and responds as a team when a SWAT mission is identified and a request is made for SWAT assistance. Each team consists of a team leader, a marksman, an observer, a scout, and a rear guard. Each member of the team is trained to perform all of the other team assignments.

(3) DEPLOYMENT

Since formation of the unit, SWAT personnel have been utilized on more than 100 occasions. SWAT personnel have provided security for visiting dignitaries including the President and the Vice President. For these details, officers wear regulation police uniforms and are primarily deployed in high ground and perimeter positions.

SWAT personnel have been deployed to protect officers engaged in crowd control details during campus disorders, rock festival disruptions, and other civil disturbances. Teams have frequently been called to incidents involving barricaded suspects. In every such instance, SWAT personnel have successfully prevented these suspects from injuring additional victims or escaping suspects.

Marksmen from SWAT have also successfully rescued wounded officers and hostages. They have been particularly useful in assisting regular officers investigating armed strongholds. When necessary, SWAT officers effect forcible entries, and apprehend suspects at these locations. SWAT personnel have also been utilized to serve search warrants at heavily-armed and fortified headquarters of a militant organization.

The unit has proven to be a definite asset to the Department by providing a pool of highly trained and disciplined marksmen to assist officers in the field. At the same time, they are a reserve, able to respond in the event of a civil disturbance, to provide the field commander with a versatile resource in restoring control to an area that is under attack.

(4) PERSONNEL AND TRAINING

In order to provide a well disciplined and trained unit capable of accomplishing special tactical missions, the following factors should be established:

1. Each SWAT team should be a permanent, self-sufficient unit which trains together and responds as a disciplined, flexible team.

2. Each SWAT team should be composed of sufficient force to accomplish the mission, yet small enough to achieve effective infiltration.
3. Each SWAT team should be provided with the weapons to effectively deliver disciplined, balanced firepower to neutralize opposing firepower and to defend itself when under attack.
4. Each SWAT team member should be selected on the basis of special skills that can be utilized in the unit. Each member should demonstrate characteristics of initiative, job interest, and dedication in the police field.
5. Each SWAT team should regularly qualify with the special weapons employed by the unit.
6. Each SWAT team member should be capable of performing all other team assignments.
7. Each SWAT team should be capable of responding to emergency situations with the necessary equipment to deploy immediately for resolution of the situation.
8. When a single team is not large enough to accomplish a given objective, organization should be such that teams may be combined to form squads or platoons.

In considering personnel for assignment to SWAT, the following minimum experience should be required of the applicant:

1. The applicant should have not less than three years experience on the police department, with assignment to a patrol division preceding a tactical force position.
2. The applicant should have been rated among the top 25% of department personnel for a period of one year before assignment to SWAT.
3. The applicant's service record should indicate a low sick record, a low traffic accident record, a low personnel complaint record, and good physical condition.
4. He should have demonstrated strong characteristics of initiative, job interest, and dedication in the police field.
5. Prior military experience is highly desirable.

Each SWAT team member should receive intensive training in the history of guerrilla warfare, scouting and patrolling, night operations, camouflage and concealment, combat in built-up areas, ambushes, rappelling, first aid, and use of chemical agents.

This training should be supplemented by field exercises, with emphasis on discipline and team integrity.

(5) EQUIPMENT

The SWAT team officers should be equipped with firepower capability to suppress concentrated weapons fire from opposing forces. The SWAT teams are equipped with a special dark uniform, boots, military web gear, first aid kit, gloves and gas mask. Each team is armed with one high-powered, anti-sniper rifle, two shotguns, and two .223 caliber semi-automatic rifles. Each SWAT officer carries a service revolver in a shoulder holster.

(6) LOGISTICS

Highly specialized equipment such as rope, rappelling gear, maps, manhole cover hoods, and pry bars are available for SWAT use. This equipment, as well as additional armament, ladders, and communication equipment should be maintained in a logistics truck. This truck should have the capability to be used as a SWAT command post.

3. NEW YORK P. D. STREET CRIME UNIT

The New York City Police Department's Street Crime Unit (SCU) fills the gap between routine, visible police patrol and after-the-fact criminal investigations. The unit focuses on street crimes—robbery, personal grand larceny, and assault. Its primary strategy employs officers disguised as potential crime victims placed in an area where they are likely to be victimized. A plainclothes backup team waits nearby, ready to come to the decoy's aid and make an arrest. Careful screening of applicants, extensive training, and close liaison with precinct commanders are marks of SCU's able management. Here is its 1973 record:

- 3,551 arrests (85 percent felonies)
- 76 percent of robbery arrests led to convictions
- 95 percent of grand larceny arrests led to conviction
- Average man-days per arrest: 8.2 (departmental average for all uniformed officers: 167)
- Cost: nominal increase per arrest and conviction, due to equipment costs
- Risk: virtually no increased danger to police or citizens.

4. SUMMARY

The TAC Units of Philadelphia (Stakeout Unit), Los Angeles (SWAT Section), and New York (Street Crimes Unit), are model TAC Units for other departments.

The best TAC Units are those whose personnel and tactics enable the unit to maximize arrests of violent criminals and to lower crime rates.

Most of the equipment recommended for TAC Units in this chapter can be carried in the trunk of a squad car. Bulk ammo and equipment should be kept at headquarters in a vehicle similar to SWAT's "war wagon". The TAC Unit personnel, however, *never* should waste their time in headquarters waiting for an assignment. They belong where crime is—on the street.

The next units of instruction (18 and 19) will concern themselves with the most productive anti-crime tactics a TAC Unit can implement against crime—Decoys and Tactical Holdup Alarm Systems.

5. QUESTIONS FOR DISCUSSION

1. What could your department use from the Philadelphia Police Department's TAC Unit? (Stakeout Unit)
2. What could your department use from the New York Police Department's TAC Unit? (Street Crime Unit)

3. What could your department use from the Los Angeles Police Department's TAC Unit? (SWAT Section)

4. How are the SWAT members on TV deployed prior to an emergency assignment? How could they be more effectively used in the war on crime?

5. Discuss the arrest and conviction rate of NYPD's Street Crime Unit?

6. What specialized equipment should your TAC Unit carry in the rear of their patrol car? In headquarters support van?

7. When should your TAC Unit be called in to support the regular patrol force?

8. What crimes should your TAC Unit target for reduction? Why?

UNIT 18

USE OF DECOYS

Use of police decoys to trap criminals is one of the most misunderstood and underutilized tactics in the police arsenal against crime.

Perhaps understanding will increase the use of this tactic which is the most effective operation a police administrator can deploy against the criminal. The key to the misunderstanding as far as use of decoys goes, is just what constitutes entrapment.

I. ENTRAPMENT

"Entrapment" is a term commonly used, and even more commonly misused, in the criminal law and police circles. Under certain circumstances entrapment may constitute a valid defense to criminal charges of various kinds, but it is not generally understood that in many instances entrapment by police is a perfectly legitimate law enforcement practice.

In its commonly used sense of unlawful entrapment, it applies as a defense only when an innocent-minded person has been incited or persuaded by law officers to commit a crime which he had no previous purpose or design of his own to commit. The same tactics applied to a person already entertaining the criminal design. Thus merely affording him opportunity to put his criminal purpose into effect, would not be a defense.

Entrapment, strictly speaking, is not actually a defense, even though commonly referred to as such for convenience. On ground of public policy the courts hold it would be unconscionable and unjust for the government to prosecute and convict a person for a crime conceived and instigated by its own officers and agents. Out of regard for the state's own dignity, the courts refuse to permit officers of the law to consummate illegal or unjust schemes designed to foster rather than to prevent and detect crime. Thus the state is barred from proceeding because allowing such a scheme to succeed would offend the common sense of decency and justice. In the language of the United States Supreme Court:

> "The defense is available, not in view that the accused though guilty may go free, but that the Government cannot be permitted to contend that he is guilty of a crime where the government officers are the instigators of his conduct." [1]

But the law is well settled that if the criminal purpose originates in the mind of the accused, the fact that officers of the law afford him opportunity for accomplishment of his purpose does not constitute unlawful entrapment. In such cases the officers are not soliciting or persuading an innocent person to do something he would not have done otherwise. They merely furnish him the occasion to do what he already had in mind to do if and when he has the chance. In other words, officers of the law must not manufacture or "artificially propagate" a crime.

Entrapment is a defense in a criminal case only when it has been perpetrated by officers of the law—"only when the criminal conduct was the product of the creative activity of law enforcement officials." Ordinarily, entrapment as a defense does not extend to acts or inducements practiced by private persons, unless they are acting in concert with or on behalf of law officers, such as decoys, or those whose activities are known to and adopted by the officers. Also, it is immaterial whether the entrapment was done by federal or local officers; the defense is available in any prosecution based on the act so instigated.

There is a clear distinction between (1) inducing or persuading a person to commit an unlawful act and (2) setting a trap to catch him in the execution of a criminal plan of his own conception. The former is unlawful entrapment, the latter is not. Opportunity and inducement to commit a crime are quite different in their implications, as are detection and instigation of crime.

It is well established on the highest authority that officers, acting in good faith and with a view to detecting the commission

---

1. C.J.S. Criminal Law, § 45. Sorrells v. United States, 287 U.S. 435, 53 S.Ct. 210, 216, 77 L.Ed. 413, 86 A.L.R. 249, 259 and note p. 263 (1932).

of crime, may make use of deception, trickery, or artifice in presenting a criminally minded person with the opportunity to accomplish his purpose.

The rule as stated by the Supreme Court of the United States in 1932 has been followed consistently by the courts, both state and federal, since that time:

> "It is well settled that the fact that officers or agents of the government merely afford opportunities or facilities for the commission of the offense does not defeat the prosecution. Artifice and stratagem may be employed to catch those engaged in criminal enterprises." [2]

In a concurring opinion, Justice Roberts added:

> "Society is at war with the criminal classes, and courts have uniformly held that in waging this warfare the forces of prevention and detection may use traps, decoys, and deceptions to obtain evidence of the commission of crime. Resort to such means does not render an indictment . . . a nullity nor call for the exclusion of evidence so procured." [3]

Twenty six years later, referring to the above case, the Supreme Court said:

> "The intervening years have in no way detracted from the principles underlying that decision. The function of law enforcement is the prevention of crime and the apprehension of criminals. . . . Criminal activity is such that stealth and strategy are necessary weapons in the arsenal of the police officer." [4]

In any event the defense of unlawful entrapment is not available to one who denies commission of the offense, since invocation of entrapment as a defense is in the nature of a confession and avoidance, necessarily admitting the defendant committed the unlawful act or acts charged but claiming he is not properly chargeable with guilt thereof.

2. Ibid. (53 S.Ct. 217, 86 A.L.R. 259).
3. Ibid. (53 S.Ct. 217, 86 A.L.R. 259).
4. Sherman v. United States, 356 U.S. 369, 78 S.Ct. 819, 820–21, 2 L. Ed.2d 848 (1958).

2. TYPES OF DECOYS

Once the entrapment issue is finally put to rest, the police administrator should realize he has a "Carte Blanche" opportunity to trap criminals. Decoys can be used to combat the following crimes in descending order of practicality:

—Robbery (including purse snatch)

—Rape

—Larceny from auto

—Larceny of auto

Use of police decoys presents a lot of tactical problems, foremost of which is the safety of the officer. Training, equipment and tactics can minimize the danger. Cost-effectiveness-wise it is still the most productive apprehension method available to police service.

Robbers, muggers, and pursesnatchers are the best targets for your police decoy. The following anti-robbery decoys have been used by the Philadelphia Police Stakeout Unit with much success:

—Granny

—Insuranceman

—Grandpa

—Watermelon vendor

—Ice Cream salesman

—Pizza truck vendor

—Cab driver

Although they are all successful decoy operators they are listed from most effective to least effective as far as producing arrests. Other decoys could be utilized depending on the nature of the crime problem. The "Granny" decoy detail should have a K–9 team in its backup crew because of the nature of the crime. Shooting is rare in this detail and a trained dog is needed to pur-

Unit 18 USE OF DECOYS 233

PRETTY POLICE OFFICER MAKES FINE RAPE
DECOY AT TRAIN STATION

"MASHER" IS CORNERED

Unit 18 USE OF DECOYS 235

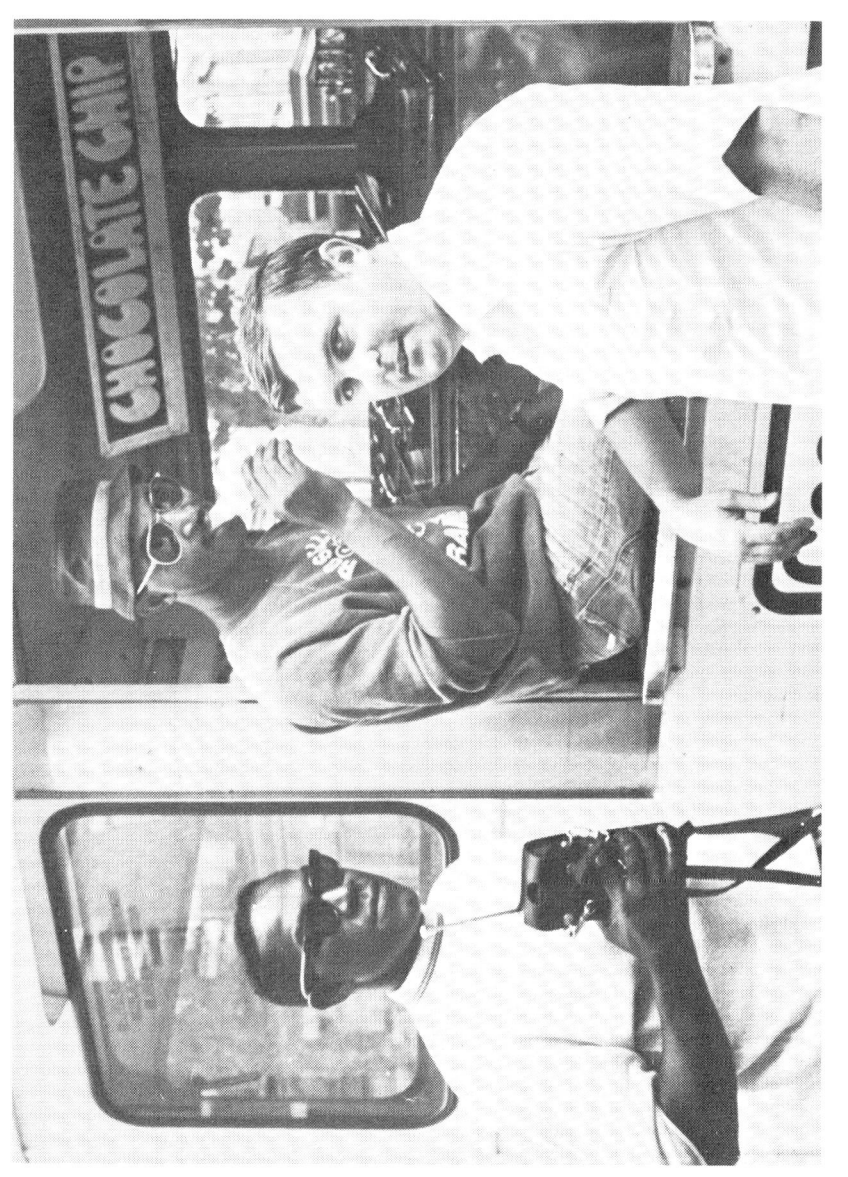

"GOOD HUMOR" POLICE ICE CREAM MAN DECOY

Sutor Police Operations Cr.J.S.—17

BACKUP TEAM AWAITS HOLDUP

Unit 18 USE OF DECOYS 237

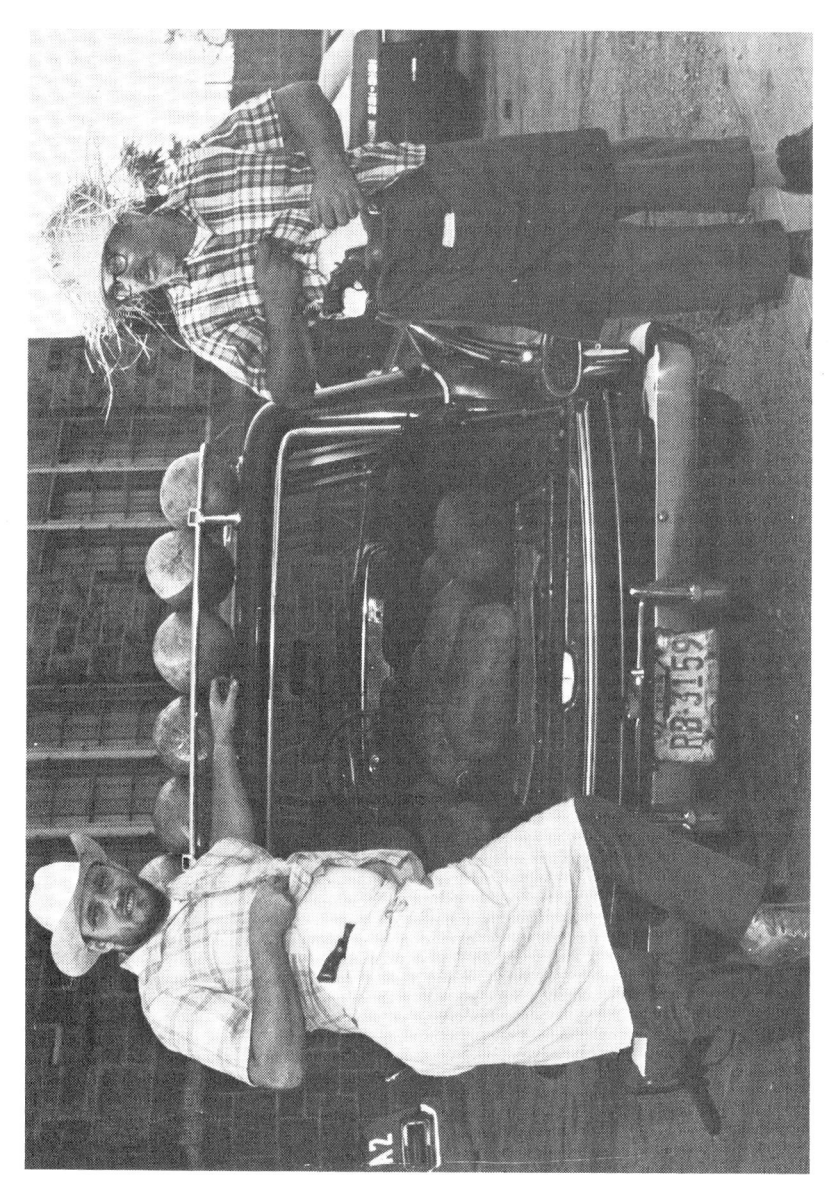

THESE "WATERMELON DETAIL" OFFICERS ARE LOADED FOR BEAR

NOTE THE "WATERMELON" DETAIL'S "MICHIGAN BANKROLL"

Unit 18   USE OF DECOYS   239

POLICE "WATERMELON" DETAIL PATROL VEHICLE

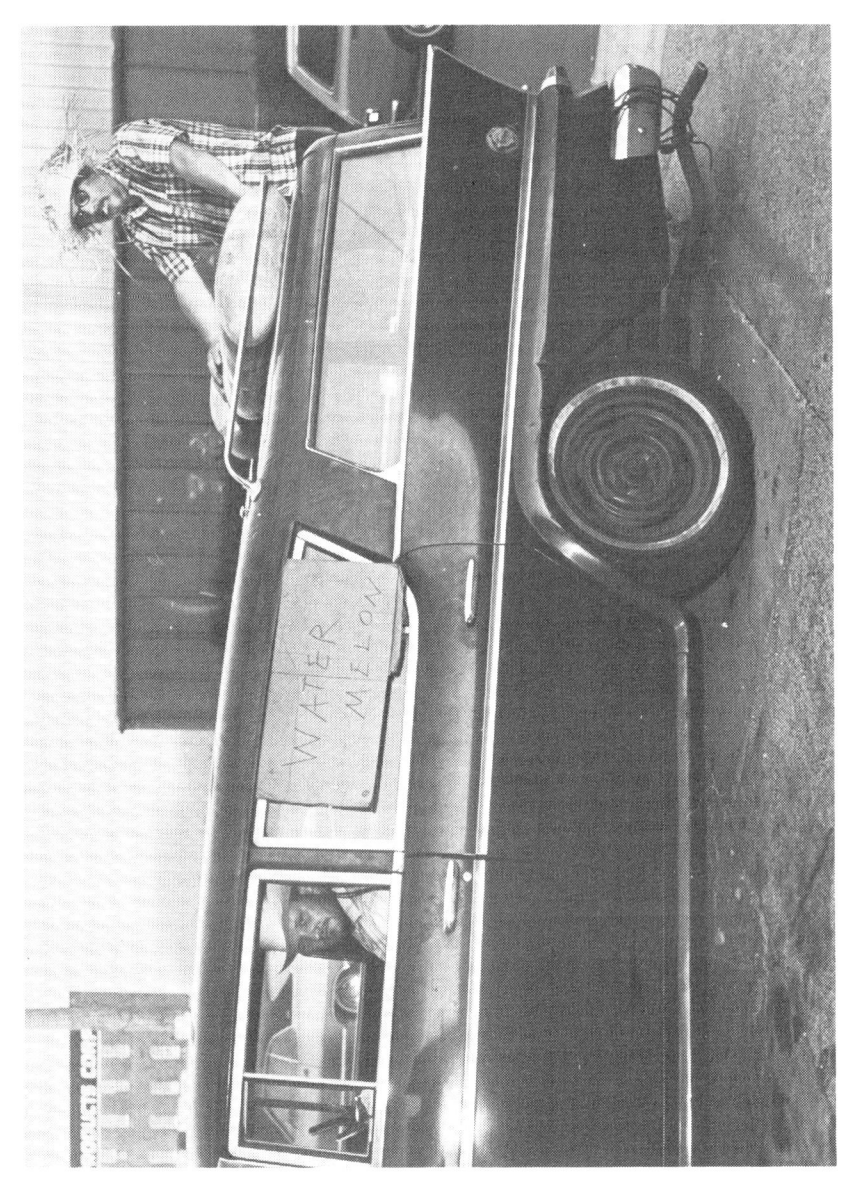

240 PROACTIVE CRIME FIGHTING TACTICS Sec. 4

"WATERMELON" DETAIL IN ACTION

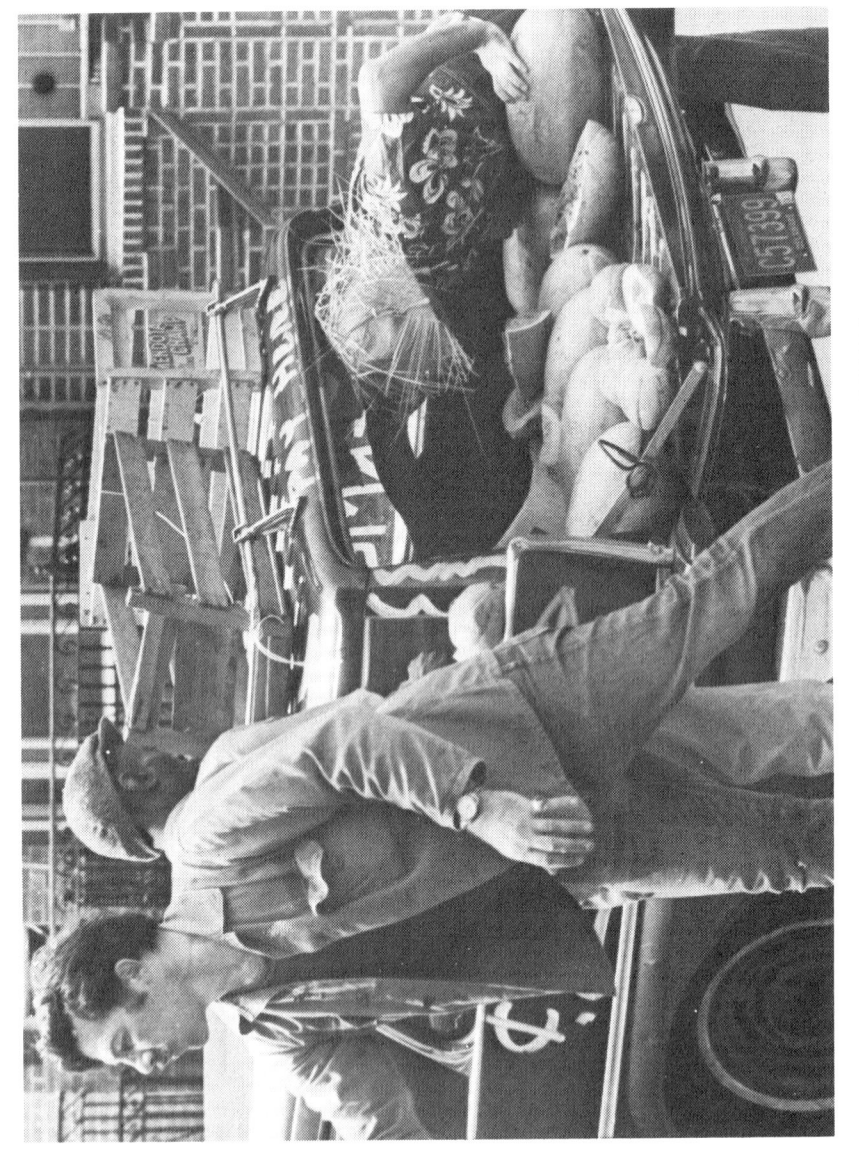

Unit 18 USE OF DECOYS 241

POLICE "WATERMELON" DETAIL AWAITS HOLDUP

POLICE "WATERMELON" DETAIL "TROLLING" FOR A HOLDUP

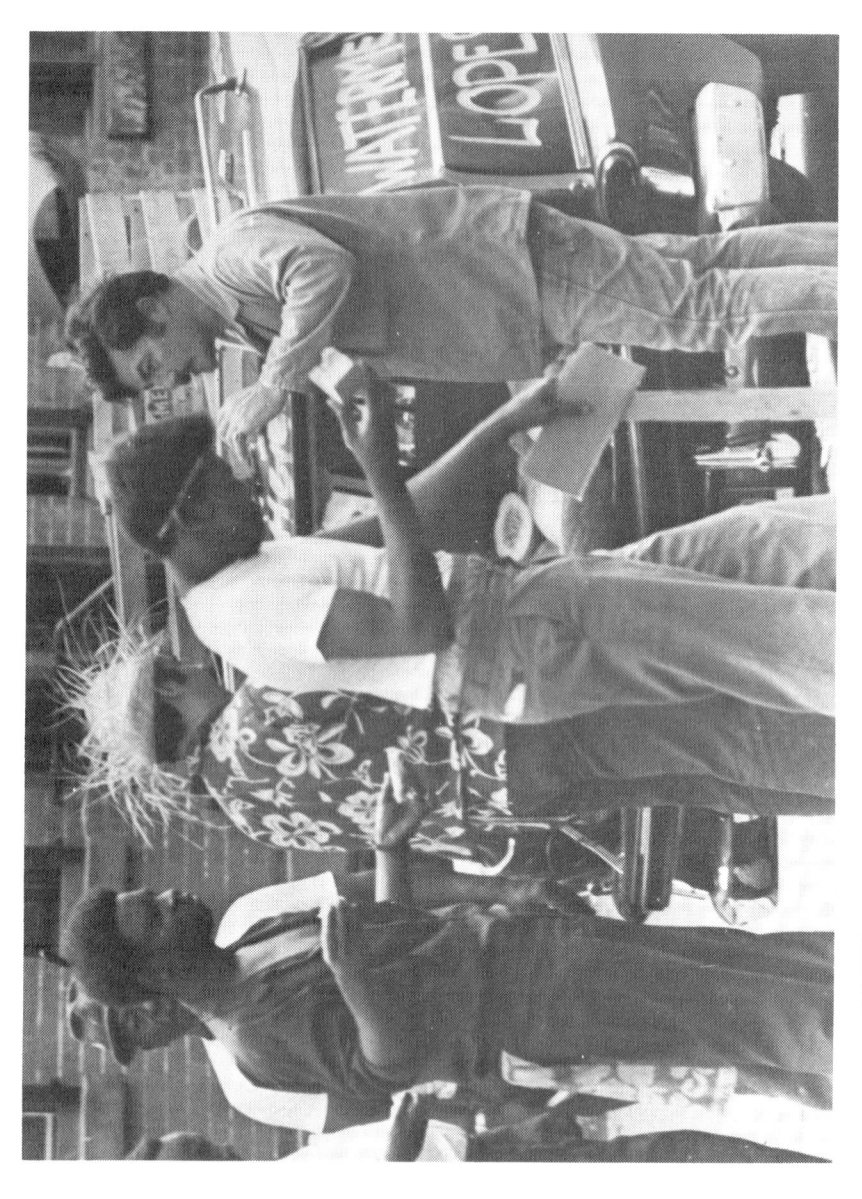

POLICE "INSURANCE MAN" DETAIL
Photo by Philadelphia Daily News

BACKUP MAN SURVEILLS "INSURANCE MAN" DECOY

Unit 18　　　USE OF DECOYS　　　245

PHILA. POLICE GRANNY SQUADS

A PURSE SNATCHER'S VIEW OF POLICE GRANNIES

Note: Grannies usually work apart

Photo by The Evening Bulletin (Philadelphia)

sue the escaping thief. The other decoy details rarely need a K-9 backup. They are, more often than not, shooting circumstances with the police officer "victim" looking down the barrel of a hold-up man's gun or being confronted by a knife. Instead of a dog, the decoy-officer needs trained marksmen for his backup.

A. GENERAL CONSIDERATIONS

The "decoy" and his backup men must dress the part and try to duplicate the circumstances that contributed to the original crimes.

For example, if the crime under consideration is the mugging of or pursesnatching from elderly ladies then a "granny" decoy is needed. If the victims are black, then you need a black "granny" decoy. Sometimes when the victims are white and the neighborhood primarily black, it is helpful to have black officers as backup men and vice-versa.

The mannerism of the "decoy" is very important. Not all willing officers can duplicate the actions and walk of an elderly granny. Policemen must master the role prior to going out on the street. Another dead giveaway is a police officer posing as a decoy who is alert and looks for suspects, at passing cars, and up and down cross streets and alleys. Also, prior to the "hit", he may have been alerted by his backup team that a mugging or pursesnatch is imminent—but he still must not look back. As you know, if he takes defensive precautions too soon, he looses the arrest. It takes a man with nerves of steel to hear the footsteps coming up behind him and wait for the "hit".

As was mentioned earlier, dress is very important to the detail. When you see an officer report to work for undercover duties wearing:

—Clean khaki or dungaree trousers

—A wristwatch

—A clean sport shirt (tail out)

—A bulge on his left hip

—A pen and pencil in his shirt pocket

—A wide black belt

—Black socks

—Clean grooming

you can bet he will be made in a minute on the street. A man dressed like this looks like he is going to an F.O.P. clambake or other police outing. He is comfortable but rarely successful in catching criminals. The best decoys and backup men dress and act the part. It is truly an art.

B. INSURANCEMAN DECOY

This detail should be utilized when you have a pattern of robbery of insurancemen and door-to-door salesmen in a particular area. You need one trained volunteer as the "decoy" and two or three backup men. The K-9 backup is optional, depending on the crime pattern.

A surveillance vehicle gives flexibility to the backup men who may trail the decoy by car or on foot.

(1) EQUIPMENT

The backup men should be armed with their service revolvers and a breakdown type 12 gauge shotgun loaded with 00 buck. The decoy should have a 2" revolver mounted in an ankle holster.

Naturally, the insuranceman should carry a briefcase and/or insuranceman's book. Bait money (Michigan bankroll) should be carried. The best is a large number of fake or one dollar bills covered with a twenty dollar bill on the outside of the roll. The serial numbers of the real money should be listed in advance for later investigative purposes.

If the policemen on the detail alternate between this type duty and uniformed patrol and are well groomed, then wigs, mustaches, beards and sideburns are necessary. The wig is beneficial in concealing the radio earjack in the decoy's ear. Eyeglasses are recommended to present a more "vulnerable" target to the criminal. If the decoy does not normally wear glasses he can wear them with clear plastic or no lens at all.

An undercover protective vest is necessary covering not less than 11" by 14" of both front and back. It should weigh about three to five pounds. Sometimes the vest is hot and uncomfortable but it is most important to wear it. Backup men should also have vest coverage in the front of their bodies.

(2) COMMUNICATIONS

Each man on the team should have a walkie-talkie with two frequencies. One frequency person to person, the other to police radio. The decoy officer should have a "button" type transmitter or similar device. He should place the radio inside the pocket of his suitcoat with the transmitter wire running down his non-shooting arm. The transmitter should be taped to the thumb. A mini-microphone should be placed behind the decoy's tie, near the knot, with the wire running inside his shirt.

Code words should be developed in advance for use when a transmitter goes bad or in case of a surprise attack on the decoy officer.

(3) THE DECOY

The following discourse is from one of the most effective "decoy" officers ever involved in the "Insuranceman Detail":

> "They have a crime with holdups and muggings and they want it stopped. You are picked to do it. Feel pretty good about it? You should, they don't pick anybody for this type of assignment. You were picked because they thought you a mature, stable, physically fit, serious minded, heads-up kind of police officer who needs little supervision and can draw on his experience instead of his gun in *most* situations. This detail is by no means child's play. When you reach this point of law enforcement you are past the prevention and deterrence stages.

It is all apprehension. They have taken you and put you on the street to be a victim of an atrocious crime. Now the criminal has you on his terms—or at least he thinks he does. You become the common denominator—the target."

"Vulnerability is the key for robbery decoys. Being liable to attack and assailable. Here is how you get set up for the insuranceman detail, wear the vest under your shirt; rig your radio equipment and test it. Place some change in your right trouser pocket, then place your "Michigan bankroll" in the same pocket. Also carry two dimes in separate pockets for emergency phone calls. If you are right-handed, wear your 2" fully loaded revolver in an ankle holster on the outside of your right leg. Flare or wide trouser cuffs are a must for an ankle holster. Carry the insurance book in your left hand (your transmitter and non-shooting hand).

Do not carry any identification card, badge, handcuffs, blackjack or personal effects. If you must carry keys make sure you remove your handcuff key."

(4) WORKING THE STREET

"Vulnerability is a difficult characteristic to master, chiefly because you are a police officer and no matter what clothing you don, you are still a policeman. You have to remember that you are now on the opposite side of that gun—tentatively speaking."

"Slow your walk down—take 20" steps instead of 30 or 36" steps. Drop your shoulders a little, let your glasses slip down your nose some. Sound ridiculous? It's hard on your posture, but it gets results. Remember you are trying to present a target and holdup men won't move if all the odds are not in their favor."

"Let your backup team lead you into your target and audience. They are your eyes and ears. You are nothing more than a passive target up to this point."

"Knock on doors and give the occupant the insurance company's door opener i. e., a pack of flower seeds, sewing needles, nail files (any insurance company will be glad to supply you with plenty of these items). Ask the occupant if they would be interested in some insurance—their answer is generally no—if yes, tell them you are a Staff Manager and you'll have an agent out to them shortly."

"Your backup team informs you that there are three males who seem interested." NOTE: Generally the decoy knows who is interested in him by their actions or reaction of them before his backup unit.

"Recorder of the backup team should be writing down a full description of the interested males."

"The decoy officer after ascertaining the location of the interested males must make every effort to locate himself in the most desolate spot available. Go into your routine, act confused pretend you are trying to locate a certain house (being sure you know your exact location and time). Let the insurance book start slipping in your left hand giving the appearance of being uncoordinated."

"The holdup men eat this up, by your actions you have eliminated a major obstacle for them—*No Trouble From The Victim— Easy Prey*. Even if there is only one holdup man—he still feels he can take you. Your job now is to let them move on you."

"This can be done by simulating making change by placing the insurance book under your left arm pit. Reach in your right pocket and take out the 'Michigan bankroll' place it in your left hand, then take out your change and leave it in your right hand. If you are uncertain as to them seeing the bankroll, let a few coins slip from your hand. Take your time picking them up—act as though you can't walk and chew gum at the same time."

Whatever you do—don't overact. The culprits sizing you up are masters of deception and extremely cunning and street wise.

All they want is the money. You've let them see it—now it's their move. Be prepared.

   (1) After you let them see the bankroll, start moving away from them. (Don't think cop—they're after you) Remember your backup team should have a spot they want you to go to.

   (2) Don't turn around to see what the culprits are up to. Again your backup unit will inform you.

   (3) Then you should head for a predetermined location conducive to a robbery. Generally this would be a phone booth, a desolate street, or alley. You could attempt to get into an auto, but be unable to locate the keys. (Act this out by patting yourself down) Another play would be to deliberately drop your insurance book and pick up the forms. When prospective robbers see you in any of the aforementioned positions and situations they become interested. Get ready because it is going to happen now.

   (4) If you use the drop the insurance book routine, drop on your left knee when picking up the forms etc., thereby having ready access to your revolver on your right ankle.

   (5) "Here they come." Those words will sound like music to you. You've worked had acting like a superficial nitwit, but you pulled it off. Now your reward is pounding down the street heading right for another defenseless victim—you—and also to one of the biggest mistakes of their lives.

(5) THE ACT . . . ROBBERY

Robbery, whether by strongarm, simulated weapon, point of knife or gun is a very serious and vicious crime. They come on fast, strong and very aggressive to put it mildly. No one can tell you, the decoy officer, how to react during this attack. However, if I may suggest, based on actual past experiences, I would highly recommend the passive role.

The decoy officer is going to have to take the hit. As soon as you are approached, open your transmitter key, thus allowing your backup unit to know that a holdup is in fact taking place. If it's a strong-arm robbery it will be obvious to them. But frequently, neither you nor your backup unit will see a weapon.

(1) In the case of a holdup by simulated weapon, chances are good that the culprit doesn't have a weapon, but don't you make that assumption during the commission of the crime—fingers have been known to go off. Generally if he has a weapon, you will be the first to see it.

(2) If at all possible have your back up against a wall. Even though you have a vest, strongarm artists love to grab their victim around the neck from behind.

(3) If it's a holdup by knifepoint, just remember if he starts swinging and slashing, keep him from the center of your body. Let him or them have your limbs until you can get to your gun or your backup unit arrives. Don't kid yourself you *are* going to be cut or nicked. This is the time your passive role stops and the professional police officer emerges.

(4) If he produces a gun, do as you are told, no T.V. dramatics enough said.

Your transmitter key should be open. Now is a good time for a code name or word, or one brief sentence description of what they have on you. Example: You don't need that *gun* mister, take the money, its insured, I'm not!

Many times your backup team will be unable to see if the robbers have any weapons on you. By telling them this, they'll know how to go up against him. NOTE: Don't try to do it all. You'll have some of the best cops in the city behind you. Use them. This is much too sensitive an assignment to be anything less than total team effort. Believe me.

(5) Let the robbery take place. Don't try for attempts; that's not your job. By this I mean don't draw your

revolver on their approach—even if you know you're going to be hit. Let them perform the act and let them take the bait money from you.

Chances are they will find the radio on you while rifling your pockets. Tell them you are hard of hearing (they see the earjack on you) and you need the battery—you might even plead a little with 'please don't take that, it takes weeks to get another one', or whatever you want to. Use a little ingenuity.

The backup team moves in:

(1) If the robbery is still in progress when the backup arrives, and most times it is, you should automatically slump to the ground. You'll hear three (3) words—'freeze—Police officers'. If the backup unit has to open up, they don't want you in their line of fire. So don't move.

(2) If the robbery is over and your backup unit isn't on the scene—generally a holdup lasts between 20 seconds to a minute—then do what is required of you to avoid the escape of a fleeing felon. As we said your job also has its moments.

(3) After all the felons are in custody or whatever, recheck your time, exact location, and all pertinent information before leaving the scene.

3. SUMMARY

The use of police decoys to trap criminals is one of the most misunderstood and underutilized tactics in the police war against crime. One of the main reasons is because of the "entrapment" issue. A knowledgeable member of the criminal justice system who checks up on the matter will soon learn that police have an almost *"Carte-Blanche"* opportunity to trap criminals. In the language of the United States Supreme Court "giving a criminally minded person an opportunity for the accomplishment of his purpose does not constitute unlawful entrapment".

Perhaps, once police administrators resolve the "entrapment" misunderstanding and experiment with a couple of granny and insuranceman decoys, they will allocate substantial resources to catching-em-in-the-act. Large departments have enough manpower to commit dozens of decoy teams to high crime areas. Surveillance vehicles parked unattended in high crime areas could have suitcases, cameras, typewriters, etc. on the backseat. The theft patterns can be eliminated by these tactics. Like Cedar Rapids' "mousetrap" the surveillance "rat traps" ensure a 100% conviction rate.

4. QUESTIONS FOR DISCUSSION

1. Explain "entrapment" and relate what difficulties, if any, it raises as far as use of police decoys are concerned.
2. What crimes could police decoys be effective against?
3. Prepare a list of anti-robbery police decoys that could be used against robbers in your area. Where would they operate?
4. How should the backup men to a police decoy be dressed?
5. Can police use a "Michigan Bankroll" to lure criminals to action?
6. Discuss the movie "Death Wish". What could police learn from actor Charles Bronson's methods?
7. Differentiate between the police decoys with possible shootouts and those without such potential. (Key here is gravity of crime and danger to officer)

References
1. Edward C. Fisher, Laws of Arrest, (Evanston, Ill.: Northwestern University Traffic Institute, 1967).

UNIT 19

TACTICAL HOLDUP ALARM SYSTEMS

Staking out a holdup target waiting for a robber can be compared to a man fishing in a pond waiting for a fish to bite. The fisherman's likelihood of success depends on his selection of a good fishing spot, his equipment, and his skill. The stakeout teams chance of success depends on very similar factors.

The fisherman's methods have been proven through the years, that's why he is still fishing. So, too, has the one-site stakeout proven successful, especially if the right "hole" has been selected.

What could the fisherman do to increase his catch? Well he could "go commercial" and instead of using one pole he could conceivably utilize twenty. Thus his chance of a bite is multiplied twenty times.

Now then, what can the stakeout team do to increase their chances for a "bite"? They, like the fisherman can use their stakeout site as a base and install twenty silent alarms in nearby holdup targets. If a "fish" comes in the base target they catch him. If a "fish" bites at one of the other nearby targets they immediately proceed there and net their catch. This tactical holdup alarm system is no "fish story". It works!

I. A NEW ANTI-HOLDUP SYSTEM

Due to the multiple types and numbers of assorted prime holdup targets in the City of Philadelphia and of the limited number of stakeout policemen available for selected sites, a wireless alarm system has recently been set up in order to cover multiple sites by one team.

This alarm system has a maximum capability of covering twenty sites. The alarm is triggered by a floor treadle or money clip or both. We were successful in apprehending two bank robbers within two hours of installation on the first day the alarm was in

Unit 19 TACTICAL HOLDUP ALARM SYSTEMS 257

service. Since then, we have had many incidents where robbers were apprehended in the act.

The alarm system has the capability of overcoming the serious problem of the victim or other civilians between the police and the holdup man. We do not necessarily have to sit in the back of a store; we can take any tactical position feasible. In most cases stakeout men can approach the holdup scene from a nearby external source. The console can even be placed in a vehicle and the men can cruise the target area.

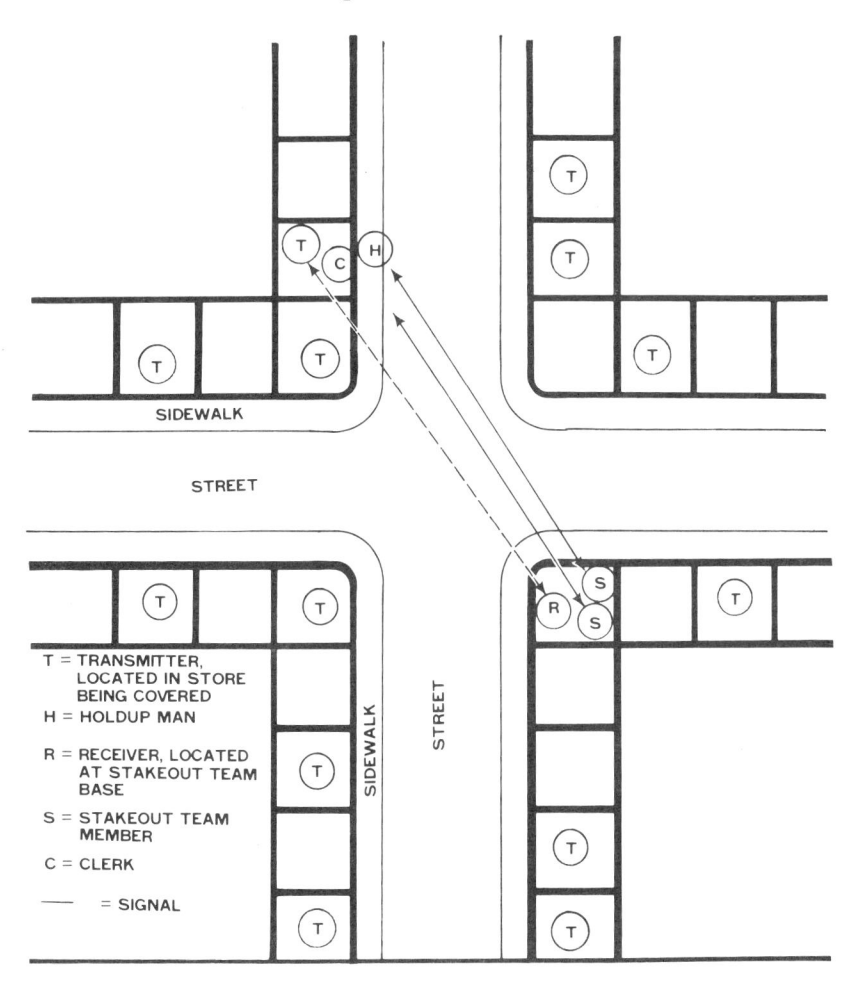

T = TRANSMITTER, LOCATED IN STORE BEING COVERED
H = HOLDUP MAN
R = RECEIVER, LOCATED AT STAKEOUT TEAM BASE
S = STAKEOUT TEAM MEMBER
C = CLERK
——— = SIGNAL

258 PROACTIVE CRIME FIGHTING TACTICS Sec. 4

rf alarms

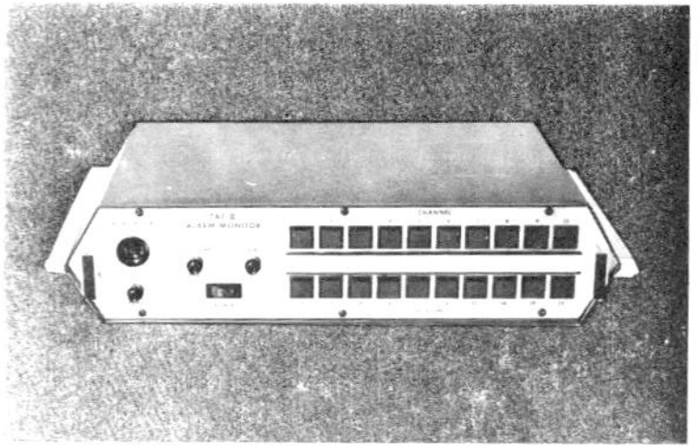

TWENTY CHANNEL RECEIVER/DECODER
One or Two Receivers (Optional) (Model 727-20)

The highly sensitive FM Receiver hears a two tone sequential signal from any one of a number of remote special applications transmitters, decodes the call and reflects to the control panel, with both audio and visual alert, which transmitter has alarmed.

One RF Channel will serve any number of alarm channels, or a separate Receiver may be installed, *in the same package,* for each of the ten alarm channels.

The Alarm Decoder offers unique opportunity to accomplish economical security without the burdens of wiring cost, leased lines, or power failures.

UNIQUE CHARACTERISTICS

- TOTALLY PORTABLE
- VEHICULAR MOUNT OPTION
- 110 VAC AND 12 VDC (220 VAC AND 24 VDC OPTIONAL)
- BUILT IN EMERGENCY BATTERY SUPPLY (30 TO 40 HOURS STANDBY)
- TONE OPTIONS (ONE OR TWO TONE CALL)
- DECODERS TIMING OPTION (FROM 0.5 TO 10 SECONDS)
- TEN, TWENTY, OR SIXTY CHANNEL MODELS
- INTERFACE WITH MOST SENSOR DEVICES
- EASILY SERVICEABLE SLIDE OUT CHASSIS AND MODULE CONSTRUCTION

APPLICATIONS

- PERIMETER SECURITY
- AREA SECURITY
- PUBLIC SAFETY (STAKE-OUT ALARM)
- WALKING POST (GUARDS)
- V.I.P. PROTECTION
- SABOTAGE ALERT (PIPELINES, OIL WELLS, ETC.)
- REMOTE POST AND/OR HAZARDOUS DUTY ALARM

BELL & HOWELL
COMMUNICATIONS COMPANY

BELL & HOWELL'S FAMOUS TAC II

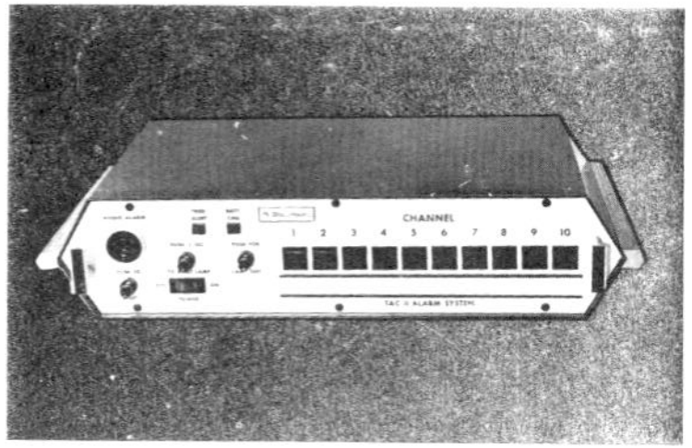

TEN CHANNEL RECEIVER/DECODER
(Model 727-10)

TOTALLY PORTABLE, VERSATILE, HIGH RELIABILITY, FALSE FREE, SOLID STATE DECODERS and matching Receivers in low profile for convenient desk top or vehicular mountings.

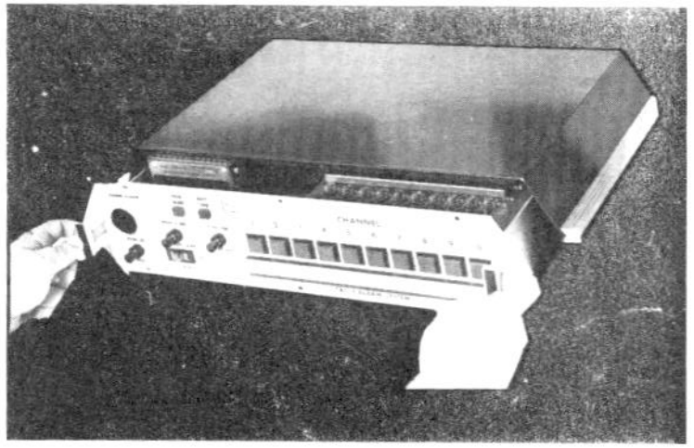

EASILY SERVICEABLE CHASSIS
Modular Construction (Model 727-10)

FIGURE 19.2

Unit 19   TACTICAL HOLDUP ALARM SYSTEMS   259

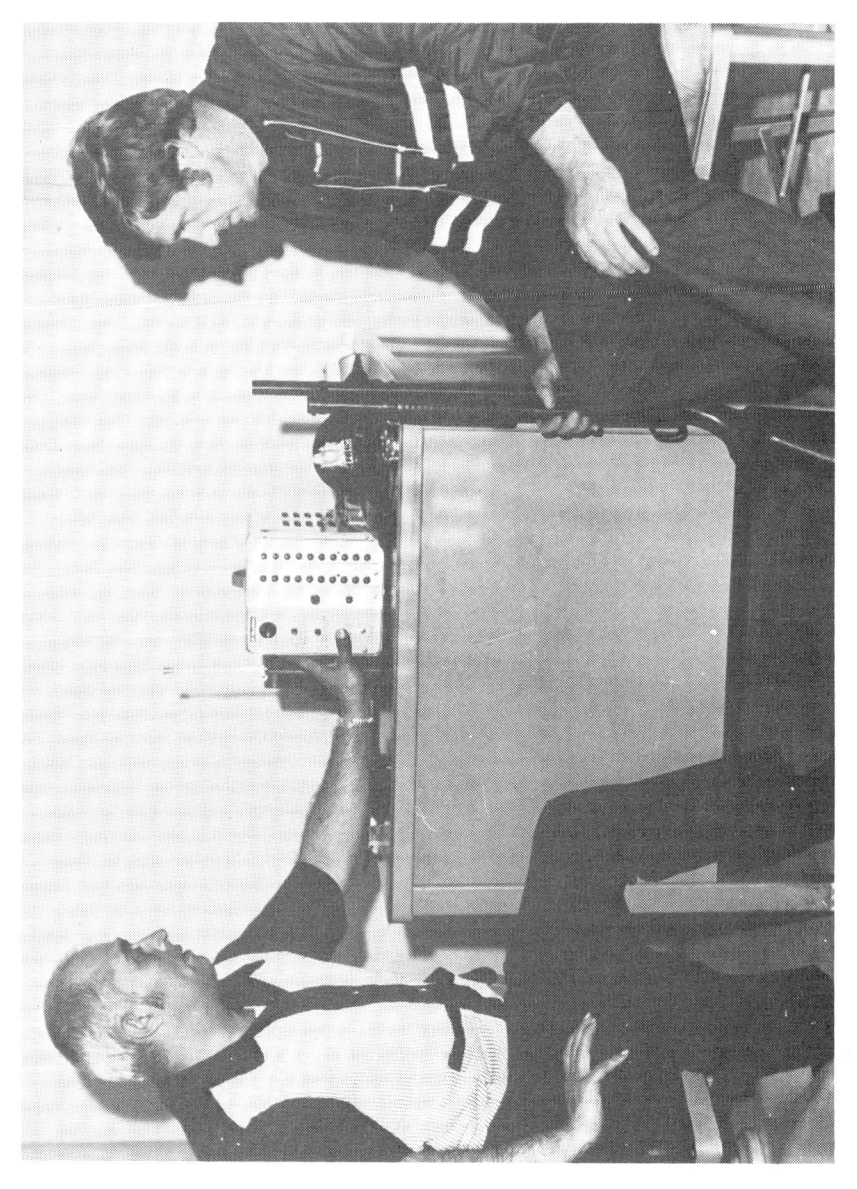

POLICE TACTICAL HOLDUP ALARM SYSTEM

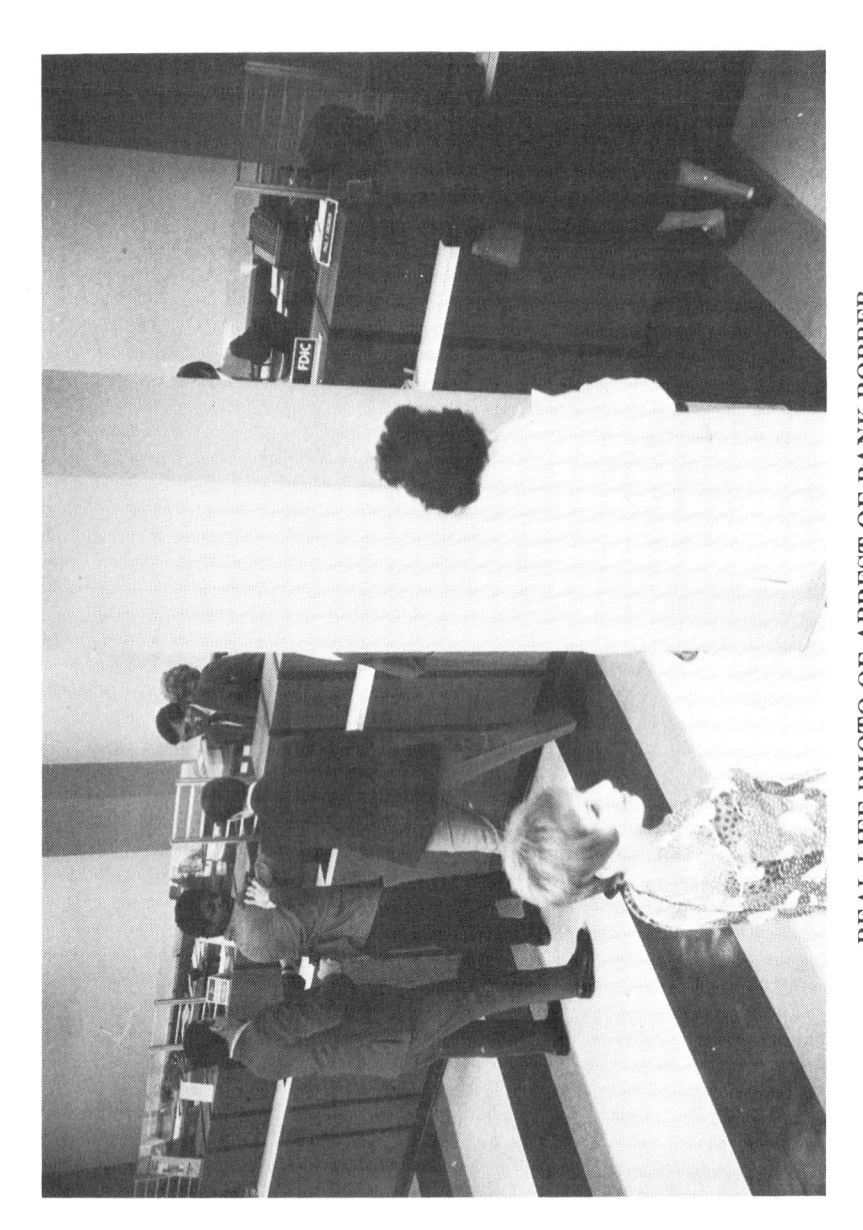

REAL LIFE PHOTO OF ARREST OF BANK ROBBER BY POLICE TACTICAL HOLDUP ALARM TEAM

Unit 19 TACTICAL HOLDUP ALARM SYSTEMS

#1 of 4

#2 of 4

#3 of 4

#4 of 4

TAC II DISGUISES

TAC II DISGUISES

It costs over $100.00 per day for a two-man stakeout team to cover a potential holdup site. Normally, to cover 20 sites would therefore cost over $2,000.00 in salaries per day. This alarm system lowers the cost by lowering the manpower need.

The Philadelphia Police Department recently received a LEAA grant of $146,445.00 to purchase ten wireless alarm systems.

Included in the items purchased were ten decoders, 150 transmitters, 700 alarm activators, three mobile radios, five four-band radios, 26 two-band radios, 30,000 feet of fire, 110 lightweight armored vests, 110 wig disguises and funds toward the purchase of two vans and one sedan.

The device is portable and should be removed and placed elsewhere once the holdup problem subsides or the detail becomes "burnt".

Other alarm systems operating on the basic principles of the TAC II system can be effective in reducing response time in any jurisdiction. And as you know, a reduction in response time means more apprehensions.

2. TACTICAL ADVANTAGES

The stakeout officers have a definite tactical advantage in utilizing the TAC II. Figure 19.3 represents a typical state store (liquor store). Notice how the clerk (figure c) is between the line of fire of the stakeout team (figure s) and the holdup man (figure h).

Figure 19.4 is the same holdup target. Notice how the stakeout men are in a better tactical position and the clerk is out of the line of fire.

3. SUMMARY

The stakeout of a potential holdup target has to be long proven an effective anti-robber tactic. However, this tactic could easily

264   PROACTIVE CRIME FIGHTING TACTICS   Sec. 4

be enhanced to cover even more targets by utilization of a police tactical holdup alarm system such as the TAC II program.

Although some systems are very expensive, others could be rigged up with bellwire. The whole idea is to cover as many hold-up targets with as few TAC Unit police as possible (but remember, at least 2 officers on all anti-holdup stakeouts). Proper selection of targets has to result in apprehension. Even if you have only one "7-11" type convenience store in your area and it is

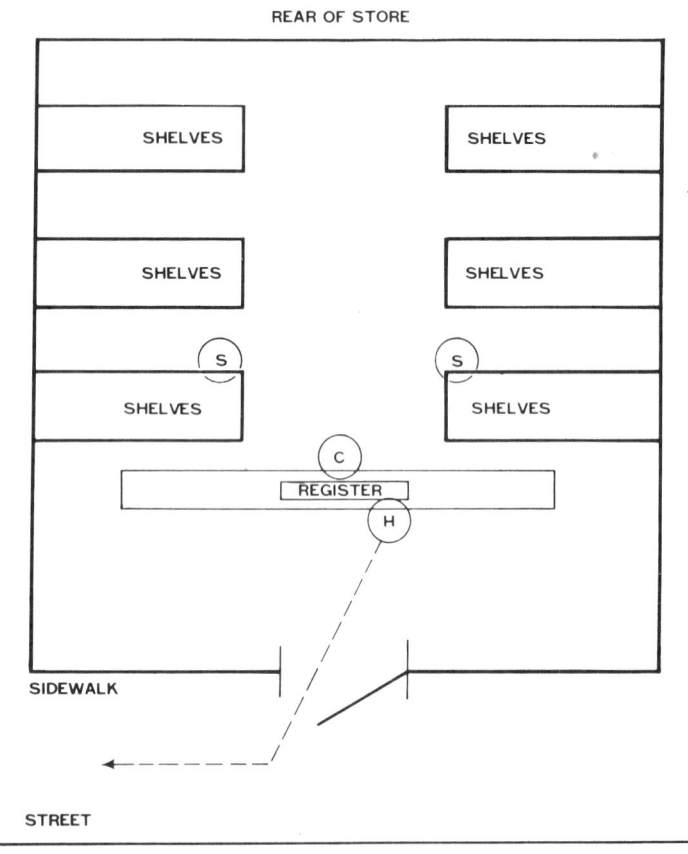

FIGURE 19.3
TYPICAL LAYOUT OF A STATE STORE WITH 'STANDARD' STAKEOUT

S = STAKEOUT MAN
H = HOLDUP MAN
C = CLERK

Unit 19 TACTICAL HOLDUP ALARM SYSTEMS

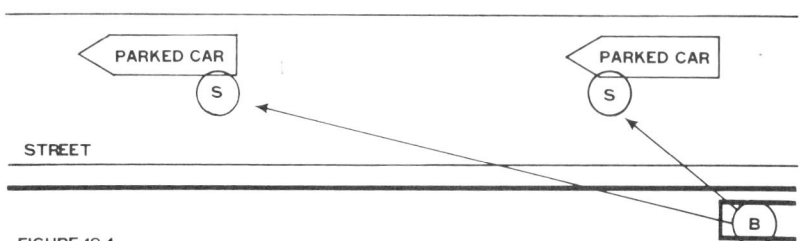

FIGURE 19.4

TYPICAL EXAMPLE OF STATE STORE WITH ALARM SYSTEM COVERAGE

S = STAKEOUT TEAM MEMBER

B = STAKEOUT TEAM BASE

H = HOLDUP MAN

C = CLERK

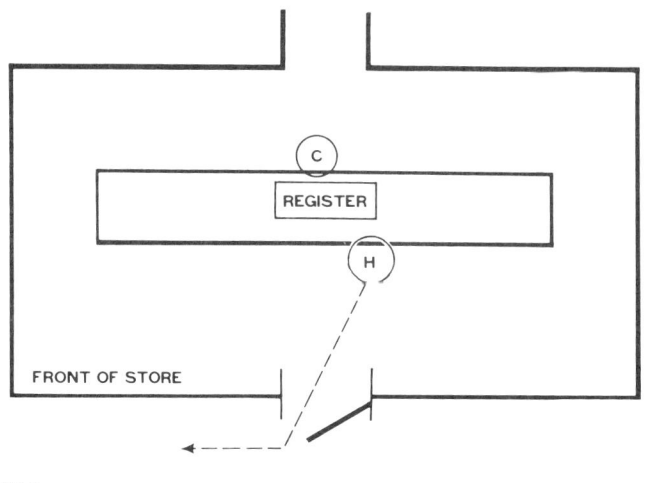

HOLDUP MAN STARTS TO LEAVE AFTER TRIGGERING SILENT ALARM

Unit 19   TACTICAL HOLDUP ALARM SYSTEMS   267

STAKEOUT MAN GETS DROP ON ROBBER

Sutor Police Operations Cr.J.S.—19

268 PROACTIVE CRIME FIGHTING TACTICS Sec. 4

"YOU'RE UNDER ARREST"

Unit 19 TACTICAL HOLDUP ALARM SYSTEMS 269

STAKEOUT PARTNER APPROACHES FROM REAR

270 PROACTIVE CRIME FIGHTING TACTICS Sec. 4

PHYSICAL ARREST IS CONSUMMATED

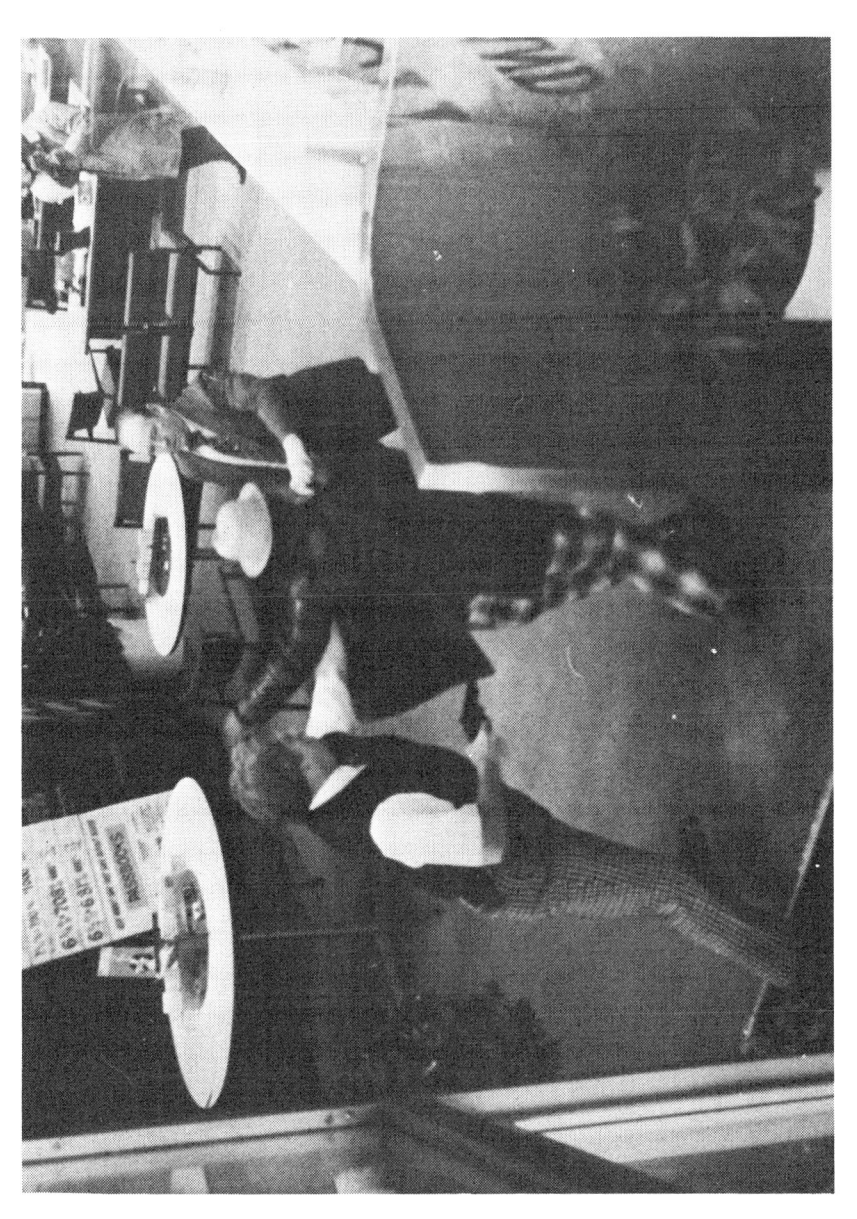

Unit 19   TACTICAL HOLDUP ALARM SYSTEMS   271

PREPARATION FOR SEARCH INCIDENT TO ARREST

HOLDUP MAN IS FRISKED

Unit 19   TACTICAL HOLDUP ALARM SYSTEMS   273

HOLDUP MAN IS HANDCUFFED

HOLDUP MAN IS TAKEN TO JAIL

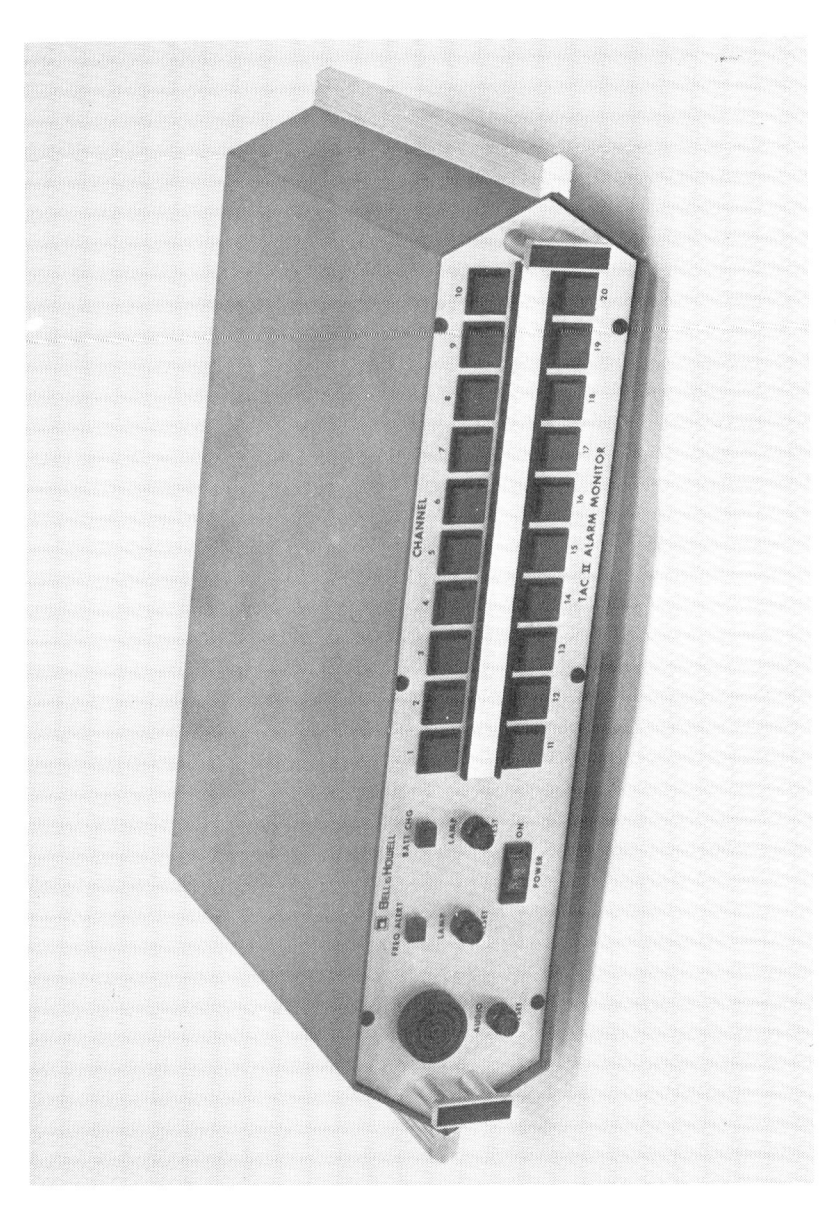

Unit 19 TACTICAL HOLDUP ALARM SYSTEMS

THIS TACTICAL HOLDUP ALARM FITS UNDER DASH OF POLICE VEHICLE

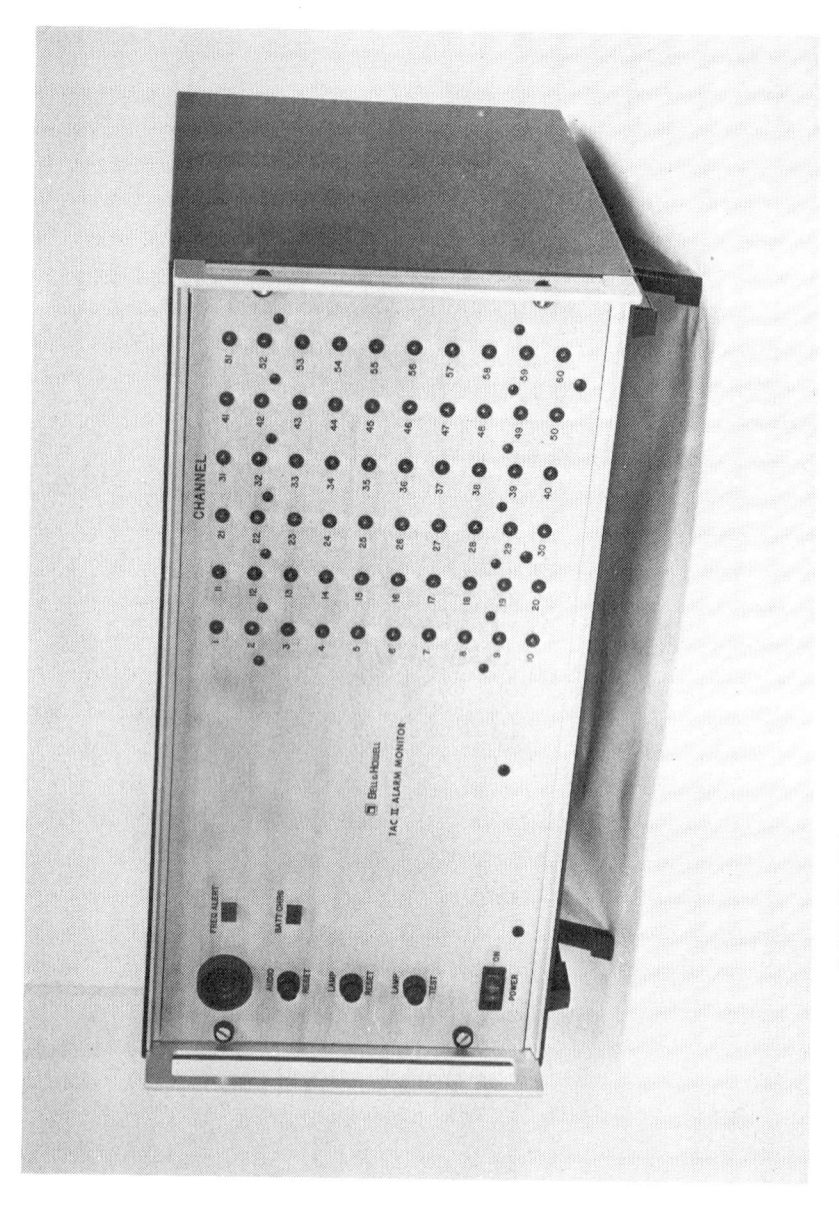

POLICE TACTICAL HOLDUP ALARM SYSTEM CAPABLE OF COVERING SIXTY TARGETS

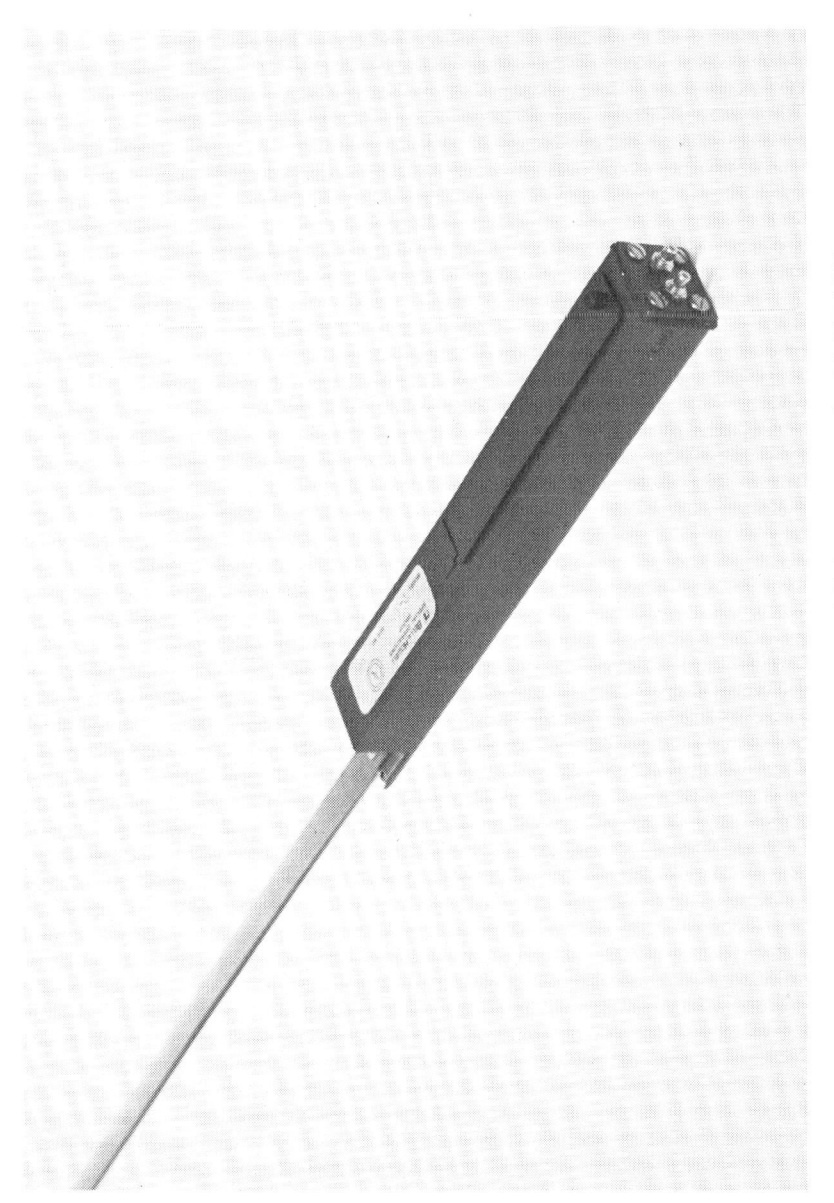

Unit 19   TACTICAL HOLDUP ALARM SYSTEMS   277

EACH HOLDUP TARGET HAS A SILENT RADIO TRANSMITTER LIKE ONE PICTURED ABOVE

robbed 3 or more times a year it is a "goldmine" to harvest robbers. Imagine having 10–20 such targets close enough to be wired-up and covered by 2 TAC Unit officers.

4. QUESTIONS FOR DISCUSSION

1. How would you select holdup targets for special Tactical Holdup Alarm Systems?
2. How would you write a request for financial aid in deploying a Tactical Holdup Alarm System?
3. Could you use a TAC II type holdup alarm system in your area? Could you do it with wires on contiguous groups of stores?
4. What tactical advantages do the officers have with the TAC II over the conventional one to one stakeout? Are the officers and passersby safer?
5. When is the best time to engage holdup men? What happens if you engage them outside and they get back inside with their weapons?
6. What other crimes could a TAC II type alarm be effective against?

UNIT 20

MANAGEMENT OF SPECIAL TAC UNITS

A separate book would be necessary to cover all the ramifications of successfully managing a special TAC Unit within a police department. However their are several fundamental considerations that are so essential to success that they cannot be dealt with later. These considerations are:

—Selection of personnel for a TAC Unit
—Leadership
—The relationship between trust and performance
—Incentives

I. SELECTION OF TAC UNIT PERSONNEL

TAC Units are likely to become glamorous and much-sought-after assignments, especially if the unit is successful. It is amazing how many policemen desire "to get back to the basics" and fight crime. A wise TAC Unit Commander will tap this reservoir of talent and resist all efforts to have new men assigned on a "political" (internal or external) basis. In fact, even the TAC Unit commander himself should not take total control of this highly sensitive and important selection process. Supervisors and/or members of the unit should have a say in who becomes a member of the unit. Specific standards will have to be developed and adhered to.

One prime characteristic necessary for a good TAC Unit Officer is "intestinal fortitude". It is extremely hard to measure in an interview or with a paper and pencil. One good criteria is the past performance and experience of the officer. Since it is likely that he will be involved under fire once he is accepted to the job, the following considerations are important:

—Has the candidate been exposed to fire in either police or military service?

—How did he perform? Department commendations or medals may be an indicator. Candidates who surrendered their weapon, shot a bystander or performed poorly should be disqualified.

—Just what type of police or military service did the candidate experience? Experience has shown that men with Army Special Forces and Marine Corps combat experience make ideal candidates.

When selecting new members remember the old adage "the past is prologue to the future". You can expect performance reflected in the officer's military and personnel record to be his performance in your TAC Unit.

Just as important as selection of new men is the "weeding-out" of non-productive officers. Careful analysis of activity records will identify those men needing improvement. These men should be counseled by their supervisor and given a chance to improve their performance. Remember no pro football team ever won the Superbowl with "deadwood" on the team. If the improvement doesn't materialize the officer should be returned to regular patrol duties and a new, highly-qualified, enthusiastic officer given a chance to prove his effectiveness.

2. LEADERSHIP

One criteria for measuring leadership of a TAC Unit commander and TAC Unit supervisors should be the results they achieve or fail to achieve. Men will work for their Sergeant and/or Captain if they respect him as a leader. The greatest quality a leader, supervisor, or TAC Unit officer can have is enthusiasm.

"Enthusiasm is the greatest business asset in the world. It beats money and power and influence. Single-handed the enthusiast convinces and dominates where a small army of workers would scarcely raise a tremor of interest.

Enthusiasm tramples over prejudice and opposition, spurns inaction, storms the citadel of its object, and like an avalanche overwhelms and engulfs all obstacles.

Enthusiasm is faith in action; and faith and initiative rightly combined remove mountainous barriers and achieve the unheard of and miraculous.

Set the germ of enthusiasm afloat in your business; carry it in your attitude and manner; it spreads like a contagion and influences every fiber of your industry; it begets and inspires effects you did not dream of; it means increase in production and decrease in costs; it means joy and pleasure and satisfaction to your workers; it means life real and virile; it means spontaneous bedrock results—the vital things that pay dividends."

Author Unknown

The dividends a TAC Unit Commander is interested in are higher arrest and lower crime rates for selected crimes.

3. HIGH TRUST—A KEY TO HIGH PERFORMANCE

In his book "Communication and Organizational Behavior", Dr. William V. Haney, Professor of Business Administration, Graduate School of Business, Northwestern University sums up what he considers the nature of an organization and the growing trends of largeness, complexity, demand for greater efficiency, and concludes:

"Today's organization requires communication performance at an unprecedented level of excellence. And chief among the demands made upon our organizations is the increasing necessity for an *organizational climate* compatible with the psychic needs of the organization's members."[1]

In his work Dr. Haney espouses the need for a "supportive climate", or one which according to Likert, develops

"a climate that ensures that each member will, in the light of his background, values, and expectations, view the experience (his job) as supportive and one which builds and maintains his sense of personal worth and importance."[2]

---

[1] William V. Haney, Communication and Organizational Behavior, (Homewood, Illinois: Richard D. Irwin, 1967), p. 11.

[2] Rensis Likert, New Patterns in Management, (New York: McGraw-Hill Book Co., 1961), p. 103.

The key to Likert's idea and Haney's management theory is "trust". In fact Haney makes it quite clear in his diagrams on the relationships between trust and performance.

Haney claims that "High Trust" on the part of the manager greatly encourages "High Performance" on the part of the employees. Conversely "Low Trust" begets "Low Performance". Throughout his entire work which includes many case histories involving organizational climate and communication (one of the means of displaying trust), Haney makes his point again and again.

Haney's theory gains support from other renowned management experts including Maslow, Herzberg, and McGregor. In fact he utilizes McGregor's famous Theory "X", and Theory "Y" management philosophies in showing how management use of external controls contributes to the feeling of "Low Trust" on the part of the employee:

> "The theory of 'Theory X' in essence holds that the so-called average man is inherently (and thereby unalterably) immature—that he is inately lazy, irresponsible, gullible, resistant to change, self-centered and thus indifferent to organizational needs, and so forth." [3]

The managerial practice in dealing with such persons is to apply external controls. Haney makes comparison of what he means by external controls with an analogy of "managing an infant" in relation to directing employees.

External controls can be interpreted as management so bent on controlling individuals that the managers forget the legitimate organizational goals and supplement them with restrictive, demeaning, meaningless reports, checks and close supervision practices. These practices succeed only in demotivating individuals and have them spend the bulk of their working day building "defenses" instead of working towards legitimate production goals.

---

3. Douglas McGregor, The Human Side of Enterprise, (New York: McGraw-Hill Book Co., 1960), p. 15.

Haney offers hope for progressive managers and employees alike. He offers advice on breaking the destructive "Low Trust/Low Performance" cycle and converting it to the healthy "High Trust/High Performance" cycle. Haney has this to say about McGregor's "Theory Y":

> " 'Theory Y' is the merging theory which promises to integrate the goals of the organization and its members." [4]

From experience, I can personally vouch on the management theory I prefer to work under and utilize myself. It is unquestionably "Theory Y". I like being given goals and let to utilize my own talents on achieving them. I like being trusted with a difficult task. Once given the trust I feel compelled, to give my all, not to violate it. It does not occur too often enough for me.

We have been discussing "organizational climate" from manager down to mid-management. From my level to employees in my charge, I can also see results.

For example, I have had charge of the Philadelphia Police Department's "Granny Squads". These squads consist of two teams of three men each. One team is black; one white. A male member of each team poses as an elderly female decoy for muggers and purse-snatchers. I would like to show how implementation of Dr. Haney's theories of: Supportive Climate, High Trust/High Performance, Personal Worth, and Communications greatly aided them in contributing to the goals of police service.

First, though, just what are the legitimate goals of police service? They are basically the protection of life and property. One measurement of accomplishment is the actual absence of crime and disorder from our community. But to what degree? Prevention is extremely hard to measure, certainly now, considering the social condition and criminal justice system we have today. Police undertake many activities in trying to accomplish these goals including the last-resort function of apprehension. This is the goal of the Granny Squad. This particular function is measured by arrests of which I have feedback in data form. As

---

4. Haney, op. cit., p. 15.

to their effect on muggings and purse-snatches, I can only offer a limited amount of subjective data in form of comments by local District Commanders that certain crime patterns have ceased to exist after an arrest by the Granny Squad.

The Granny Squad's success can be attributed to the way the operation is conducted. Team members are volunteers and are not paid anything extra for their hazardous duties. These duties that require long hours of patrol and walking the streets during (less desirable) evening hours which the squad works steady throughout the six-month cold season.

People often ask: "Why does Granny do it?" I believe because higher level needs are fulfilled in the operations. The men know they are doing a good job ridding the streets of criminals. They receive much recognition in the form of departmental citations, publicity throughout the mass media, and last, but not least, respect from their peers.

In addition to these rewards which contribute to the "supportive climate" under which they work, other management techniques enabled them to turn a successful operation into an extremely successful one. One year the grannies did not seem up to par. There was talk of "not walking this year". Coupling Haney's theory on "Trust/Performance" with Herzberg's theory on "Job Enrichment" the grannies were given raw computerized data on crime patterns and allowed to select their own beats and hours. Then they went out to prove they were right. They walked "where angels feared to tread" and came up with the amazing combined record of 73 arrests in 42 separate robberies.

If external control, on the other hand, became my goal under a "Theory X" climate, I am sure that if I selected small, ridged beats and inflexible hours, (the Granny Squad changed theirs to correspond with daylight hours) and loaded them up with direct supervision and many supervisory checks, the results would have not have been the same. Contacts with uniformed or plainclothes supervisors would have "burned" the undercover operations. If hourly "pulls" (telephone contacts with headquarters) were made, a large portion of time would have been spent coming and going from telephones.

Most of all, I feel, the lack of strict external controls contributed to a feeling of "High Trust" on the part of the members of the Granny Squads which was, predictably under Haney's theory, followed by "High Performance". This cycle continued throughout the season and the results are now a matter of public record.

It is my belief that the same management techniques will apply to any organization that has goals and to any employees that have hearts in their chests.

4. INCENTIVES

Many departments are experimenting with incentive programs to increase performance. Orange, California initiated a program where members of the city's 139-man police force received a 2 percent "bonus" wage increase for a 17.6 percent reduction in rapes, robberies, burglaries, and auto thefts.

On the other hand, members of the Cleveland Ohio Police Department were threatened with a decrease in salary if they did not reduce crime by 5 percent in a given period. While these department-wide crime reduction/incentive programs are in the experimental stage they should be pursued further to determine if they work.

On the TAC Unit level I know of two successful incentive plans that worked well. Members of the Ohio State Patrol received decals for posting on the side of their patrol vehicle when they made a stolen vehicle arrest and recovery. The decals are similar to the "Zero decals" U. S. pilots received for shooting down Japanese planes in World War II. The trooper who has got 5 was known as an "ace" and the trooper who made the most was given the highest award the OSP "Blue Max" with sole operations rights to new squad cars. These kind of programs worked in World War II and they work today.

The Stakeout Unit of the Philadelphia Police Department had a "Pinch of the Month" award where members of the squad selected the team for the most outstanding arrest of the month.

A fund set up where the officer recipients and their spouses/girlfriends were honored with a dinner at a first-class restaurant. The team with the best pinch of the year was honored with a special trophy awarded before all unit members at the Stakeout Unit Annual Banquet. If you feel incentives don't work, you should see the faces of the recipients as they receive the award. The key element is peer group recognition. They know it is for real and they earned it.

A. MONETARY INCENTIVES

Some form of extra remuneration is in order for members of TAC Units because of the following reasons:

—They work less desirable (high crime) hours including weekends.

—They are (should be) the best qualified people in the department.

—They are the most productive members of the department and you want to keep it that way.

—Their high productivity (arrests) results in frequent court appearances.

—Their job is most hazardous.

—Often they have to travel further than regular officers.

Therefore extra compensation in the form of one of the following is in order:

(1) PAID OVERTIME (ESPECIALLY COURT)

There is no departmental money spent better than on overtime for court. If the officer is there with a felon in tow it is worth triple-time to society. Remember the Judges, Prosecutors and Correctional people get their clientele handed to them on a "silver platter". The arresting officer is the only man who has "proven" his effectiveness up to this point. The reward system should encourage others to do likewise. One good measure of overtime well spent is to compare productivity (arrests) with the IRS W-2 (earnings) Form at the end of the year. If there is a positive correlation between high producing officers and the highest paid officers, you have a fair compensation system designed for success.

(2) INCENTIVE PAY

Special pay for highly trained and qualified officers. Avoid the use of the term "hazardous duty" pay because it insults the regular patrol officers who are often "ducking bullets" on the street too.

B. PERSONAL CAR PROGRAM

A personal car program modeled after Indianapolis Indiana Police Department or Prince Georges County Maryland Police Department can pay direct dividends in productivity in addition to being a morale building incentive. Under the program officers are allowed to take either marked or unmarked patrol cars home with them and use them off-duty. Many fine arrests and lower crime rates will result. If it is not possible to issue police vehicles to officers, putting police radios in the officers private vehicles and issuing a gas allowance will suffice.

C. 4 x 10 PLAN

The 4 x 10 plan, four 10 hour workdays per week with 3 days off can be an effective schedule. Careful study is needed to "plot" the crime patterns. If the majority of crime can be covered with these hours it is an excellent incentive to TAC Unit officers. The department gains by one or two less roll calls and lunch hours per week and a reduction in sick leave use. Usually everyone but the criminal benefits from this plan. The Huntingdon Beach, California Police Department, Cherry Hill, New Jersey Police Department and the Harrisburg, Pennsylvania Police Department have used this system with success. An example of a schedule would be to have a TAC Unit work 3 p. m. to 1 a. m. on Wednesday thru Saturday. Sunday, Monday, and Tuesday would be regular days off unless commanders deemed it necessary to work a "skeleton crew" on days with the least crime.

5. SUMMARY

The fundamental considerations essential for success in the management of special TAC Units are: Selection of personnel for a TAC unit, Leadership, Understanding the relationship between trust and performance, and Incentives.

The "cream of the crop" of your personnel should be selected for the TAC Unit duty. It is essential to get input from other members of the TAC Unit on whom they choose to work, and perhaps die, with.

An enthusiastic TAC Unit leader can infect other members and achive amazing results. A good check on the quality of leadership in a TAC Unit is the morale and the production of its members.

High trust invariably leads to high performance. If the men trust their supervisors and leaders they will move mountains for them. This is turn gains the supervisor's respect of the men. It is a healthy cycle.

Incentives for members of TAC Units are in order because they are the best qualified members of the department working the least desirable hours and doing the most important and hazardous police job.

Put these ingredients together and you have the makings of a successful TAC Unit.

6. QUESTIONS FOR DISCUSSION

1. Name three of four fundamental considerations for successful management of a TAC Unit. What do you feel is the most important management consideration?

Unit 20 MANAGEMENT OF SPECIAL TAC UNITS

2. How do you pick good men for TAC Unit duty? Who should participate in the selection process?
3. How do you measure a good TAC Unit leader?
4. Explain the relationship between trust and performance?
5. What motivates you to do a good job? Do you think you could apply what motivates you to others?
6. List some incentives for members of a TAC Unit. Which do you recommend?
7. Why should you avoid the term "hazardous duty pay" for members of a TAC Unit?
8. Explain the advantages and disadvantges of the 4x10 plan. From the standpoint of the officer; From the standpoint of management.

UNIT 21

HELICOPTERS ON PATROL

The helicopter may prove to be the most outstanding police patrol vehicle of this century. It possesses an omnipresence which no other police vehicle ever had before. Chart 21.1 illustrates law enforcement and related missions performed by helicopters for selected agencies.

It is the policeman on the street who will benefit most from the helicopter. It will not be out of service on miscellaneous calls when the officer on the street needs a back-up on a felony car stop. It can respond quickly and in any direction while police cars are bogged down in traffic.

The helicopter will virtually eliminate the high speed chase. It will "lock-on" to the subject vehicle and stay with it until the ground units can cut off its escape routes. Once the police officer breaks off the pursuit the subject auto will probably slow down eliminating the dangers to pedestrians and motorists charteristic of the high speed chase. This will definitely be a plus factor for police community relations. Although it will be unusual for the helicopter to land to accomplish its mission it does have the ability to land almost anywhere.

A police helicopter is a natural airborne command post. It is an excellent observation post during fires, disasters or other emergencies. There is even the possibility of mounting a closed circuit TV under the copter to provide command personnel with the opportunity to observe an incident within minutes or even seconds after it takes place. A Commanding Officer could direct ground operations or effect traffic control without leaving his office. This is of tremendous value to the police administrator who must evaluate a potentially dangerous situation as quickly as possible.

Unit 21 HELICOPTERS ON PATROL

LAW ENFORCEMENT AND RELATED MISSIONS PERFORMED BY HELICOPTERS FOR SELECTED AGENCIES	CHICAGO P.D.	DENVER P.D.	FORT WORTH, CITY OF	HENNEPIN COUNTY SHERIFF, MN	Illinois State Toll Highway Auth.	Indianapolis Airport Authority	KANSAS CITY P.D.	L.A. COUNTY SHERIFF	L.A. P.D.	Home Office Police, London	MEMPHIS P.D.	NASSAU COUNTY P.D. NEW YORK	NEW JERSEY STATE POLICE	NEW YORK CITY P.D.	NEW YORK STATE POLICE	PENNA. STATE POLICE	ROYAL CANADIAN MOUNTED P.D.
COMMAND POST		•					•		•		•		•	•	•	•	
CRIMINAL APPREHENSION																	
HIGH SPEED CHASE			•	•	•		•	•	•			•		•		•	
PATROL-rural or vacant areas			•				•	•	•	•			•			•	
PATROL-seasonal areas in off seasons			•				•	•	•				•			•	
Providing intercept direction/control			•		•	•	•				•		•			•	
To surface vehicles or foot personal																	
RESPONSE TO ALARMS				•		•	•	•			•	•				•	
ROAD BLOCK - SET UP											•		•			•	
SEARCH FUGITIVES			•		•	•	•	•	•	•	•		•	•		•	•
SEARCH VEHICLES			•		•	•	•		•		•		•	•		•	
SURVEILLANCE - COVERT	•		•		•		•	•	•	•				•	•	•	•
SURVEILLANCE - GENERAL	•	•	•	•	•	•	•	•	•	•	•	•	•	•	•	•	•
SURVEILLANCE - ROOFTOP			•		•		•		•		•			•			
TRACKING FLEEING SUSPECTS			•		•		•			•	•		•			•	•
NARCOTICS DETECTION						•			•					•		•	
OBSERVATION POST			•				•				•		•	•		•	
Preventative night patrols with lights	•	•		•			•	•			•			•			
RIOT CONTROL	•	•			•			•	•		•		•	•		•	
SECURITY-valuable surface movements										•							•
TRANSPORT PRISONERS										•	•						•
Transport specialists to crime scene	•	•	•					•			•			•	•	•	•
VIP SECURITY			•						•					•		•	
VOICE CONTROL of ground events				•		•	•	•	•	•	•		•	•	•	•	•
AERIAL PHOTOGRAPHY		•	•		•	•			•	•	•	•	•	•	•	•	
WATER AREA PATROL	•		•						•			•	•	•			•

1. SURVEILLANCES

The helicopter comes into its own during a surveillance. No other police vehicle has the three dimensional concept of observation. If a copter is available there will be no need for a police officer to crawl through a dark alley to look for a suspect. The copter with its search light can light up the entire alley on command. The officers in the copter can observe the entire area as ground troops seal it off. In a dark alley a felon may try to assault or even kill an officer in a bid to escape. There is little likelihood of any offensive action from a felon as he stands bathed in the light of a searchlight from a hovering police helicopter. As for surveillance the copter again has attributes which cannot be matched when it comes to following a suspect.

In a foot surveillance a helicopter can cover both front and rear exits when a subject enters a building.

In a vehicular surveillance the helicopter can maintain speed and maintain a surveillance of any ground vehicle.

2. ADVANTAGES AND DISADVANTAGES

Any discussion about the use of helicopter patrol would not be complete without properly looking into the advantages and disadvantages of such patrols.

A. ADVANTAGES OF POLICE HELICOPTER PATROL

(1) Improved response time.

(2) Increased apprehension of offenders.

(3) Increased prevention of crime.

(4) Improved efficiency of regular patrol units through airborne information.

(5) Increased ability in conducting roof searches for suspected felons.

(6) Improved surveillance capability, a helicopter can watch both front and rear exits of a building.

(7) More efficient rescue operations and emergency ambulance service.

(8) A better system of floodlighting areas at night.

(9) Information can be broadcast to large areas through airborne loudspeakers.

(10) Rapid emergency transportation of personnel.

(11) Added security to patrol officers through "backup" offered by aerial patrol.

B. DISADVANTAGES OF POLICE HELICOPTER PATROL

(1) The major disadvantage of the use of helicopters is the high cost of initial investment in equipment, training and maintenance.

(2) Normal patrol time is limited to about 2 hours before refueling and to about 5 hours during an 8 hour tour.

(3) The most frequently purchased craft, the more economical piston engine helicopter can carry only 2 people and are limited in performance. The larger more efficient jets are disproportionately more expensive. (About 3 times the purchase price and twice the operating expense.)

(4) There is a strong potential for a tragic accident due to pilot error or mechanical failure.

(5) Weather conditions will limit the operating time.

(6) Smog and light or intermittant clouds might affect vision.

(7) There is a danger from high wires, trees and similar objects.

(8) There can be difficulty in landing in urban areas.

(9) Pilots get fatigued and must work shorter periods of time than regular police shifts.

(10) Special facilities are required for housing and repair.

(11) There are many tactical problems to overcome such as location of police units on ground, and the exact locations of addresses from the air.

(12) Adverse public reaction due to noise.

(13) Criminals can hear the helicopter coming and surprise is lost.

3. TURBINE HELICOPTERS FOUND MORE COST-EFFECTIVE

A study by the Los Angeles Police Department comparing the cost effectiveness of turbine-powered helicopters with reciprocating-engine aircraft indicates that air patrol service could be provided more economically by the turbine-powered units.[1]

Through 17 police divisions, the department is responsible for patrolling 469.4 square miles. Police helicopters now operate regularly in five divisions, offering 105.6 square miles of the city regular air patrols.

Preliminary results indicated that 16 turbine-powered helicopters could patrol the entire area of this sprawling metropolis. Acquisition costs would be about $441,000 more a year, but operational costs would be about $740,000 less annually. If turbine-powered helicopters were used, the city could be divided into eight patrol areas with two aircraft serving each area.

Use of the reciprocating-engine helicopters would require that the city be divided into 13 patrol areas rather than eight. This is because the slower piston-powered aircraft cannot cover as large an area. The 13 smaller areas would require 22 helicopters in a mixed fleet.

Figures from the Los Angeles police have shown a strong relationship between response time and helicopter effectiveness.

The speed of the turbine-powered helicopter would allow the response time to be reduced and increase effectiveness. In some police divisions with large areas and low population densities,

---

1. Robert R. Rapelewski, "Police Find Helicopter Effective", Aviation Week And Space Technology, Vol. 97, (Los Angeles: July 17, 1972) p. 50.

turbine-powered helicopters would be a requisite for achieving a good response time.

If helicopter coverage were provided for the entire city, the department would sell three or four of its present piston-engine aircraft and retain about the same number. The piston-powered helicopters are considered necessary for some photographic and surveillance tasks.

The department also kept some piston helicopters to give it limited capability if, for example, a component failure were to ground its entire turbine fleet.

4. ARREST/HELICOPTER RESPONSE TIME [2]

Two-month survey by the Los Angeles Police Department of response time to valid radio calls shows relationship between response time and arrests. Use of helicopters to cover wide areas could require that turbine-powered units to be employed to reduce response time and increase effectiveness. In table below, the "Air 3" includes two densely populated adjacent urban divisions. The 11th patrol area also includes two adjacent police divisions that are somewhat less densely populated. The last area, Air 10, is a sprawling suburb in the San Fernando Valley. The valid radio call designation excludes false alarms.

	Air 3	Air 11	Air 10
Average response time	66 sec.	83 sec.	128 sec.
Square miles in area	21.2	29.6	54.8
Arrests per valid radio call	0.336	0.330	0.178

The helicopter section's records for a single year show that helicopters were involved in 1,601 arrests (not including 109 arrests at a single major disturbance) in the Astro function, plus 273 arrests in the investigative function. Helicopter/patrol car teams effected felony arrests 62% of the time they were deployed, compared to 30.5% for patrol cars acting alone.[3]

---

2. Ibid. p. 53.   3. Ibid. p. 53.

5. POLICE PATROL IN FIXED WINGED AIRCRAFT

In some jurisdictions the size of the area to be patrolled necessitates a different type aircraft for police patrol.

The Henrico County, Virginia Police Department utilizes fixed winged aircraft to patrol a high-crime corridor adjacent to the city of Richmond. Because of the large area to be covered a fixed-winged aircraft is more efficient than a helicopter. In fact that TAC Unit (Special Action Force) utilizes the TAC II in the aircraft. Ground units are coordinated by the air crew in their response to robberies and burglaries in progress.

A. STOL AIRCRAFT

The Dade County Public Safety Department (Florida) conducted an experiment in comparing the use of helicopters and STOL's (Short takeoff and landing) in police patrolling.[4]

The STOL aircraft used in the experiment is a single-engine six-place light aircraft. It can land, or take off over a 50-foot obstacle, in only 610 feet. Its top speed is 165 mph, but its special wing configuration permits it to be flown under complete control as slow as 30 mph.

The one-year project was partially funded by the Law Enforcement Assistance Administration (LEAA), an agency of the U. S. Department of Justice. Increasingly, police jurisdictions are applying to the Federal government for financial assistance in purchasing aircraft. Usually these are helicopters, but LEAA raised the question as to which missions a STOL craft could perform as well or better than a helicopter, and how cost-effective the STOL would be.

The comparison aircraft was a helicopter which the Dade County police had been using for 10 years. Both the STOL and the

4. Cornell Aeronautical Laboratory, Inc. "Research Trends", (Autumn 1971) p. 50.

helicopter were assigned to fly 10 different types of patrols, including general surveillance; special patrols over the waterfront, rooftops, vacant land, parks and other recreational areas, and rural areas; fire detection, and search for stolen vehicles.

In one test period, the STOL flew 63 patrols totaling 126 hours, the helicopter flew 50 patrols totaling 71 hours.

The helicopter during its 50 missions assisted in at least 24 arrests. Its crew discovered more than 15 fires, 10 automobile accidents, 9 stolen or abandoned automobiles, two areas where narcotic plants were growing, and assisted at the scene of two drownings. The helicopter also provided illumination to assist in night rescue operations after a stolen car, pursued by a police ground unit, plunged into a canal in a rural area.

The STOL during 63 missions assisted in at least 8 arrests. Its crew discovered 11 fires or more, 8 stolen or abandoned automobiles, and two auto accidents: at one major fire it dispersed the crowd by using its high-intensity searchlight.

Helicopters are preferable, analysists found, when missions are no longer than two hours, the jurisdiction is compact in area and there is need for hovering as during rescue, evacuation, crowd control, or delivery of tear gas.

The STOL is preferable to a small piston-engined helicopter when the area to be patrolled is large or is distant, requiring a flight of more than 5 or 10 minutes to arrive on station; when anticipated missions are longer than 2 hours, and when the required payload may be large in terms of personnel and/or equipment, as in evacuating victims of a serious accident. In the Dade County experience, the STOL had a marked edge in its ability to remain aloft; the STOL could fly continuously for 8 to 10 hours, compared with a maximum of about 2 hours 20 minutes for the piston-engined helicopter which the Dade County police have. This endurance gives the STOL an advantage as an aerial command post directing ground forces during a prolonged civil disturbance.

The ability to land in a restricted space is a plus for the helicopter, but not as large a one as might be thought. Because of the danger of striking unseen objects such as wires, the helicopter would not make off-airport night landings unless the pilot was very familiar with the obstructions surrounding the landing areas.

(l) COST EFFECTIVENESS

One of the major reasons for evaluating STOL aircraft for police use is that certain STOLs are considerably cheaper to operate than any of the helicopters now used by police agencies. During the test period, fixed and direct expenses came to $16.99 per flight hour for Dade County's STOL and $28.94 per flight hour for its helicopter.

One way of evaluating costs is against "significant discoveries" —events discovered from the aircraft and requiring police action (events to which the aircraft responds by direction of the dispatcher are excluded). The helicopter made approximately 48 such discoveries, at a cost—giving each discovery equal weight— of about $30 each; the STOL made 32, at a cost of about $41 each.

As an alternative, if direct costs are divided among arrests— again giving each discovery equal weight—the helicopter's 24 arrests can be considered to have cost about $59 apiece and the STOL's eight to have cost approximately $160 apiece.

On the basis of their respective performance in Dade County, the helicopter would appear to have been more cost effective. However, this must not be considered a conclusive result because of the differences in pilot experience, the brevity of the test period, the single sample from each vehicle type, and the tendency to assign the STOL (because of its longer range) to rural and wilderness areas.

Coverage from the air will never replace squad cars. The cost of providing around-the-clock patrol for a year, by a two-man police car, has been estimated at $100,000. On that basis the Dade County STOL cost about 3.7 times as much as a patrol car, per hour of patrol, and the small helicopter cost about 4.4 times as much.

Partly offsetting this higher cost is the fact that the air vehicles cover a much greater area. The big difference, however, is that the air vehicle and the patrol car accomplish different types of tasks: police aircraft serve as aerial platforms to supplement and enhance the effectiveness of ground units.

References

Beall, James R., and Downing, Robert C., Helicopter Utilization in Municipal Law Enforcement: Administrative Consideration, (Springfield, Illinois: Charles C. Thomas Co. 1974)

Burden, Chief Earl, "Helicopter Patrol Services", Law and Order, (New York: November 1, 1973), p. 67–69

Stinson, Captain Palmer, "A Police Helicopter Program", FBI Law Enforcement Bulletin, Vol. 40, No. 7 (Washington, D.C.: FBI, July 1, 1971) p. 2, 6 and 32.

6. SUMMARY

The police helicopter possesses an omnipresence which no other police vehicle ever had before. It has both deterrence and apprehension capabilities. Modern and progressive TAC Units will certainly take more advantage of this police tool in the future.

Another type aircraft—the STOL has a place in law enforcement. Depending on the geography of your jurisdiction this aircraft may be even more productive than the helicopter. Criminals of the future are in for a tough time from on the ground and in the air.

7. QUESTIONS FOR DISCUSSION

1. What are the principal advantages of a police helicopter on patrol?

2. What are the principal disadvantages of a police helicopter on patrol?

3. Could your department use a police helicopter for patrol duty? Would you use it in your TAC Unit?
4. Could your department use a fixed winged aircraft for police patrol? How would you deploy it?
5. Discuss the pros and cons of using police firepower from aircraft.
6. What crimes could a police helicopter on patrol best combat?
7. How could police helicopters on patrol aid in "Operation FIND"?
8. How can police helicopters on patrol enhance the effectiveness of ground units?

SECTION 5

TACTICAL APPROACHES TO SELECTED CRIMES

UNIT 22

TACTICAL APPROACHES TO ROBBERY

No other crime deserves more police attention than the crime of robbery. Robbery is the highest (most serious) "repressible" crime in the hierarchy of Part I Offenses.

This unit is concerned with "putting it all together" in combatting robbery. A unit by unit analysis will follow:

—Units 1, 2 and 3 demonstrate the robbery problem in relationship to the Crime Problem in America.

—Unit 4 "Victims" focuses in on robbery victims mainly by several "real world" case histories. This unit clearly demonstrates the horror of the robbery problem in America.

—Unit 5 "Police Victims" points out the extreme danger to police involved in apprehending robbers.

—Unit 6 "Crime Reporting and Clearance" concerns itself with the need for accurate reporting to establish robbery patterns; the elements of the crime of robbery; and robbery as the most serious "repressible" crime.

—Unit 7 "The Goals of Police Service" spells out what a policeman should do, *Catch Robbers*. Also the effectiveness of preventive patrol against robbery and other crimes is questioned.

—Unit 8 "Reactive vs Proactive Response to Crime" emphasizes methods necessary to catch robbers "in-the-act". Relationship of anti-robbery TAC Units with the Detective Bureau is demonstrated as essential for success in combatting robbery.

—Unit 9 "A Day Without Police" covers the preventive aspects of policing. Robbery and other crimes increase tremendously without police presence.

—Unit 10 "Role Implementation" spells out goals and objectives. Crime specific goals are necessary to have and measure a successful anti-robbery program.

—Unit 11 "Resource Allocation" is about deployment of men, material and systems against the crime problem in general and robbery problems in particular.

—Unit 12 "Communications" involves radio, alarm, and roadblock systems to be utilized against robbers,

—Unit 13 "Holdup Information Systems" relates how response time is the key to success in apprehending robbers. A systematic approach to getting the necessary information out is emphasized.

—Units 14 and 15 "Surveillances" and "Searches" are concerned with "How to do it" techniques in dealing with robbers.

—Units 16 and 17 "Special Crime Tactical Forces" and "Model TAC Units" points out the importance of having a special anti-robbery TAC Unit.

—Unit 18 "Use of Decoys" puts "entrapment" in perspective and documents the most successful police anti-robbery operations.

—Unit 19 "Tactical Holdup Alarm Systems" identifies an innovative technological program in expanding a TAC Unit's capability for catching robbers.

—Unit 20 "Management of Special Squads" deals with the leadership and motivation techniques necessary for success.

—Unit 21 "Helicopters on Patrol" illustrates the practical deployment of aircraft against a robbery problem.

Put it all together and you have to be successful in combatting robberies.

1. HELPFUL TECHNIQUES

Proactive Approach to Robbery

1. Establish robbery patterns (via computer if available) so that TAC Unit members can visually observe the problem and develop tactics to deal with it.
2. Maximize communications and intelligence flow on robbers and robberies between members of the TAC Unit and:
    - —Detective Bureau
    - —Regular Patrol Forces
    - —FBI
    - —Other police jurisdictions
    - —Bank security officials
    - —Informants
3. Once a robbery problem is identified, select the tactic that has greatest potential for success in combatting it:
    - —Decoy
    - —Tactical holdup alarm system
    - —Stakeout
    - —Surveillance of robbery suspects
    - —Use of Helicopter
4. Count pursesnatches as robbery when planning corrective operations.

2. RESPONDING TO A ROBBERY IN PROGRESS

1. Cut lights and sirens at least three blocks from the scene.
2. Drive with caution and observe all exit routes from scene.

3. A route should be followed that will keep the police car hidden from the criminal until the last possible moment.
4. Only one or two cars respond to the scene of a "Report of a Robbery"—all other cars be on the lookout for suspects. In the case of a "Robbery in Progress" or "Silent Alarm" all available cars should close in on the scene.
5. On approaching the scene have personal walkie-talkie on ear jack so that robbers can't hear your approach. Noisy equipment such as handcuffs and keys should be secured.
6. The police officer should approach the scene on foot from an angle and in a manner (using cover) that will allow him to approach the scene without being seen.
7. Be on the lookout for the lookout man or getaway vehicle.
8. Observe what is going on through the window of the holdup target, if possible.
9. *Never* enter a holdup target building alone. (Holdup in progress or silent alarm)
10. Treat all silent holdup alarms as the "real McCoy". Be aware of diversionary tactics by robbers.
11. If plainclothesmen are responding to a robbery scene they should notify the police dispatcher so that other units may be so advised. This will reduce the possibility of an accidental shooting.
12. When encountering holdup men still on the scene, try to wait until they make their exit before challenging them. They are most vulnerable coming out a doorway and are a lot less likely to take a hostage.
13. When announcing "halt police" make sure you have already taken cover and they can see no more than a portion of your eye and the barrel of your gun. It should be a shotgun-sized barrel if you have one.
14. Even though you may have a right to use firearms, avoid it if passersby are endangered. It is better that a guilty person escape than an innocent person be hurt.

15. If the holdup men are not stopped short in their tracks and weaponless after step # 13, shoot them.
16. If your partner or a bystander is taken hostage, *never give up your weapon*. (If you do, you know for sure they have a real and loaded one.)
17. Once a holdup is established and the holdup men have fled, give out "flash" information on perpetrators as soon as possible.
18. Get an open telephone line to the police dispatcher.
19. Utilize your holdup information system to get the fastest and best description out. Look for unusual characteristics on description of suspect and getaway vehicles.
20. Take victim and/or witness on ride of getaway route.
21. Check neighborhood bars.
22. Tenacity pays off.
23. If you did not catch them the day of the robbery get the victim and/or witness to "ride along" on succeeding days.
24. Keep M. O. (Modus Operendi) and wanted photos and composites on all holdup suspects.
25. Be ready for the next one. It will happen.

3. SUMMARY

The main thrust of the proceeding units of this book has been directed against robbery because it is the highest crime in hierarchy of Part I Offenses that can be affected by police. The same tactics and principles apply to other crimes as well.

Helpful techniques in establishing a "proactive approach" to the robbery problem are offered as the best chance to get the problem under control. As you know under 30% of robberies are cleared and detectives only clear between 10 and 30% of those that are cleared. Therefore the TAC Unit picks up prime responsibility for fighting this crime and its little sister, pursesnatching.

The police decoy is the most effective anti-robbery tactic in the law enforcement arsenal against crime. This is closely followed by the police tactical holdup alarm system. Both tactics should be performed by highly trained members of a TAC Unit.

Officers whose duties include responding to robberies in progress should review the 25 steps suggested in this unit. Then practice. Playing "cops and robbers" sounds like childsplay but it is for real. It could mean the difference between life and death.

4. QUESTIONS FOR DISCUSSION

1. Explain why the robbery problem should be dealt with prior to other crimes.
2. Define a "Legalistic Style, Proactive, Apprehension Oriented Approach" to the crime problem and relate how this form of policing can reduce robberies.
3. List some cooperative sources that members of TAC Units can rely upon to gain intelligence information on robbers. Which are the most effective sources?
4. Once a robbery pattern has been established, what tactics are available to the police to combat it?
5. List as many of the steps to follow when responding to a robery that you can and identify the most important steps.
6. If the robbers have fled the scene, how do you get the fastest and best description of the doers out over the air?
7. Explain the "ride along" technique in fighting robbery.
8. Explain why an officer confronting armed robbers should never surrender his gun, even if hostages are involved.
9. What is the present clearance rate for robberies in your area? How does it compare with the national average? How could you improve your clearance rate?

UNIT 23

TACTICAL APPROACHES TO BURGLARY

Burglary is the second most serious "repressible" crime challenging police. It is recommended that you focus in and correct your robbery problem first because of the violence involved in that type of crime. Once robbery is under control you can set up systems to deal with the burglary problem.

Don't sell burglary short on its potential for violence. Many burglary victims and police officers wind up as assault or homicide victims.

1. BURGLARS

Most burglars fall into the juvenile and adult amateur categories. They are opportunists who usually just take what happens to be of immediate use or value. Because of their lack of planning and crude operations, they are the easiest to catch.

The most dangerous type of burglar is the one who enters a building to fulfill sexual desires. Often they are quite sadistic and vicious. A secondary aim of this type burglar would be the theft of valuable articles.

The "professional" burglar is the hardest type to apprehend. When he strikes the take is usually big. He utilizes planning and cunning to his best advantage. He represents a true challange to the expertise of law enforcement personnel.

2. THE "PROFESSIONAL" BURGLAR

Who is a professional burglar? He may be anyone. He may be the man standing next to you in the bar, part of the foursome following you around the local golf course, or the individual sitting next to you on the bus. In any of these circumstances he could be collecting information for his next job. What better place is there to collect information than where people gather and talk unguardedly about their personal problems and exploits. People like to brag about their possessions and the possessions of their relatives or friends. This is just what the burglar is looking for. However, he doesn't take this information at face value; if he did he would not have reached professional status. The professional takes the information and begins to do some checking in order to satisfy himself that the score is worth the time and effort.

The "good" burglar is contemptuous of the police and others, and feels that society exists to supply his needs for a good life and to amuse him. Most often, the burglar's education is mediocre or below average but his instinct for survival is high. He believes he is smarter than the police, but this does not mean he does not respect them. There are certain policemen for whom he has high regard, and because of this he avoids them.

Those individuals who consider themselves "professional" burglars are not usually vicious; although they have been known to commit acts of violence when cornered. The average burglar relies solely on good planning, stealth, instinct and knowledge of his subject. Usually he is unarmed and will flee rather than face a showdown.

3. CASING THE JOB

To effectively use the information obtained, the burglar will "case" the job, (i. e., examine the location and its surroundings). There is much that he must know before he can effectively plan and carry out his crime. Among the questions he may ask himself are:

Where is the house?

What surrounds the house?

Does the residence have a burglar alarm?

Does the house have outside lighting?

What type of doors and locks are on the house?

How are the rooms situated?

Where and how many avenues of escape exist?

What kind of traffic frequent the area?

How many people are in the house?

What are the habits of the occupants and neighbors?

How much time is spent at home?

When are they out most often?

How many and what kind of cars are used by the occupants?

What are the habits of the police and do they have any particular custom which would aid or inhibit the burglar?

This list of questions looks impressive. But in reality, many of them can be simply answered by driving past the house or just walking around the block and observing—especially when one knows what to look for. For example, activity of the household members can be easily checked by telephone, vehicles can be observed in the driveway or in front of the house, vehicle registration can be checked out by telephone, questions concerning the police can be answered by locating and following them for short periods, phony calls may be placed to determine response time or as a diversionary tactic.

Most commercially installed alarm systems have a control box in an inaccessible but conspicuous location and when the alarm is activated a bright red light shows up on the control panel. The installers and the owners are not interested in apprehending the burglar but merely in scaring him off. The burglar is not anxious to get involved with an alarm system or a dog; however, he has been known to by-pass or disable both. Neither is adequate protection.

Door locks are not a hindrance, as most commercially installed locks can be easily snapped or slipped. Professionals are skilled in the use of picks and other lock picking devices. Sliding doors are especially vulnerable, since most locks on these doors are inferior. At best, "locks are made to keep honest people honest and only hinder thieves."

4. POTENTIAL BURGLAR TOOLS

After an examination of the location, the burglar will pick a minimal number of tools to attain his goal. Here is a list of the more common ones:

1. Crow, pinch or pry bars
2. Thin metal strips—6 to 12 inch lengths (celluloid strips)
3. Glass cutters
4. Adhesive or scotch tape
5. Various types of hammers
6. Drills
7. Burning equipment
8. Wire
9. Screwdrivers
10. Wire cutters
11. Bolt cutters
12. Pipe wrenches
13. Wood or metal saws
14. Lock picks

5. PLANNING

Depending on the type of burglary planned, the burglar will require assistance. Cohorts are relatively simple to find. Many burglars have their regulars who they can trust and who will work for a set fee or a percentage of the take. If the main purpose of the burglary is obtaining small items, only one confederate will be needed to act as a lookout and driver.

The burglar and his accomplice maintain communications so they can coordinate their actions. This can be accomplished by using the walkie-talkie radio, which has a built-in call signal.

These radios are often sold across the counter to anyone requesting them.

Using a call signal, the radio-equipped burglar will operate as follows: When the transmitter button on the walkie-talkie is depressed it activates a beeper or buzzer in the other unit. A code system is worked out in advance making it unnecessary for either operator to speak through the set. These radios are small in size, (smaller than a carton of cigarettes), and can be hidden in many places. They will fit in glove boxes, can be mounted under dashboards, carried in pockets, hung on a belt, placed under seats, etc.

6. VEHICLES USED

Some type of motor vehicle is a necessity. It can be borrowed or stolen just prior to the burglary and discarded immediately afterwards. Rented automobiles may also be used. If the rented auto is identical to the vehicle belonging to the homeowner, the burglar can drive right up to the house and park the car with little chance of arousing suspicion.

Rental trucks and moving vans should be investigated whenever seen loading or unloading goods. Remember, burglaries of residences usually occur during daylight hours. Encourage local citizens to report all suspicious activity with particular emphasis on suspicious vehicles on a neighbor's property.

7. THE BURGLARY

Everything is ready: the tentative time has been set, equipment gathered, accomplice found, and all that is necessary to ensure there are no occupants on the premises has been done. At the appointed time, a phone call is placed to the house; if there is no answer, everything is go. Just before reaching the house another call is put through; if everything is still go, the burglars drive past the house to check the driveway and lights. When all looks good, one or more of the culprits are dropped off to make the approach. Here we find variation because each man operates in a different manner. Each burglar is a creature of habit. He finds a way that works well for him and uses it repeatedly. This applies to avenues of approach, methods of entry, articles taken, modes of transportation, etc.

Time spent on the premises and the tools carried are kept to a minimum. Thieves go directly to the primary objective and in doing so may take any other "attractive" item which can be easily carried. The longer the burglar spends in the building, the greater are his chances of being caught. When leaving, he has to carry his loot until he reaches his car or truck; *it is during this departure time the burglar is particularly vulnerable.*

8. RESPONDING TO A BURGLARY IN PROGRESS

Utilize the same techniques as responding to a "robbery in progress" (Unit 22) with these additional measures. Burglaries in progress calls can be in the form of alarms or calls from the victim or witnesses.

(1) Surround the area and block off all exists. The first car on the scene should observe the situation with all lights out until the arrival of backup personnel. It is possible for two patrol cars to cover a small square building. This can be done by each patrol car taking diagonal corners of a buiding. At night, both patrol cars could direct their headlights down one side of the building and their spotlights down the other side. Then each side will be covered with light.

(2) Be on the alert for the lookout. All persons around the target building should be detained until you establish if a "break" was made (either forced or surreptitious entry). Be particularly suspicious of occupied autos parked or circling the scene. Sometimes females are used as lookouts and/or drivers of getaway vehicles. Do not neglect coverage of the roof especially if the building is connected with others.

Unit 23					TO BURGLARY					313

- (3) *Have the radio dispatcher notify the owner to come to the scene.* He knows the property best and can be of valuable assistance in establishing if there was a break. He will also be helpful in the search by providing keys and information on lighting.
- (4) *Call for supervision and support prior to building search.* Presence of a supervisor will help in organization of the search and be valuable if breaches of police integrity are charged after the search. Also special support such as K-9 can prove invaluable.
- (5) Thoroughly search the building. Refer to "Searches" (Unit 15) for further details.

9. TIPS FOR THE POLICE TO AID IN APPREHENSION

1. DO NOT form bad patrol habits. Be irregular, use your rear view mirrors, backtrack, ask what people are doing if you don't know or understand, and look above the ground level.
2. Know the cars/trucks of residents.
3. Know the area behind and around the buildings in your sector.
4. Be alert for loitering strangers.
5. Look for strange vehicles with two-way radios mounted in unusual places.
6. Pay particular attention to noises, movements, etc., which are not normal.
7. Investigate the occupants of vehicles which park or stop with their motors running; especially during the hours of darkness. If the vehicles are unattended, await the arrival of the driver and interview him.
8. Know which buildings on your sector have burglar alarms.

9. Investigate heavily laden cars and trucks during unusual hours.
10. Know and utilize proper tactics in responding.
11. Utilize proactive measures (police alarms, stakeouts, helicopters and surveillances) whenever possible.

10. TRUANCY AND BURGLARY

The American Federation of Teachers estimate that 2 million of 50 million students are absent from school daily throughout the U.S. Many of these are truants who are responsible for daytime burglaries of residences and auto thefts.

A good anti-truancy system (coordinated with the school authorities) could pay handsome dividends in form of lower burglary and auto theft rates.

11. CURFEW AND BURGLARY

Juveniles account for even larger proportions of nighttime burglaries (mainly businesses) and auto thefts. Strict enforcement of curfew laws are a valuable police tool in lowering more serious crime rates. If your Department does not have a good curfew law it behooves police administrators to lobby for one.

12. SUMMARY

Burglary is the second most important "repressible" crime facing police. Once robbery is brought under control you can set up systems to combat the burglary problem.

Burglary, with over 3 million reported offenses a year in the United States, is a problem in most communities. Fortunately it is a repressible crime but not as repressible as robbery and auto theft. Because of the high rate of recidivism with burglary, you have an opportunity to reduce the crime if you incarcerate some burglary repeaters. Also, once a jurisdiction gets the reputation as "being tough on burglars" they (the burglars) will avoid you like the plague.

There are basically two kinds of burglars: amateur (juvenile and adult) and professional (usually adult). In order to combat the burglary problem in your jurisdiction it helps to know what type of burglar you are fighting. The amateur is rather easy to catch; but the professional presents a real challenge to the expertise of law enforcement.

It is important to know how the burglar cases the job, what kind of tools you can expect him to carry, how he plans the burglary, what kind of vehicle he uses, in combatting burglary.

Adjust police tactics to met the challenge of the burglar and you will have an opportunity to raise the rather low clearance rate on burglary (18%). Stakeouts, surveillance of known burglars and police tactical alarm systems are proactive methods of fighting burglary.

Two other programs have potential for combatting burglaries by amateurs: An anti-truancy program and a curfew program.

If you can raise the clearance rate to 25% or better and duplicate Cedar Rapid's "mousetrap's" conviction rate (100%), your burglaries have to go down.

13. QUESTIONS FOR DISCUSSION

1. How many burglaries are reported in the United States each year and how many are solved (cleared) by police?
2. What is your local burglary count, rate, and clearance rate?
3. Identify the two basic types of burglars and explain which is the most difficult police challenge.
4. List the tools you could expect a burglar to be transporting and explain where to look for them.
5. When is the burglar most vulnerable to arrest? Why?

6. What steps do you take in responding to a burglary in progress?
7. What "tips" could you offer to aid in the apprehension of burglars?
8. Enforcement of what other laws have potential for lowering burglaries?
9. What do you think is a reasonable clearance rate for burglary? How do you improve the conviction rate on this crime?

UNIT 24

TACTICAL APPROACHES TO AUTO THEFT

Since there is one reported auto theft every 34 seconds, officers will have plenty of opportunity to deal with this type crime.

Some people do not view auto theft as a serious offense. Think of how much you have invested in your own car and you get some idea of the value of the 1 million autos stolen in the United States last year.

There are other reasons for police to be concerned with auto theft. Frequently stolen vehicles are used in other offenses such as robbery and burglary. Many deaths and injuries result from crashes of stolen autos.

One reason often overlooked why police should give prime attention to auto theft is the locale in which they occur. It is hard to conceal a stolen car. Car thieves usually operate them on the street, and that is the police domain. Since we have the opportunity to catch them, why not make the most of it. Stolen vehicles give the police administrator an opportunity to evaluate the quality and effectiveness of his police patrol.

Quality police patrol can be measured by analyzing the clearance rate for auto theft and the recovered auto rate. If you are not clearing more auto thefts than the national 15% average, or recovering over 85% of the stolen vehicles, your patrols are not up to par. A 25% apprehension rate and 90% recovery rate are reasonable goals.

Chart 24.1 gives you some idea about where stolen vehicles are being taken from.

I. PROACTIVE APPROACH TO AUTO THEFT

There are two prime considerations in catching auto thieves:
—The quality of NCIC auto investigation
—The quantity of NCIC auto investigation

MOTOR VEHICLE THEFT BY LOCATION
September - October, 1974

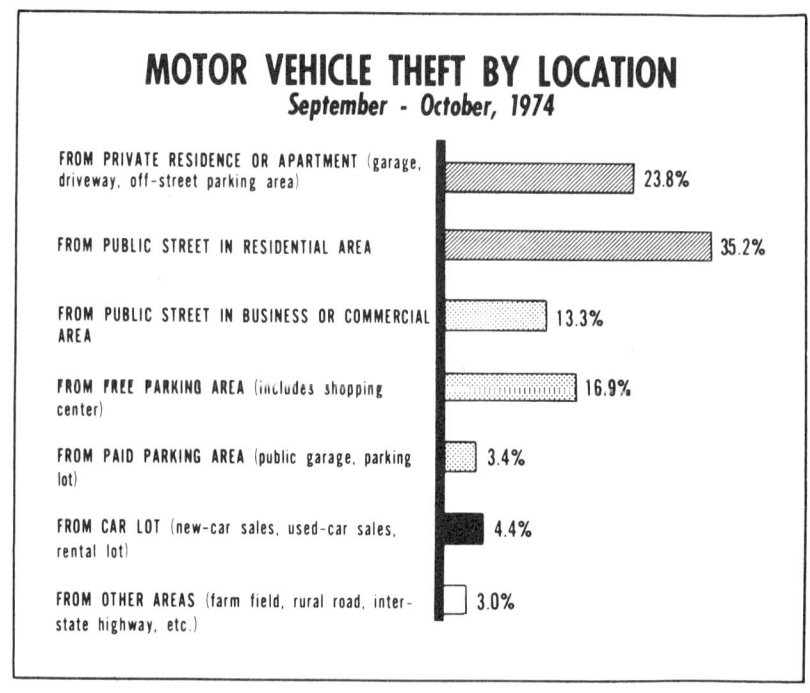

Location	Percentage
FROM PRIVATE RESIDENCE OR APARTMENT (garage, driveway, off-street parking area)	23.8%
FROM PUBLIC STREET IN RESIDENTIAL AREA	35.2%
FROM PUBLIC STREET IN BUSINESS OR COMMERCIAL AREA	13.3%
FROM FREE PARKING AREA (includes shopping center)	16.9%
FROM PAID PARKING AREA (public garage, parking lot)	3.4%
FROM CAR LOT (new-car sales, used-car sales, rental lot)	4.4%
FROM OTHER AREAS (farm field, rural road, interstate highway, etc.)	3.0%

CHART 24.1   FBI CHART

The National Crime Information Center (NCIC) computer has approximately one million active stolen vehicle records on file. These records should be readily available to the officer on the street who needs the information to perform.

Since persons under 21 years of age constitute 74 percent of the persons arrested for auto theft, officers should be particularly suspicious of youthful operations. "Moving NCIC checks" can be made without stopping the suspect vehicle simply by following an auto until police radio either confirms the auto stolen or clears it via NCIC. You do not need a lot of probable cause to make inquiry. If the officer is reasonably selective and makes many inquiries he will be successful. Another benefit to this method is that it is almost impossible for a complaint against police to be made because there is no personal contact between the officer and suspected driver.

Vehicles bearing out-of-town tags should be subject to inquiry because of the high mobility of the criminal element today. Rob a bank and kill a cop in St. Louis today and drive your stolen getaway through Chicago tomorrow.

Moving NCIC checks can pay dividends in these type cases. Imagine being a Chicago officer and receiving the wanted reply on the aforementioned situation. *Now* you have probable cause to intercept the auto!

Other proactive approaches would include:

—Utilization of TAC II Alarm System (Unit 19) to "wire-up" twenty or more "decoy" cars (police surveillance or personal cars of patrolmen) in a given shopping center, parking lot or high-theft street. The doors or seats should be wired so that nearby police could respond to a "hit". Thefts from vehicles could be also handled in the same fashion.

—NCIC inquiry terminals in police vehicles for a massive amount of inquiries.

—Daily checks of automobile junk yards, automobile disposal facilities (crushers) and body shops.

—Investigations of:
- Any car being towed.
- Persons having difficulty entering a car or who attempt to avoid being seen by a policeman.
- Persons changing license plates or removing tires or parts from a vehicle.
- Persons looking into windows of a series of parked cars.
- Vehicles driven recklessly or at high speed.
- Vehicles operating without lights at night.
- Vehicles bearing evidence of forced entry. (example: broken vent window or missing door or trunk lock mechanism)

- Vehicles with license plates that are cleaner or dirtier than the car, or with front plates that do not match rear plates.
- Vehicles with temporarily fastened license plates, altered license plates or wrong type license plates.
- Vehicles left for a long period of time as evidenced by debris, dust or citations on windshield. Any recovery of unoccupied stolen vehicle presents an opportunity for a covert stakeout. The thief or "car strippers" often return.

—Hangouts of known criminals and juvenile delinquents should be checked periodically including:
- Area around schools
- Horse racing track parking lots
- Drag racing areas
- Dancehalls and pool halls
- Drive-in restaurants

—Vehicles that obviously do not match their operators should be the subject of inquiry. Examples would be a difference in race of operator with ethnic flag decals or a person in seedy clothing driving a shiny cadillac.

—Also, known car thieves could be tailed until they do what they are known for.

2. HIGH-SPEED PURSUITS

By definition, high-speed pursuit is pursuit in which the police car reaches speeds of perhaps 70 MPH in municipalities and 85 MPH on county or state roads. Each department should establish its own definition of high-speed pursuit and develop policy that will protect both the officer and the public.

A. PROBLEMS INVOLVED IN PURSUITS

The practice of high-speed pursuit by police officers has come under considerable fire in the past few years. In a study done in 1968 by the Physicians for Automotive Safety, it was estimated that 500 Americans die every year in pursuit crashes. One out of every 25 of these is a police officer.

Pursuit driving presents several concerns to the police officer. He is concerned, first of all, with enforcing the law. Far and away the most common incident which sparks pursuit is the traffic violation. The vehicle is already in motion, the violation is detected, the patrol officer signals the violator to stop, and the motorist steps on the gas pedal and flees. What motivates a person to run instead of stop? The police officer doesn't know if the suspect has a body in his trunk, a stolen car, narcotics under the front seat, or a warrant for armed robbery on his head. And so he pursues, and in most cases, apprehends him. This is his duty, and it is part of what the public expects of him.

But during the pursuit, a number of other concerns present themselves. The police officer is jeopardizing his life; the fleeing suspect is jeopardizing his life and those of his passengers; the lives of innocent third parties are endangered. There are times when, as a result of high-speed pursuit, an accident occurs and a civil or even a criminal suit is filed against the police officer and his employers. In many instances, the very public that has demanded that the police department pursue, intercept and apprehend violators of the law becomes severely critical of that department for actions of its officers in pursuing suspects.

Clearly, there must be an understanding about the level of enforcement effort which should be undertaken by an officer in an individual case. It is not advisable to set specific limits on pursuit activity, e. g., X number of mph on expressways and X number of mph on city streets. Besides giving fleeing suspects an incentive to exceed these limits and elude their pursuers, it is inflexible and does not allow the individual officer to exercise his discretion.

B. CONTROLS FOR HIGH-SPEED PURSUITS

Typical of the kinds of controls which can be imposed by administrative decision and enumerated in a policy statement as well as incorporated into departmental training are the following guidelines:

1. A decision by an officer to initiate high-speed pursuit, and to continue to successful apprehension, must reflect:
    a) a consideration for the type of violation committed;
    b) weather and road conditions;
    c) visability;
    d) dangers to other motorists and pedestrians;
    e) availability of assistance;
    f) probability of successful apprehension in light of these risk factors.
2. The driver of a police vehicle shall inform the radio dispatcher immediately when he is chasing a fleeing violator and is likely to reach "pursuit speeds".
3. The driver of a police vehicle, when in high-speed pursuit of a violator, shall maximize control over his vehicle by adjusting his speed to traffic, vehicle and roadway conditions.
4. When a police vehicle is engaged in pursuit the operator or passenger shall not, for reasons of personal and public safety, shoot at the fleeing car except in the most extreme cases. Even then, weapons in the typical police arsenal have been proven very ineffective against vehicles. The 12 gauge shotgun loaded with rifled slug is the most practical police weapon against a vehicle.
5. Bumping maneuvers intended to force the fleeing driver to stop his vehicle are prohibited except when the suspect has taken aggressive action with his vehicle, attempting to force a pursuit vehicle off the road or to ram it.
6. Only those police vehicles which are subject to a regular preventive maintenance program—those in which alignment, brakes, tires, lights, doors, driver-restraining de-

vices, steering mechanism and emergency equipment are in prime condition—and which are capable of a top speed equivalent to or above that of the average car, shall be used in high-speed pursuit.

7. Only officers who have successfully completed a program of testing, training and skill evaluation designed to provide an awareness of their limitations as drivers; a knowledge of their vehicles' performance characteristics (acceleration, cornering, deceleration); and their ability to respond correctly to hazards shall be authorized to engage in high-speed pursuit.

8. Emergency lights and sirens should be used only by the first police car in pursuit or the closest car if the first car has broken-off the pursuit. Sirens should not be considered capable of clearing cross-traffic at intersections. All other cars involved in pursuit should use emergency lights.

9. The pursued driver who stops his car must be considered dangerous and should be approached with extreme care.

3. SUMMARY

Auto theft belongs to the police because most cars are stolen from, and afterwards, operated on the streets. Since this is where the police are supposed to be working, the crime is highly repressible. The cost of the million vehicles stolen each year is astronomical.

There are other reasons why police should combat auto theft: Stolen autos are used in other crimes and many deaths and injuries result from crashes of stolen autos.

Two prime considerations in catching auto thieves are the quality and quantity of NCIC auto investigations. An increase in this area certainly has the potential for raising the 15% national average for clearance of auto theft. In addition to clearances, recovery of stolen vehicles is another measure of the effectiveness of police patrol.

Because tactics involved in apprehending auto thieves often result in high speed pursuits, it is necessary that the officer be properly trained and equipped to perform such duties.

All in all, auto theft is a rather easy crime to combat. By utilizing proper tactics and concentrating on youthful offenders, a 25% clearance rate and 90% recovery rate are achievable goals.

4. QUESTIONS FOR DISCUSSION

1. How many autos are stolen in the United States each year? What is the clearance rate?
2. Compare the above figures with your local auto theft problem and clearance rate. What is your local recovery rate for stolen vehicles?
3. How can auto thefts best be combatted? Why?
4. Who is responsible for most auto thefts?
5. Where are autos likely to be stolen from?
6. Why is it important for police to fight the crime of auto theft?
7. Discuss the implications of a high-speed pursuit of a stolen auto.
8. What is a reasonable clearance and recovery rate for stolen vehicles?

INDEX

References are to Pages

AGGRAVATED ASSAULT
Clearance of, 23
Defined, 22
Nature of, 23
Police officers, 53

AIR PATROL
Helicopters, 291
STOL aircraft, 296

ALARM SYSTEMS
Burglary, 135
Robbery, 134
Tactical, 134, 147, 256

AMARILLO, TEXAS
Police department, 203

ARRESTS
Firearms violations, 210
Gun, 210

ATLANTA, GEORGIA
Police department, 207

AUTO THEFT
Defined, 32
Locations, 318
Nature of, 32
Repeaters, 60
Tactical approaches to, 317

BASIC POLICE FUNCTIONS
Apprehension, 68
Deterrence, 68
Prevention, 68

BERTILLION, ALPHONSE, 155

BURGLARY
Clearances, 29

BURGLARY—Cont'd
Defined, 28
Nature of, 28
Repeaters, 60
Tactical approaches to, 312

CASE STUDIES
Mr. Rauer, 39
Mrs. Slawnyk, 36

CEDAR RAPIDS, IOWA
"Mousetrap", 315
Police department, 135

CHERRY HILL, NEW JERSEY
Police department, 287

CHICAGO, ILLINOIS
Police department, 203
Special operations group, 206

CINCINNATI, OHIO
Police department, 80

CLARK, RAMSEY
Crime in America, 2, 55

CLEVELAND, OHIO
Police department, 285

COMMUNICATIONS
Alarm systems, 134
Dispatchers, 131
"Flash" information, 147
Holdup information systems, 147
NCIC, 318
Police radio, 131
Telephone, 132

INDEX

References are to Pages

COMPLAINTS AGAINST POLICE
Brutality, 208
Corruption, 208

CRIME
Against property, 28
Clearance of, 55, 57
In America, 1
Index, 3
Part I offenses, 3
Rates, 6
Reporting of, 55
Repressible, 62
Types of, 2
Unfounded, 5
Violent, 9

CRIMINAL INTELLIGENCE
Methods, 80

CRIMINALS
Repeaters, 60

CURFEW
Arrests, 210
Violations, 314

DADE COUNTY, FLORIDA
Police department, 296

DECOYS
Disguises, 233, 261
Granny squad, 283
Types of, 232
Use of, 229

DEPLOYMENT
Four-ten plan, 208, 287
Non-emergency services, 111
Police manpower, 110
RDO volunteers, 115
Resource allocation, 109
Stack cars, 116

DESCRIPTION
Of persons, 155
Of vehicles, 157

DETECTIVE WORK
Study on, 79

DETROIT, MICHIGAN
Police department, 115, 206
S.T.R.E.S.S., 206
Tactical mobile unit, 206

ELEMENTS OF CRIME
Act, 61
Defined, 58
Intent, 61

ENGLISH MODEL OF POLICING
See Foreign Police Systems.

ENTRAPMENT
Defined, 229

F.B.I.
F.B.I., 3, 47, 98, 303

FEENEY, FLOYD, 80

FORCIBLE RAPE
Defined, 15
Locations of, 16
Nature of, 15

FOREIGN POLICE SYSTEMS
British, 68
English model of policing, 68
French Surete, 155

FORT LAUDERDALE, FLORIDA
Police department, 115

GOALS
Development of, 89
Internal publication, 93
Of police service, 67

HANEY, WILLIAM V., 281

HARRISBURG, PENNSYLVANIA
Police department, 287

HENRICO COUNTY, VIRGINIA
Police department, 296

HOMICIDE
See Murder.

HONOLULU, HAWAII
Police department, 203

INDEX

References are to Pages

INCENTIVES
"Blue max", 285
Cleveland, Ohio Police Department, 285
Four-ten program, 287
Monetary incentives, 286
Orange, California Police Department, 285
Personal car program, 287
Philadelphia police stakeout unit, 285

INFORMANTS
Use of, 81, 303

KALAMAZOO, MICHIGAN
Police department, 203

KANSAS CITY, MISSOURI
Metro squad, 207
Patrol study, 71
Police department, 93, 104, 115

KELLEY, CLARENCE M., 47

LABELING THEORY
Theory on deviance, 56

LANCASTER, PENNSYLVANIA
Police department, 115

LARCENY–THEFT
Defined, 30
Nature of, 32
Types of, 31

LAW ENFORCEMENT ASSISTANCE ADMINISTRATION
Study, 55, 80

LEE, ADRIAN, 36

LIKERT, RENSIS, 281

LOS ANGELES, CALIFORNIA
Metropolitan division, 206, 221
Police department, 74, 115, 203, 205
SWAT, 221, 223

McGREGOR, DOUGLAS, 282

MASLOW, ABRAHAM, 282

MASSACHUSETTS INSTITUTE OF TECHNOLOGY, 13

MONTREAL, CANADA
Police department, 84

MURDER
Circumstances, 12
Clearances, 12
Defined, 9
Nature of, 10
Projection of, 13
Weapon used, 11

MURPHY, PATRICK V., 72

NATIONAL ADVISORY COMMISSION
Standard, 8.1, p. 94
Standard, 8.2, p. 98
Standard, 9.8, p. 201

NCIC
See Communications.

NEW YORK, NEW YORK
Family crisis intervention unit, 62
Police department, 109, 203
Street crime unit, 226

OBJECTIVES
Development of, 89
Internal publication, 93

OFFICERS KILLED
By hour of day, 50
By type of activity, 49
Circumstances, 51
Weapons used, 51

OHIO STATE PATROL
Blue max, 285

OPERATION F. I. N. D.
Techniques, 141

ORANGE, CALIFORNIA
Police department, 285

PART I OFFENSES
See Crime.

INDEX

References are to Pages

PATROL
Deployment of, 116
Service priorities, 97

PEEL, SIR ROBERT, 68

PHILADELPHIA, PENNSYLVANIA
Police department, 141, 256
Stakeout unit, 208, 214, 285

POLICE STRIKE
Montreal, Canada, 84

PORTRAIT PARLE, 155

PURSUITS
Procedures, 320

QUEBEC PROVINCIAL
Police department, 84

RAPE
See Forcible Rape.

REPEATERS
See Criminals.

RESOURCE ALLOCATION
See Deployment.

RESPONSE TIME
Defined, 147
Schematic, 148
Study on, 98

RESPONSE TO CRIME
Proactive, 78
Reactive, 78

RIZZO, FRANK L., 141, 214

ROADBLOCKS
Operation F. I. N. D., 141

ROBBERY
Comparison of, 22
Defined, 17
Nature of, 19
Persons arrested, 21
Repeaters, 60
Responding to, 303
Study on, 80
Tactical approaches to, 301

ST. LOUIS, MISSOURI
Police department, 207

SAN FRANCISCO, CALIFORNIA
Police department, 204

SANTARELLI, DONALD E., 42, 55

SAVANNAH, GEORGIA
Police department, 203

SEARCHES
Communications in, 179
Control of, 180
Objectives of, 178
Organizing, 179
Planning for, 178
Types of, 182

SPECIAL CRIME TACTICAL FORCES
Defined, 201
Deployment of, 203
Organization, 205
Part-time units, 207

STACK CARS
See Deployment.

STYLES OF POLICING
Legalistic, 74
Service, 74
Watchman, 74

SURVEILLANCE
Automobile, 170
Defined, 160
Equipment, 163
Fixed, 165
Foot, 166
Helicopter, 291
Locality of, 162
Moving, 164
Preparation for, 161
Use of, 161

SYRACUSE, NEW YORK
Police department, 203

TAC II
See Alarm Systems.

INDEX

References are to Pages

TAC UNITS
Activity of, 210
Leadership of, 280
Management of, 279
Model units, 214
Operations room, 211
Selection of members for, 279
Weapons, 211

THEFT
See Larceny-Theft.

TRUANCY
Arrests, 210
Violations, 314

UNIFORM CRIME REPORTS
Defined, 3

VICTIMS
Case studies, 36, 39

VIOLENT CRIMES
See Crime.

WEBSTER, JOHN A., 97

WEIR, ADRIANNE, 80

WILSON, O. W., 1